W9-CZJ-936

Sports Collectors Digest

All Sport
Autograph Guide

By
Mark Allen Baker

Published by:

 **krause publications**

700 E. State Street • Iola, WI 54990-0001

Please call or write for our free catalog of sports publications.
Our Toll-free number to place an order or obtain a free catalog is
800-258-0929. Please use our regular business telephone number
715-445-2214 for editorial comment or further information.

Library of Congress Catalog Number: 94-77502

ISBN: 0-87341-316-4

Printed in the United States of America

Dedication

To Matthew Robert Baker, my godson and youngest brother:

If wealth was measured by the honesty, sincerity and love in a man's heart, then you would be the richest man I have ever met.

Contents

Preface

According to one industry analyst, $60 million is spent annually on autographed sports memorabilia, with industry-related advertising alone exceeding $6 million dollars in hobby publications. Large corporations are now fueling the market too, through a variety of channels, including satellite shopping networks, regional cable television, national retailers, national catalogs, hobby stores and even through corporate promotions.

The two main companies producing and marketing autographed sports memorabilia are the Score Board Inc. and Upper Deck Authenticated, a division of the Upper Deck Co., and an affiliate with McNall Sports Entertainment.

The Score Board, a publicly-held corporation, designs, markets and distributes sports and entertainment products. It has two primary businesses - selling specialty sports trading cards and selling sports and entertainment memorabilia and games. The company, founded in 1987, has seen its revenues grow in excess of $108 million for fiscal year 1994. Sales of sports memorabilia, the division of the company that includes autographed sports items, amounted to $15.7 million in 1993, accounting for 21 percent of the company's fiscal 1994 revenues.

In 1992, Score Board faced its first true competitor in the market, Upper Deck Authenticated. This division markets a variety of autographed memorabilia, including balls, jerseys, hats, *Sports Illustrated* magazine covers, cards and commemorative card sheets. During the last 12 months the company has been very aggressive in the market, challenging many of the marketing channels developed by Score Board.

The success of both companies in marketing autographed sports memorabilia will depend on their ability to control marketing channels, procure licensing, and expand product offerings by signing exclusive contracts with top athletes.

It is through these marketing channels that you, the collector, will initially purchase one of these companies' fine products. Both companies, as dominant factors in this hobby, will have a significant impact on its growth and direction. Nowhere is this better illustrated than by picking up a copy of *Business Week's* Annual "List of the 100 Best Companies," which undoubtedly will include Score Board for its fourth consecutive year.

One of the biggest concerns to the average sports autograph collector is players who sign exclusive agreements with one of these firms; this impacts the signature's value and its supply. This exclusivity, however, benefits the collector because a player's signature may now only be a phone call away, but it does so at an expense that is often significantly higher than market value or beyond an average collector's budget. Yet another advantage of exclusivity is that it has provided collectors with many new and creative limited-edition collectibles.

Score Board's personal service contracts with approximately 50 current and former professional athletes and entertainers allow the company to purchase autographs on a per signature basis. In some cases, personal appearances are also required. But these arrangements do not come without a significant cost. For the fiscal year ending January 31, 1994, the company had commitments in future payments under these contracts in the amount of $8.6 million.

Exclusivity can benefit the collector in other, often unexpected ways. As previously stated, exclusivity involves a contractual length and an associated amount of signatures. If, for example, a company using this method loses a significant distribution channel - a shopping network or national retailer - to one of its competitors, it does not release the company from its contractual obligations with the athletes.

Thus, the company is forced to expand inventory levels, which is an unpopular concept among owners and stock holders, because unsold goods do not pay bills or dividends. If new sales outlets are not found, the company may be forced to liquidate the items at dramatically reduced prices, prices which may be more conducive to an average collector's budget.

Remember, however, that an exclusive player contract does not mean that if you approach Troy Aikman for an autograph in an airport that he must refuse the request. It also does not mean that a player must stop making public appearances or stop signing autograph requests made through the mail. It is merely a marketing method used by corporations to guarantee inventories and decrease competitive product offerings.

The growth in sales of autographed sports memorabilia has led to increased competition; with each passing year new companies are entering the market. During the next few years, the collectors should benefit from this increased growth.

Today's sports autograph collector is considerably smarter than his predecessors and is a lot better organized. He is less likely to make foolish purchases and is more creative and committed to his autograph pursuits. The collector realizes that a player such as Wayne Gretzky, who is entering his 15th NHL season, is still only 33 years old, and thus may be facing another five years worth of autograph requests.

More knowledgeable of his trade, today's collector realizes the acquisition options available and the associated costs. If a dealer is selling an autographed Jose Canseco baseball for $40, today's collector is better equipped to make a reasonable judgment of the item's true value and its future appreciation, from both a sentimental and financial perspective.

Every autographed sports memorabilia collector has an acquisition strategy that is unique to his or her needs. This book's goal is to enhance that strategy, whether it be by enlightening you with alternative acquisition methods or by educating you on factors which continue to impact the hobby.

By definition, a handbook is a compact reference manual; to be a good reference source it should be specific. I have tried to be specific where and when I could, but there are a few things that were omitted intentionally to preserve the book's integrity, such as players' home addresses.

I have several friends who are professional athletes. I believe that their public lives end when they enter their own environments. An athlete's home is his domain, not ours. However, when the season has started, and the athlete or entertainer is collecting a paycheck as a result of a public performance, then he or she is fair game to autograph seekers, as long as the approach is courteous and professional.

Publishing a handbook of this nature exposes it to possible misuse. To do so would be a tremendous injustice to the athlete, other collectors and to the hobby. Please keep this paramount in your mind, and try to be conspicuous and subtle with your autograph requests.

Unlike other sport autograph books, I have not plastered my name throughout the text and have even spared you from pictures of myself with other athletes. Like in any book, pages are precious and for your benefit, not mine. I sincerely hope you find this book extremely helpful and I welcome your insights and suggestions for ways of improving it.

There are instances in this book where I have been critical of certain professional athletes, teams and corporations. But I have not done so with just provocation. The criticism is aimed only at improving the hobby for all of its participants.

I would like to thank every professional and amateur athlete who takes time out of his busy schedule to sign an autograph. Yes, there will always be opportunists who are driven by financial reward. But please remember that for every one of them, there are two children who are awaiting your response with anticipation and sincere adoration.

During this project, I was lucky enough to be treated with a note from a player who I have always respected. I don't know him personally, but after this note, wish I did. There is a lot of truth in his words:

"For the player, signing autographs is a very real way to 'bond' with the public. There is a connection between player and fan, often denied in these times of terrorism regarding the professional ball player. I enjoy it." - Earnest Byner, Washington Redskins

Thanks, E.B.

Mark Allen Baker
P.O. Box 2492
Liverpool, N.Y. 13089

Foreword

Photo courtesy the National Baseball Library, Cooperstown, N.Y.

Ford Frick speaks during the 1939 Baseball Hall of Fame Induction Ceremony.

It is this moment that I cherish most, among the many sports autograph experiences I have had.

We can't explain the instinctive nature of man to be drawn by certain elements or environments; we can only speak to its existence. Perhaps it is a lost soul inside of us, crying in a voice that we do not understand. It is the magnetism of the soul that drives a man to be who and what he is, and it is this environment that tests his fortitude and his commitment to that task on a daily basis. Fortunately, there are rare occasions when a man's soul is complemented by his environment, resulting in a wealth of creativity, symbolism and even a glimpse of immortality.

For some of us such a place exists, nestled in between fertile hillsides so dense that the eye is given no reprieve from its vastness. Even the mirror-like surface of a lake, so divinely placed, echoes a constant hue of unbroken verdure. Supplementing this allegory of botanical majesty is the haunting stillness of the water, so solemn and at peace with itself.

It was the Iroquois Indian who first saluted this splendor by making it a gathering place and later a trading post. In its name Otsego, which means "place of the meeting," the lake was a forebearer of its future. Two centuries later, we are still drawn by its magnetism, gathering to trade stories and cards instead of food and furs.

Cooperstown, located 200 miles northeast of New York City in the central-eastern part of the Empire State, rests nine miles south from the tip of Lake Otsego. From here we can witness two births, the first of which is our national pastime - baseball. The second is of a great river, the Susquehanna, which, if you follow, leads to Oriole Park at Camden Yards, the closest active professional ballpark to our nation's capitol.

The Abner Graves family presented this baseball to the Hall of Fame.

It is from these hills, so timelessly recreated in the leather stocking tales of James Fennimore Cooper, that we are drawn not by the adventures of Natty Bumpo or the passions of Uncas and Chingachgook, but by the exploits of Ruth, Gehrig and DiMaggio. A half a century ago, in the morning sun of a mid-June day in 1939, a rural town awoke in a fashion that would become an annual ritual, to a rhythmic chatter roaring through the surrounding hillsides of the Susquehanna Valley.

Along the overgrown rusted rails of a former arm of the Delaware and Hudson railway traveled a passenger train. Although no cargo had passed over these rails in seven years, today steel wheels would leave an indelible etch upon its path.

Inside the train was virtually every great name the game had seen during its first decade, and the entourages of worshipers they attracted. From points all over this great land they assembled to make the pilgrimage in celebration of the game's centennial.

It was, as if planned, a beautiful upstate morning in July in 1989, and as the dew began to fade from the hood of my car, I, too, began my pilgrimage. Winding along the rural roads of Route 20, I estimated my arrival time in Cooperstown at just before 8 a.m.

Although I had made the journey countless times before, my anticipation had never been greater. For it had now been 50 years and 11 days since that train rolled across the beautiful countryside of upstate New York.

The significance of the event was paramount in the minds of all those who planned to attend. With each passing mile, a memory of a previous induction was resurrected, the joy of that moment once again saluted with a smile.

Characteristic of induction weekend is the increased traffic, if such a term exists in Richfield Springs. The augmentation in motor vehicles is first evident at the typically quiet intersection of Routes 20 East and 28 South.

On that Sunday morning, as I turned right onto one of the two main arteries feeding the village from the north, it was difficult to believe that there was actually more than one car at that intersection headed in the same direction. The morning sunshine sifted through the dense forest crowding the many spring-fed lakes, creating shadows that danced across the road. As if to a Vivaldi concerto, each corner's adagio-presto-adagio shadow sequencing only added to my apprehensiveness. The symphony came to a conclusion as I drifted down my final hill and into the village.

When you pass by Doubleday Field, you're getting close to the Hall of Fame.

At the bottom of the hill, leading into the village, the congestion became immediately evident. Cars had already begun parking along the village's secondary roads. In true capitalistic spirit, many opportune residents had already filled their driveways with vehicles at $5 per space. As a seasoned veteran, I read the signs, anticipated the play and immediately proceeded down Susquehanna Street, which rests parallel to the outfield fence of Doubleday Field. Overcome by the anticipation, I, too, relinquished my hopes of finding a free parking space, resorting instead to the now mobilized community parking garage.

With my leather bag at my side, filled with the standard reporter rations - three cameras, a handful of pens, assorted note pads, a bottle of extra strength Tylenol caplets, saline solution and enough film to photograph Mario Andretti on every lap at the brickyard - I double-timed it to the Hall of Fame's executive offices to pick up my media credentials. Within a few blocks from the museum, I could already hear the crowds staking plots on the beautiful grounds of Cooper Park, a whisper's distance from the headstone of James Fennimore Cooper. With my credentials in order, it was off to the grounds of the Otesaga hotel.

The class of 1939, clockwise, from top left: Wagner, Alexander, Speaker, Lajoie, Sisler, Johnson, Young, Mack, Ruth and Collins.

As I walked along the quaint tree-shaded sidewalks, I came to the same corner where, on Induction Day in 1939, Grover Cleveland Alexander enlightened a few players and fans with tales of his pitching prowess. "I threw my fast ball with a twist that rolled the ball off the inside of my middle finger," he professed. "Sort of a screwball. But when I reached spring training, my finger was tender and a blister always formed. I'd have to take it easy until the blister broke," the tall pitcher said as he looked down at an aging, freckled right hand.

"The team always went out for a beer celebration. It meant that Old Pete was ready to start throwin' 'em hard."

The majestic grounds of the Otesaga were already bustling with activity. Cars lined up along the long driveway to deliver the hotel's next guest. The lobby was filled baseball luminaries and dignitaries gathered in small groups, most awaiting escort into the hotel's dining room for breakfast. Wives and guests roamed the spacious hallways, captivated by the ambiance of the setting.

As I passed the center of the lobby, I stopped to remove my video recorder from my bag. My first glimpse of an inductee was Harmon Killebrew, who was signing a stack of Hall of Fame plaque postcards two inches thick on one side of a round oak table with an elaborate centerpiece that is centrally located in the hotel's lobby. A woman wearing a yellow blazer asked Killebrew what the gentleman was going to do with all those autographs. In a simple reply, "The Killer" said, "He's going to sell them."

I left the congested lobby and went out a back door to the porch. Despite having been all over Europe and the United States, I still believe that on a clear day the panoramic view from this porch is one of the most beautiful to be found anywhere. A large, blue-striped tent, erected to protect the players during the numerous scheduled autograph sessions, dominated the grounds of this Monticello-like setting. Just beyond the tent I spotted Charlie Gehringer, who was being interviewed by a reporter.

Just a half a century ago Casey Stengel came upon Eddie Collins, Napoleon Lajoie, Billy Herman and Gehringer huddled together. Casey turned to a nearby reporter and said, "Since when did you see four second basemen as good as those fellows collected in one spot?"

Gehringer, who I think cherished his elite membership more than any other inductee, on this day was a congruent link to our past. The "Mechanical Man" loved the serene village of Cooperstown, the game of baseball and its fans. He was noticeably apprehensive with some thoughts, but extraordinarily open with others.

"I hated everyone that wasn't on my side, especially the Yankees," he said. "Everyone wanted to beat them and we nosed 'em off a few times."

Photo courtesy the National Baseball Library, Cooperstown, N.Y.

Commissioner Bart Giamatti with a member of the class of 1989, Carl Yastrzemski.

Because he'd been inducted in 1949, there were no new questions, no new ways to regurgitate old answers from Gehringer. There was certainly little new ground to cover on the topic of baseball. But the Michigan gentleman remained patient through the entire interrogation and cordial to the interviewer.

As Gehringer stepped aside, I noticed Bob Feller sitting on one of the benches that adorns the hill overlooking the lake. It was from a similar spot, 50 years ago, that then-Giants manager Bill Terry, casting stones along the still shimmering surface of the lagoon, turned to a reporter and said, "This is the most pleasant day I've ever experienced." Ironically, he would have another pleasant day in 1954, when he took his place among the immortals.

Before I could reach "Rapid Robert" Feller, he had already started another interview. Feller's delivery was fast and furious, an auspicious and unfailing characteristic, as he expounded the virtues of his last few years.

"I retired in '56, won a few, lost a few, had a little fun, made a few friends, made a couple dollars," he said, immediately footnoting it with "Nothing like it is today, but I have no complaints. We won the war, I participated in it. I'm no hero; the heroes didn't come back." He recited this line, which some would have viewed as a trite expression, with the dignity and honor that only a veteran could possess.

The four years he spent in the Navy prevented him from winning 300 games. You could sense by his expression there was still some resentment. "I gave exercise to the crew," aboard the battleship Alabama, "twice a day and it kept me in shape. When I returned to the Indians in late August of 1945, why I was in good shape. My best year was in 1946."

Feller proved his point; he fanned 348 in 1946. I guess in retrospect one hero did make it back.

Each player slowly took his appropriate position, his name methodically and strategically placed on the back of his chair, underneath the Barnumesque tent. The mass of fans was split into three lines; each collector, with the batting order apparent, headed toward the lineup of players he wished to face. As the contest began, it was not the crisp, clear sound of the crack of a bat that was heard, but rather the thud of an autographed baseball being placed on a table.

No longer a captivating surrounding, I headed toward the lobby, where I found Marge Schott, Harry Caray, Bill White and "Yaz." As I eyed the now graying figure in his white shirt, with its red collar and blue horizontal stripes, my entire childhood passed before my eyes. I remembered living in Virginia Beach, Va., during the late 1960s, listening to my friend Paul Meyer exclaim his reverence for Carl Yastrzemski. At a time in my adolescence when friends meant more than baseball, I politely listened to Paul's praise, but could not share in his adoration; I was a devote Yankee fan.

I was also too embarrassed to admit that I struggled with the spelling of the slugger's name. As such, I sought logical comfort in the names of Ford, Howard, Mantle and Maris. Here, now, in front of me, was "Yaz." I didn't ask him for his autograph; my Yankee pride just ran too deep.

Following the autograph session, I headed back to the tent area, hoping to catch someone for an interview. I did - Stan Musial. "The Man," with seven batting titles to his credit, always reminded me of Gene Kelly, primarily because of his facial features. It was true that Musial had played in the rain, and Kelly once sang in it, but both were graceful, agile and the best at what they did. Neither were long-ball hitters, but both knew how to get the job done and were invariable performers.

Musial had all the stock baseball answers, so when I asked him what he thought about Red Schoendienst's induction he said, "Well, Red never got too high, or too excited, or too low. He always kept an even keel, and as players we appreciated it."

As a writer, this type of nondescript answer always irritated me, but I realized it was part of baseball, accepted it, and never let the frustration show during the interview.

When the Musial interlude concluded, I wandered over to where Ted Williams had been stopped by some Boston reporters.

When Williams was asked about Yastrzemski, he responded, "I had been hearing about him for a couple of years...I could see an intensity in him from the beginning. He impressed me with his keyed up determination...I saw his whole career, and still think he could have been better. But all and all he was a great player."

Hall of Famer Ted Williams attended Carl Yastrzemski's induction ceremony.

Only Ted Williams could look at a balanced player like Carl Yastrzemski and say in a voice that bears a stark resemblance to that of John Wayne, "I still think he could have been better."

The dedication ceremonies in 1939 were held across the street from the post office, where a large platform had been erected directly in front of the museum's door. Some 15,000 spectators flooded main street that day and crowded toward the red, white and blue draped platform. Photographers lined the row in front of the stage, some even atop ladders.

With a flashbulb salute, Charles J. Doyle, president of the Baseball Writers Association of America, stepped to the podium. The large microphones before him echoed his memorable words, "Today in Cooperstown, New York, home of baseball, we gather in reverence to the game's immortals - living and dead. This is the centennial of baseball."

Perhaps it was the humble Eddie Collins who summed up the meaning of Induction Day when he said, "Standing up here today on the same platform with these men, I had the biggest thrill in my life. Why, I'd have been happy as bat boy for this crowd."

The induction ceremonies, on this day fifty years later, occurred in Cooper Park, where a similar platform had been erected directly in front of the library's doors. The spectators still crowded the platform, the photographers still congregated in front of the stage and the words once again echoed through the hillside. The crowd erupted as the master of ceremony, George Grande, walked to the podium and said, "Welcome to the 1989 Hall of Fame induction ceremony. I hope your hands are ready and lungs are ready, because we've got some great people to honor today."

The induction ceremony belongs to the inductees; the weekend belongs to the fan. Ironically, the ceremony is the only part of the weekend that is rehearsed, saluting a game that is not.

After the ceremony, I returned to the hotel to meet with Hall of Famer Joe Sewell. As a player, he was a durable infielder who finished his career with a .312 batting average. During his 14 seasons with the Indians and Yankees, Sewell, known for his outstanding bat control, struck out only 113 times. If you combined the 1925, 1929 and 1932 seasons, his statistics include 1,689 at bats, with only 12 strikeouts.

I intended to thank Sewell for writing the foreword for one of my other books. We had corresponded by mail, but had never been properly introduced. Meeting him in person, discussing his career, and even his acknowledgment of my work, was indeed a precious and very gratifying moment. We talked in the Otesaga lobby about the 1932 Yankees, what it was like for him to room with Lou Gehrig, and the status of the game today.

I still remember him looking straight into my eyes, saying, "You know Mark, most of the baseball fans today have never seen a great ballplayer, because there are not many."

Twenty minutes into our conversation we took a short break; Sewell had to prepare for the annual photograph of all the returning inductees. He said we could continue our conversation by the lake where the picture was being taken. I walked on to the porch, passed Robin Roberts sitting in one of the rocking chairs, and headed down the stairs to one of the seats facing the lake.

Commissioner Bart Giamatti and Willie Stargell spoke during the 1989 ceremonies.

As I waited by the lake, I saw Commissioner Bart Giamatti walking toward me, so I got up and met him. I had a tremendous admiration for this man, not only for his love of the game, but for his depth of observation in the areas of literature and philosophy. As a scholar and philosopher, he brought to baseball a staunch sense of fundamental values, values he was being so highly criticized for, particularly when the subject turned to Peter Edward Rose.

I knew about the allegations facing the great hitter. I had even called Giamatti's office to inform him that Paul Janszen, from whom I had purchased autographed Pete Rose memorabilia, was still actively selling it through an assumed name in some hobby periodicals.

As I approached Giamatti, his tired eyes hidden behind a pair of sun glasses, Rose as a topic wasn't even a consideration. "Well, Commissioner, I guess you couldn't have picked a finer day for an induction ceremony," I said.

"I guess not," he responded. For a brief time we stood in silence, staring out across the horizon. I then asked, "Do you still love the game?" He paused briefly, and said, "Yes, there are still plenty of ways to love this game. Besides," he said as he lifted his hands upward in an almost spiritual way, "how could I possibly miss all of this?"

I then spotted Joe Sewell walking toward me, so I excused myself from the commissioner to

Joe Sewell and Bobby Doerr discuss Sewell's strikeout figures.

greet Joe.

The tranquility, especially now that the induction was over, took hold of the village, sweeping the grounds of the Otesaga. I was seated to Sewell's right on a bench by the lake. Bobby Doerr walked over and sat on the opposite side.

"Those numbers are just amazing," Doerr said, referring to Sewell's strikeout figures. "You know what? I watch a lot of television, and sit and watch those ballplayers swing and miss balls by six or eight inches," said Sewell. "If they can't hit that, they can't hit nothing."

Doerr then called over to Giamatti, "Hey Bart, what do you think about a guy striking out three times a year? I thought I read where it was 12..."

Giamatti, with a gruff laugh, answered, "That was putting three or four of them together."

"He even said one guy struck him out twice," said Doerr. "Who was that?" Giamatti asked.

"Pat Caraway, and he couldn't have thrown a ball as hard as you could," Sewell replied. With that comment, all of us broke out laughing.

As the Hall of Famers assembled for their photograph, I knew my time was ending, so I thanked Joe once more and walked away.

It was ironic. Bobby Doerr was Giamatti's hero. He even once said, "I wanted to be Bobby Doerr." My hero, at the time, was Joe Sewell.

When Giamatti had been asked why Doerr, and not Williams, his response was, "I could imagine myself playing second base, but not hitting .400. Children imagine, adults fantasize."

There does indeed come a time, in baseball, where the qualities of a man's heart and mind transcend the game itself. It is these men who should be cherished.

As I drove out of the village that day, I knew something very special had been given to me. *

* A few months later, in March of 1990, I received a phone call from Susan Sewell, who was the wife of Joe's son Jimmy. She told me Joe had passed away.

* A. Barlett Giamatti died Sept. 9, 1989.

Chapter 1

Why We Collect

Remember when the only responsibility you had was for yourself?

What possesses someone to seek the simple pleasures of life is a far greater task to determine than the evolution of any game or sport. Perhaps, as some believe, we seek them because they evoke childhood memories; so much of what we enjoy later in life is what we recall about ourselves at our earliest.

It is those memories, faded by the passing of time, that come from deep within our hearts. They are memories not only of our childhood or of a specific game, but of an era where the only responsibility we had was for ourselves.

Photo courtesy the National Baseball Library, Cooperstown, N.Y.

Who but Jackie Robinson really knew what challenges he faced?

As our entire life lay ahead of us, today's memories were unbounded hopes then. The memories came from a belief, possibly planted firmly within us by our parents, that the best was yet to come. Ironically, as we grow older with the passing of every new season, we finally realize just how close we came to realizing those dreams.

Much of what we remember was secured by the birth of a new season, and the passing of another. When we finally accepted the fact that it just wasn't going to be the Yankees in the World Series this year, we could mourn in the soft chill of an early autumn breeze, shifting our sense of optimism to the Giants.

We all, sometime, have wondered what it would be like, just for one second, to stand in the shoes of a Ted Williams, Julius Erving, Gordie Howe or Walter Payton. It is not that we wanted to be better. Rather, it was to simply say that we had played, and performed to the best of our god-given ability. To recall our best hopes is to relive them, with each new game of each new season, even long after the playing is over.

We collect to preserve a moment, to remind us that it is the human spirit, and the willingness to succeed despite all adversity, that guides us throughout our lives. Our artifacts speak without words, as no words could define them. After all, who can accurately describe the challenges faced by a Jackie Robinson or a Lou Gehrig?

Each artifact becomes a reflection of its time. Although we can't stop its deterioration, we can try to preserve its relevance. Through it we share an association with the subject - it is for our benefit. As we stare at our autographed Gale Sayers football, we remember gathering around our black-and-white television set, watching the Sunday afternoon broadcast live from Soldier Field. It's an anomaly that any man could run with the style and grace exhibited by Sayers on those frigid winter days in Chicago. Through an autographed football we are assured that those vivid memories will never end, forever evoked by a glance to the shelf where it remains transfixed in time.

Through collecting autographed sports collectibles we share in the triumphs of our subjects - it becomes success through association. It is indeed human nature to want to share in the success and happiness of others. It becomes even easier when it revolves around a professional athlete because they are so revered and accessible to the public.

It is the smart collector who remembers that the athlete, too, is only human, and that he or she should command the same level of respect as our friends and family. And it is as a smart collector that you will realize your own accomplishments are equally as rewarding, and, although they often go unrecognized, are equally as significant.

Chapter 2

What to Collect

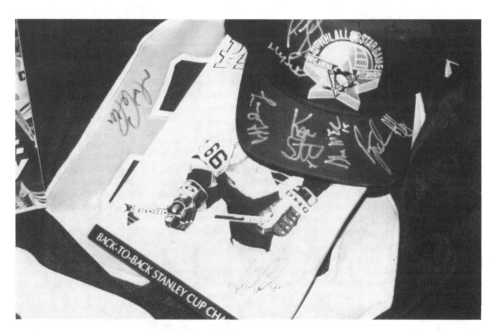

Many collectors concentrate on one team or player.

The creativity in autograph collecting begins here. What should you collect? As an autograph collector, anything that can be signed is available for your use. Most collectors build their collections around a specific individual, team, sport or type of item that is to be autographed.

For example, one collector I know collects items autographed by Mario Lemieux - from Sports Illustrated covers to golf balls. If it can be signed by the Pittsburgh Penguin captain, he wants it. Another person I know collects only autographed bats. He doesn't limit himself to a specific occupational field; his collection includes such notables as Wayne Gretzky (hockey), President Bill Clinton (politician), Stephen King (writer), John Glenn (astronaut) and Kevin Costner (actor).

Most sports autograph collectors, however, concentrate on one sport, specializing in one particular type of collectible, such as equipment, 8x10 color photographs or trading cards.

Set a goal for yourself

A friend of mine used to say, "if you don't know where you are going, any road will take you there." Well, the same adage can be applied to collecting sports autographs. If you're just doing it for fun, and are not concerned about any element of the hobby, then what to collect is irrelevant. Just enjoy yourself.

But the fact that you are reading this book indicates that, in addition to having fun, you also want to learn more about collecting sports autographs. The first step in becoming a serious collector is to set a realistic goal for yourself in collecting. Doing this will preserve your enjoyment of the hobby. The word "realistic" is paramount here. For example:

Collector A

Collects only autographed, official, NFL game-worn jerseys of the sport's greatest stars. His collection includes:

- A 1986 Dan Marino, Miami Dolphins #13, white mesh autographed jersey. Cost: $1,500; purchased from a dealer.
- A 1992 Jerry Rice, San Francisco 49ers #80, white with red trim autographed jersey. Cost: $1,400; purchased from a dealer.
- A 1993 Howie Long, Los Angeles Raiders #75, autographed black jersey. Cost: $995; purchased from a dealer.

Collector B

Collects only 8x10 autographed color photos of NFL players. His collection includes:

- Andre Reed, Buffalo Bills #83 - acquired in person while the player was doing a promotion at a local shopping mall. The photo cost $3. Reed did not charge for his signature.
- Raghib Ismail, in his Notre Dame uniform. Cost: $9.99; acquired from a dealer.
- Jim Brown, in his Syracuse University uniform - acquired in person at a local book store while Brown was promoting his book "Out of Bounds." The photo cost $3. Brown did not charge for his signature.

Both collectors have a goal for collecting sports autographs, which determines the following issues: availability, cost, acquisition or purchasing time, acquisition or purchasing method, and storage requirements. Both are dedicated collectors having fun and are equally concerned about their collections. Using this example, it is very easy to see the advantages and disadvantages each collector faces while pursuing his collecting goal.

Collector "A" is vice president of a bank where he spends more than 40 hours a week. Because collects only "game-worn" (actually worn in a real game) autographed football jerseys, he is extremely restricted by availability.

Some professional football players only wear four jerseys during a single season. Authenticating them is extremely difficult. Also, since he has budgeted himself to spend only $500 a month on collecting, he seldom adds more than five pieces annually to his collection.

Because he can't afford to spend a lot of time on collecting, he buys all of his jerseys through reputable dealers, but has never seen any jersey in his collection autographed in person. He loves football, enjoys collecting and believes that he is preserving and building a very valuable collection. His collection is stored in a large safe-deposit box at the bank for $65 each year.

Collector "B" is a junior in high school. Because he collects 8x10 autographed color photographs, he is not restricted in supply or availability. He purchases about four photographs each week for $3 each. He then mails them, along with an autograph request and a return self-addressed stamped envelope, to the player's team, hoping for a response.

He has been fairly successful at acquiring sports signatures this way, but also takes advantage of every opportunity to have a photograph autographed in person. Because he has a part-time job, his finances are limited. He does, however, have plenty of free time and doesn't mind waiting in line for an hour for a free signature. Meeting a player is part of the hobby he enjoys most; an autographed photo is a way for him to preserve that moment.

Collector "B" loves football and enjoys collecting autographs. He keeps all of his photographs preserved in individual polypropylene sheets in a binder on a shelf in his room. Each sheet costs 10 cents; he paid $6 for the binder.

By setting an autograph collecting goal, you are determining the parameters by which you will collect. The best goal is one which has definable limits, therefore making it easier for the collector to track his progress, yet exciting enough to pursue. Below is a list of collecting goals given to me by a group of sports autograph collectors.

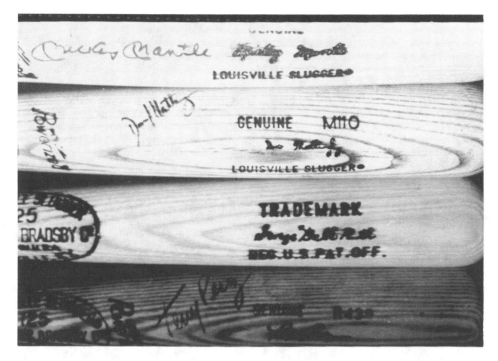

Set a goal and stick to it; you can track your progress easier.

Collecting goals

- A single-signed "official league" baseball signed by every living member of the National Baseball Hall of Fame.

- A single-signed football of every Super Bowl MVP.

- An autographed complete set of Topps 1993-94 basketball cards.

- A 1992-93 Pittsburgh Penguins hockey stick signed by the entire team.

Availability

Building a collection of single-signed "official league" baseballs from every living member of the National Baseball Hall of Fame is a realistic pursuit. Official league baseballs manufactured by the Rawlings Sporting Good Co. are in plentiful supply. They are available to the average collector for about $6 each. Another factor in favor of this goal is that most of the inductees still attend and sign autographs at sports trading card shows, with signing fees in the $10-$20 range per ball.

Trying to find a single-signed baseball from the more reclusive inductees, such as Joe DiMaggio or Sandy Koufax, will provide a greater challenge. Limited availability, or supply, often means an increased demand, and thus a higher price tag. This is the case with an autographed single-signature baseball of Joe DiMaggio, which now commands around $350. Despite the price of certain autographed baseballs, the goal still remains realistic, as the supply is still considered plentiful.

This would not be the case with a collector who wants a single-signature baseball of every member of the National Baseball Hall of Fame. Not only is supply limited by the type of item signed, but some members, particularly the pioneers of the sport, rarely ever have their signatures offered for sale in the market in any form - Mickey Welch, Charles Radbourn, Sam Thompson, Tom McCarthy, Addie Joss, Pud Galvin, Buck Ewing and Ed Delahanty.

To restrict your goal by the type of item to be signed, in this case a single-signature baseball, would make this task nearly impossible for even the advanced collector.

Cost

Availability has a reciprocal effect on cost. Therefore, a collector's goal can immediately be dismissed and deemed "unrealistic" strictly due to cost. From the beginning, it is extremely important to understand how much money you can afford to spend. In addition to signatures, the money you allocate to the hobby will be used for postage, telephone calls, traveling expenses and purchasing everything from storage supplies to reference materials.

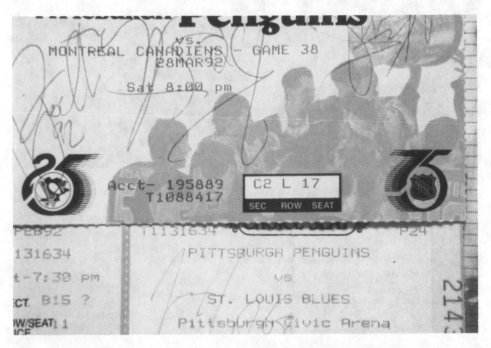

If you can't afford a Lemieux jersey, an autographed ticket will do.

The object you choose to have autographed may have the greatest impact on your costs. If you can't afford to collect autographed hockey jerseys, try sticks. If you can't afford sticks, try photographs.

Items autographed by Mario Lemieux

• Signature on piece of paper$9.00 *	• Sports Illustrated issue....$109.95
• Action-Packed postcard $34.95	• Sporting News cover $109.95
• Penguins logo golf ball........$34.95	• Authentic hockey stick ...$169.95
• 8x10 color photo $39.95	• Authentic helmet $229.95
• All-Star ticket $39.95	• Lithograph stick..............$349.95
• Official baseball $49.95	• Authentic jersey..............$369.95
• Baseball cap $49.95	• Official skates.................$895.00
• Framed crest and ticket $99.95	

Source: Penguins Authentic Memorabilia, collector's edition
* Not available in catalog

Acquisition time

Your goal determines how quickly you can add items to your collection. Collector "A" wants only "game-worn" autographed football jerseys. If he wanted a Walter Payton Chicago Bears jersey, it could take a considerable amount of time for such a jersey to enter the market. Due to its limited availability, Collector "A" can't just pick up the phone to purchase the jersey from a major dealer, even though he may have the money. Instead, he may have to wait years for a Payton jersey to surface in an advertisement or auction. During that same time period, Collector "B" may have added 100 new color 8x10 photographs to his collection.

Cost also has a major impact on acquisition time. Do you purchase an 8x10 autographed color photo of Jose Canseco from a major dealer for $23? Or do you wait outside the nearest American League ballpark where he is playing and hope to have your $3 picture signed? If you don't have $23 to spend and have the time to wait, the alternative is clear.

If money is not a factor, however, and you have chosen a common item to be autographed - such as a baseball, football, basketball or hockey stick - your acquisition is usually a simple phone call away.

Acquisition method

Collectors can add to their collections directly by in-person autograph requests, or indirectly through mail requests, trading or purchasing from dealers. Proximity is usually the factor that limits in-person requests. If you do not live in a town that supports one of the four major sports franchises, you usually have limited availability to most professional athletes.

You can always be sure of authenticity if you have the player sign in person.

Most collectors add to their collections through indirect sources. Depending upon the type of material you collect, certain methods may not be cost effective and may involve a high degree of risk. For example, if you collect authentic NFL football helmets manufactured by Riddell, you may not want to risk mailing your helmet to a player to have autographed; it may be lost or damaged. Instead, the alternative would be to purchase the helmets already autographed, or wait for an opportunity to have it signed in person.

The other risk associated with indirect sources is forgery. Unless a collector actually sees his item being signed, can he ever really be sure of its authenticity?

Expertise may also restrict a collector from purchasing various items. If you collect baseball signatures, but are unfamiliar with an authentic Lou Gehrig signature, you may want to have an expert purchase the autograph for you.

Storage requirements

Often overlooked in determining a collector's goal is storage requirements. Certain collectibles, such as paper-based products, must be stored properly to avoid environmental damage. This may require certain types of expensive storage materials. Other collectibles, such as football helmets and hockey sticks, are very cumbersome and difficult to store.

Living in an apartment or home with restricted space can quickly alter a collectors's goal. A collector I know once said, "if it doesn't fit in a safe-deposit box, I don't collect it." This collector's concern was obviously safety. The more valuable the item, the greater concern for its protection. Protection also comes with a cost; many safe-deposit box fees range from $50-$200 annually, depending upon size and availability.

Enjoyment

The reason for choosing a realistic goal for collecting sports autographs is to prolong your enjoyment of the hobby. Meeting your goal brings about a tremendous feeling of satisfaction and a sense of completeness. You will also find that the collectors who have chosen realistic goals have also assembled very cost-effective collections. Because these collectors have remained focused on the task at hand, they have wasted little time and money on unrelated material.

These baseballs have been signed by, clockwise, from top left: Johnny Unitas, Paul Kantner, Olga Korbut, Wayne Levi, Harry Caray and Joe Frazier.

Collectors without goals often accumulate haphazard, overpriced and unrelated collections.

Enjoy what you collect, and remember the gratification you receive from collecting sports autographs is in the pursuit of the task, not in its expense.

What Should They Sign?

SPORT	BASEBALL	BASKETBALL	HOCKEY	FOOTBALL
Equipment				
	baseball	basketball	puck	football
	bat	xxx	stick	xxx
	game jersey	game jersey	game jersey	game jersey
	practice jersey	practice jersey	practice jersey	practice jersey
	pants	trunks	pants	pants
	socks	socks	socks	socks
	cleats	sneakers	skates	cleats
	T-shirts	T-shirts	T-shirts	T-shirts
	cap	hat	hat	hat
	jacket	jacket/pants	jacket	jacket
	gloves *	xxx	gloves	gloves
	sweatbands	sweatbands	xxx	sweatbands
	xxx	headbands	xxx	headbands
	helmet	xxx	helmet	helmet
	------	------	------	------
	home plate	backboard/rim	hockey goal	down marker
	pitching rubber	xxx	xxx	goal post
	bases	xxx	xxx	xxx
	lineup card	xxx	xxx	xxx
	catcher's equipment **	xxx	goalie's equipment ***	
Paper based				
	index card	index card	index card	index card
	tickets	tickets	tickets	tickets
	schedules	schedules	schedules	schedules
	program	program	program	program
	yearbook	yearbook	yearbook	yearbook
	media guide	media guide	media guide	media guide
	trading cards	trading cards	trading cards	trading cards
	postcards	postcards	postcards	postcards
	magazines	magazines	magazines	magazines
	photographs	photographs	photographs	photographs
	artwork	artwork	artwork	artwork
	posters	posters	posters	posters
	newspapers	newspapers	newspapers	newspapers
	books	books	books	books
	advertisements	advertisements	advertisements	advertisements
	cachets/envelopes	cachets/envelopes	cachets/envelopes	cachets/envelopes
Other				
	pennants	pennants	pennants	pennants
	dolls/figurines	dolls/figurines	dolls/figurines	dolls/figurines
	assorted souvenirs	assorted souvenirs	assorted souvenirs	assorted souvenirs

Notes:

* = includes batting and fielding; ** includes chest protector, masks, shin guards; *** includes mask, shin guards, etc. Assorted souvenirs include plastic-based products such as cups, mugs, etc., and golf balls, banners, flags, ceramic plates, and anything that can be signed.

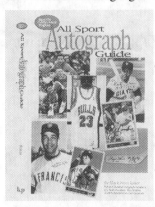

Chapter 3

The Autograph Collector's Language

Autograph collectors have developed their own language.

As a group, sports autograph collectors have evolved and have developed their own form of communication, a combination of the dialect of an autograph collector and a sports fan.

Today, abbreviations for conversations and advertising are commonly accepted in the hobby. While it is by no means as difficult as understanding ESPN broadcaster Dick Vitale, it will still take some understanding to realize that to us a "PTP Baby" means a porous tip pen.

The word autograph often refers to writing one's signature on or in something. To a sports autograph collector, what that signature is on or in is almost as important as the autograph itself. From George Brett autographed pine tar cans to Dave Schultz boxing gloves, the collector's imagination is his only limitation. Typically, the greater the significance of the subject matter or item, the more appealing it is to the collector.

The definitive sports autograph collector and many research professionals often describe their materials with colloquialisms indicative of a specific sport or era. The novice collector must therefore study not only the language of the autograph collector, but the terminology used and history of such sports as baseball, basketball, football and hockey. Here are a few sample advertisements that prove my point:

- For Sale: Turgeon, Titan TPM4020, sl. crack, auto., gm. used - best offer.
- For Sale: Ripken, H&B, K100 (Fungo), LS, auto., $35.
- For Sale: E. Smith, auto., Riddell replica helmet, n-guard facemask, large Sharpie sig., c. guard missing - $135.
- For Sale: "KJ" auto. official Spalding ball, send SASE for photo - $135.

It becomes clearly evident, especially to the novice collector, that some understanding of a sport, its players, its equipment and the hobby can facilitate his purchasing process. Therefore, official sports guides, equipment publications and hobby periodicals are always worthwhile acquisitions for sports autograph collectors.

Worth noting, and certainly adding to the confusion, is that many terms are not identically interpreted by collectors, especially regarding grading the condition of an autographed item. As a buyer or a seller, be sure that the language is clear and concise when defining or describing an item to be purchased over the phone or through the mail. This will avoid a lot of confusion and the associated costs of returned items.

Knowing certain handwriting terms can be helpful to collectors.

There are several terms that are haphazardly used in the hobby, without regard to the proper definition. For the novice collector's benefit, we will try to clarify some of them in this chapter.

Replica versus authentic

A replica item, be it a helmet, jersey or jacket, is a copy done by the maker of the original. It can be nearly identical in every way to that of the original, or it can have subtle differences. For example, a Riddell authentic game helmet, which can range in price from $130 to as high as $170, is not the same as a Riddell replica helmet, which is a lightweight reproduction that costs between $40 and $60. The price of these items alone should indicate a possible difference, which is most often the result of a material exchange.

Another example would be a Spalding official NBA synthetic ball. As a collector of sports autographs, you will be purchasing several types of sports equipment to have signed. Understanding the differences in this equipment is useful to preserve the value and appeal of the piece. A Spalding official NBA leather basketball, signed by Chris Mullin, has far more collecting appeal than a synthetic ball signed by the Golden State star.

Collecting potential refers to appeal as well as value. Most collectors prefer to have "official league" equipment signed. After all, when was the last time you saw Chris Mullin practicing with a synthetic ball?

Facsimile

A facsimile, a term often referred to regarding signatures, is an exact reproduction or copy. A facsimile autograph is not an authentic signature. They are typically printed on items, such as footballs, basketballs and baseballs, which often include facsimile signatures of an entire team. Thus, they are marketed as "official team balls" or "replica autographed balls." For example, the New York Yankees sell "Yankee Replica Autograph Baseballs," which bear facsimile signatures of club members, for $12.

Machine-signed or ink-stamped autographs, approaches used by some popular stars, are also considered facsimiles because they are exactly reproducing an original signature. "Ghost-signed" signatures, those autographs produced by someone other than the subject to intentionally deceive the recipient of the autographs, are considered forgeries.

A limited edition

Producing a restricted number of copies at one given time is a limited edition. For example, if during a one-hour autograph session you have John Elway autograph and number 500 photographs, printed at the same time from a negative you own, you have created a limited edition.

The term seems to have evolved from book collecting; there it means an edition published only in limited or preset numbers, usually before the first edition. In book collecting, however, after the printing the plates are broken up so no further copies are made regardless of demand. Also, limited editions in book collecting are often numbered in a series, sometimes signed by the author, binder, illustrator or someone affiliated with the project.

Collectors should understand that there is no established rule for the number of copies a limited edition may comprise. However, many collectors are less enthusiastic over a limited edition with a very large issue or printing.

This term still remains vague when it refers to limited-edition autographed sports collectibles. As a buyer, you should understand that there are no parameters assigned to its use. If John Elway returns to sign 500 more photographs, which were all created and signed at the same time, another limited edition, by definition, has been created.

Notice I said "another" limited edition, as there are no set rules for the way in which these editions may be released or distinguished. Why is it still defined as a limited edition? Because the number still remains restricted and the 500 photographs were created and signed at the same time.

Many of the limited-edition autographed sports items offered in the market today are either photographs or lithographs. A photograph is a picture made from photography, which is a process that involves exposing a surface sensitive to light or radiant energy to an image. A lithograph is made from lithography, which is an offset printing process in which an inked image is transferred from a plate onto a blanket cylinder and then onto paper.

Collectors of limited-edition autographed sports collectibles prefer issues that are identified, first by the copy number, followed by the production number (135/5,000). Proof that the original printing plates, or the original itself, were destroyed after the edition and guarantees that there will be no subsequent, or similar issues, are also reassuring to the collector.

Certificate or Letter of Authenticity

A "Certificate" or "Letter of Authenticity" is a document attesting to the fact that an item is genuine or real. That is it; there are no other guarantees unless they are clearly stated on the letter or the certificate. Some companies include a "Certificate of Authenticity" (COA), some do not. There is no mandated procedure for such a process.

Upper Deck Authenticated, a firm that sells autographed sports memorabilia, has a patent-pending authentication process. Each signature is witnessed and recorded. A numbered hologram is placed on each item and logged at Upper Deck Authenticated for further verification. The

Certificate of Authenticity

It is hereby certified
that the item of sports memorabilia
which accompanies this document
has been personally autographed by
Sandy Koufax
The item was signed under the direct supervision of.
and in witness thereto, The Score Board, Inc.

The autograph is
unconditionally guaranteed
as to its authenticity.

Paul Goldin

Paul Goldin, President
The Score Board, Inc., Cherry Hill, NJ

The Score Board, Inc.

Sports and Entertainment Marketing Specialists

A Certificate of Authenticity attests that a signature is genuine.

holograms, or mirrored surface stickers imprinted with a design that appears three-dimensional, can't be removed without damage or be reused.

Each signed item Upper Deck sells comes with a certificate of ownership that has a matching, numbered hologram corresponding to the number on the actual item. Each buyer can then register the item by phone or by mailing in a registration card.

To reiterate, the inclusion of such a document is not, as of yet, mandated by law or decisive proof that an item is genuine. There is obviously no substitute for knowledge, or for first-hand autograph acquisitions. Should an autograph prove to be a forgery, such a certificate or letter could be admitted to many a court of law as an exhibit, in hopes that it could be referred to as a means of deceiving the buyer.

Nevertheless, the efforts by companies such as Upper Deck and the Score Board Inc. to include such items should be applauded.

A chart which includes a brief listing of hobby equipment terminology has been included for your reference. It is important that you become familiar with the handwriting terms on this chart; they will be constantly referred to in Chapter 10 of this book. Price ranges have also been added to many of the equipment definitions to act as a cost guideline.

Sports Autographs Collector
Hobby and Equipment Terminology

Hobby

Uniform/jersey terms

Flag tag - any tag that is attached to a jersey on only one side.

Flannel - older style uniforms often made of wool, cotton or a blend of material. For example, in baseball this term usually refers to uniforms worn before the mid-1970s.

Knits - refers to modern doubleknit uniforms made most often of polyester-based fabrics.

A manufacturer's tag helps identify the company which made a jersey.

Manufacturers tag - a tag that is sewn or attached to the uniform that identifies that product as being manufactured by a specific company. Uniform and jersey manufacturers include Chapman, Russell, Wilson, Rawlings, CCM, Goodman and Sand-knit.

NIC - a player's name is sewn, or written into, the collar of a uniform or jersey.

NIT - a player's name is sewn, or written into, the tail or bottom of a uniform or jersey.

NOB - a player's name appears on the back of the uniform or jersey.

Paper-based terms

ALS - this is a letter or a document completely written in the hand of the celebrity.

Cachet - a special design, in honor of a person or an event, printed or drawn on an envelope.

Facsimile - an exact reproduction of a person's signature which is often photographed, printed or stamped on an item. Most of these items are paper-based.

F.D.C. - a First Day Cover, or an envelope, usually bearing a cachet with a stamp affixed and canceled on the first day it was available for public sale.

Sometimes a tag gives a player number and year the jersey was made.

Holograph - a writing sample in the hand of the subject.
Legal size - 8.5x14 standard paper size (U.S. Government 8x12.5).
Letter size - 8.5x11 standard paper size (U.S. Government 8x10.5).
Lot - a group of materials sold at one time.
LS/DS - most often a typed letter or document signed by the celebrity.
SIG - this usually refers to the actual signature itself on a card or album page, or possibly cut from a letter or a document.
SP - typically a color or a black-and-white signed photograph.
UV coated - a high-gloss finish applied to an item that protects it from environmental damage. The coating has limited adherence qualities, making it difficult to sign.

Handwriting terms

Arm - the part of a letter that extends even or upwards from its stem.
Ascender - the segment of a letter that extends above the main body or lowercase letter height.
Baseline - an often invisible line that a subject's signature seems to rest upon.
Character formation - the way in which the subject typically forms a letter, usually in conformance to known writing methods. Character formations often include loops which may be closed (touching strokes) or open.
Descender - the segment of a letter that extends below the baseline of a signature.
Height - refers to the distance above the signature's baseline. The two common forms of height are lowercase and upper case (capitalization).
Leg - the part of a letter that extends downward from its stem.
Provenance - the record of ownership of an item or collection.
SASE - a self-addressed, stamped envelope, often included with autograph requests.
Signature break - a common characteristic of most signatures, it refers to the space between where a stroke ends and another stroke begins.
Slant - the direction and degree to which signatures vary from perpendicular or 90-degree plane.
Stroke - the main ingredient of every signature, it begins at the point in which ink, or a similar substance, is applied to a surface and continues until the ink or substance is discontinued from application.

Equipment

Baseball

Batting helmets - actual game model helmets worn by the players are currently manufactured by ABC. Helmets are available with right or left ear flaps. (Price range: $40-$55).
Official league baseballs - these balls, manufactured by the Rawlings Sporting Goods Co. since 1977 (American League) or 1978 (National League), are used by Major League Baseball. The league president's

signature is stamped on the ball opposite of the sweet spot, where most collectors of single-signature baseballs prefer to have a player's autograph. (Price range: $5-$8).

Official league baseball bats - bats are manufactured in a variety of shapes and sizes. Most professional players order their own "model" bats precisely made to their specifications. The primary manufacturers of bats for Major League Baseball are Hillerich & Bradsby (Louisville Slugger), Rawlings (Big Stick), Worth (Tennessee Thumper), Cooper (Pro 100) and Mizuno. There are four characteristics of bats: authentic cracked or uncracked game-used bats; Mint or authentic non game-used bats; model or retail bats; and commemorative bats. Each classification has unique characteristics that identify the bat as such. (Price range: $12-$25).

Authentic Major League Baseball jerseys - these are uniforms currently being manufactured by Russell Athletic, although over the years they have been manufactured by a variety of companies.

Basketball

Spalding NBA - Spalding manufactures a leather game ball with the NBA logo stamped on it (Price range: $50-$70). The company also manufactures the same ball made of a synthetic material. (Price range: $30-$60).

Football

Authentic Wilson NFL jerseys - these are Wilson jerseys made from the same material and construction as used by each NFL team. (Price range: $80-$90).

NFL game football - same model used in all NFL games, "Wilson" logo in gold. (Price range: $50-$60).

"1001" college football - same model used in most college football games, with the "Wilson" logo in gold on one side and the "AFRCT" logo on the opposite side. (Price range: $53-$63).

Riddell helmets - Riddell manufactures the helmets worn in the NFL, WLAF and the Canadian Football League. Helmets are shipped with a specific team's logo and a facemask - most often the quarterback model. (Price range: $130-$170). Riddell also manufactures a variety of other helmets, including replica helmets, which are lightweight reproductions of official league helmets, and old style and logo throwback helmets, which are nostalgic reproductions of helmets worn in the early days of the NFL.

Super Bowl footballs - same as NFL game footballs, except the "Super Bowl" logo is on the side panel. Wilson has manufactured this football since Super Bowl XX. (Price range: $60-$95).

Hockey

Authentic CCM NHL jerseys - CCM currently manufactures the jerseys worn in the National Hockey League. For fans and collectors, the company offers a wide range of sizes and materials for replica jerseys. Collectors should be aware that authentic jerseys may be limited to certain sizes and teams. (Price range: $150-$180, includes customizing in most cases).

NHL official pucks - official NHL pucks, some include a team logo on top. (Price range: $4-$8).

NHL hockey helmets - hockey helmets are also manufactured in a variety of shapes, sizes and colors. Both Jofa and Cooper are popular helmet manufacturers. (Price range: $55-$65).

Official league hockey sticks - hockey sticks, like baseball bats, are manufactured in a variety of shapes and sizes. Many professional hockey players order custom-made or custom combination (shaft and blade) sticks. The primary manufacturers of sticks for the NHL are Easton, Louisville, Titan, Koho and Sherwood. There are also numerous blade manufacturers. (Price range: $50-$130, includes shaft and blade).

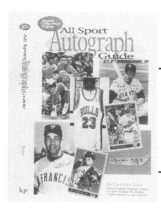

Chapter 4

The History
of Writing Instruments

The correct writing instrument makes a difference in autograph preservation.

Having a basic understanding of writing instruments and materials can enhance a collector's knowledge of authenticity, because writing can be dated. Choosing the correct writing instrument to use on a particular material can also help to preserve the piece. Both are critical elements of collecting and of paramount concern to the collector.

Similar to other inventions, writing instruments have developed in many stages. By understanding these evolutionary stages, you can determine what types of writing instruments were used by Red Grange, Albert Spalding, Eddie Shore or Bob Pettit. Although the Bible's Old Testament refers to the existence of ink, the reference point for most sports autograph collectors begins with the use of iron gall inks, used into the 20th century.

Historians typically divide writing instruments into four categories: quills, durable pens, reservoir pens and pencils. Since the problems with quills and their eventual solutions led to the development of metal pens by the 19th century, a discussion of their evolvement would be impertinent to the majority of sports autographs collectors.

Pencil, although a popular writing device since its "lead strip" discovery in 1564, has decreased in popularity. It is not often used by today's collectors. Limited adherence qualities and erasability limited pencil use for informal, non-permanent applications. Although ink was a bit more troublesome during its evolution, it was the favored and accepted medium.

The writing instruments of greatest interest to sports autographs collectors are durable and reservoir pens. The "steel pen," which was a durable pen, was fully accepted as a writing instrument by 1845, when the first acknowledged organized baseball club, the New York Knickerbockers, was formed by one of it members, future Hall of Famer Alexander J. Cartwright.

Durable pens

Steel, gold and glass pens are considered durable pens. The use of these began in the late 1700s, dominated the 1800s, and later gave way to the more practical reservoir pens. The durability of metal and glass logically replaced the quill, but still required an independent ink reservoir.

Steel pens

Only isolated references to metallic pens were made before the end of the 18th century. The steel pen, with its conflicting date of origin, was successfully reintroduced in England in 1780. It was best described as a sheet of steel rolled in the form of a cylinder, with one end cut and trimmed to a point (similar to the quill). The seam, where both edges met, formed the slit of the pen.

The first patent in England for metal pens was awarded in 1808 to Bryan Donkin. Machine-made pens were introduced in about 1822. A United States patent for a "metallic writing pen" was issued to Peregrine Williamson in 1809. Although the steel pen was commonplace by the mid-1840s, it wasn't until 1858, the year after Henry Chadwick invented the box score, that the first steel pen company was established in the United States by Richard Esterbrook Jr., a former pen salesman.

A steel pen can be readily discerned by examining strokes under magnifications. In contrast to its predecessor, the quill, a steel pen is distinguished by the presence of "nib tracks," which are the result of the pen's point (nib), a metal slit, separating under pressure on the downstroke and digging into the material it is touching. Nib choices naturally and predictably effect the line quality in writing.

Special types of steel pens produced distinctive line quality, due to the flow of the ink into the nib. For example, the "stub pen" produced a slightly outlined, yet uniform, stroke that became lighter as the ink neared its end inside the nib. The stub pen, although of limited use in the 1870s, grew in popularity and represented about one third of the total pen consumption entering the 1930s.

Gold pens

The "gold pen," which was a method of giving quills a metallic cast by dipping them into a solution of nitromuriate of gold, was patented in 1818 by Charles Watt. It was a natural evolution to the guiding of quills to increase durability. Although the gold was useful in resisting the corrosive tendencies of acidic ink, the points still lacked sufficient hardness and quickly broke.

Glass pens

Glass was one of the many materials experimented with in the making of pens - found as early as 1850. A United States patent of 1890 describes it as "a pen formed of a piece of round glass drawn out to a point and having grooves running spirally down the sloping sides and meeting at the point."

Many early glass pens were sold as "marking pens" for writing on fabric, and used indelible inks. Its ink permanence was a favorable factor for many applications, but the pen was never very plentiful and has been used in only isolated instances.

The demise of the durable pen was ironically attributed to its lack of extended durability. The problem was the frequent need to replenish the pen's ink source, requiring repeated dipping into the inkwell.

Reservoir pens

Dip pen writing, produced by durable pens, identifies itself with the words graduated in intensity, "from dark to light, to dark again." The "ink failure," which is also an identification characteristic, acted as the motivation for the development of reservoir pens. Fountain, ballpoint and porous tip pens are examples of writing instruments which use a reservoir ink system. These instruments, most still popular today, are the writing instruments of greatest concern to the sports autographs collector.

Fountain pens

Attempts to solve "ink failure" included a "solid ink" fountain pen, circa 1870s, that held a stick of concentrated ink which was dipped into water for writing. Fountain pen patents were profuse, being regularly advertised in periodicals by the late 1870s. During this time, "stylographic" pens also became popular. These pens had a plunger that was pushed back while writing, allowing ink to flow out. Stylographic pen writing is characterized by its thick strokes of uniform diameter. Interchangeable pen points allowed the user to vary the diameter of its strokes.

In 1864 Lewis E. Waterman marketed the first truly successful fountain pen. Witnessing Waterman's success, George S. Parker was enticed into establishing his own company in 1888. With several patents for improving ink feed design, Parker became the leading American fountain pen manufacturer by the end of the 1930s.

Ballpoint pens

The highly successful fountain pen, with its numerous variations in style, was eventually displaced in popularity in the late 1940s by the ballpoint pen. Although ballpoint pen patents can be traced as far back as 1888, it wasn't until 1935 that two Czechoslovakians, Frank Klimes and Paul Eisner, began producing a modern-style ballpoint. Two Hungarian brothers, Ladislao and George Biro, also developed a rotatable ball pen in 1938. The Eberhard Faber Co. eventually obtained rights to it. When the United States Army expressed interest in purchasing large quantities of the pen, Scheaffer outbid its competitors to share the American rights with Faber. The Biro pen became so popular that one American businessman sold almost 25,000 pens through just Gimbel's department store in New York City.

Early ballpoint pen writing is easily recognizable by its blotting and skipping. These characteristics were attributed to the ink, which was a dye solution in a base of oil, that, although smooth flowing, dried very slowly. Also worth noting is the fading of the ink when exposed to light. This characteristic is most noticeable with pens produced before 1954.

Most of the deficiencies in the ballpoint pen design were remedied by Parker's introduction of the "Jotter" in 1954. The Jotter, made entirely of stainless steel, wrote five times as long as its competitors and also offered a variety of point sizes.

Parker also introduced the "Liquid Lead Pencil" in 1955. This pen contained a liquid graphite solution that was erasable. Failing to gain acceptance, this pen was phased out of production in the 1960s. Ironically, the Paper Mate division of the Gillette Co. introduced the "Eraser Mate" pen in April 1979, capturing what was thought to be a non-existent portion of the market.

Porous tip pens

The ballpoint pen faced competition in the early 1940s when a "porous paint" pen was introduced. It was composed of fibrous materials that acted like a nib, while storing ink in a spongy material. By the early 1950s, these pens, known as "markers," included airtight leakproof stems that fed ink into a wedge-shaped wick. After some Japanese enhancements, the pen was reintroduced and popularized around 1964. Additional varieties of colored inks were subsequently introduced, but many of the inks were not permanent and faded badly after a few days' exposure to sunlight.

Sanford's "Sharpie," a highly water-resistant, permanent, large fiber tip market that writes on virtually every surface, found a home in the collectibles market in the mid-1970s. Although the marker was available in 1963 (black) and 1964 (blue), it did not gain popularity until nearly a decade later. This writing device soon became a hobby standard, due to its surface adherence qualities and ease of use.

Over the years, concerns about its deterioration characteristics surfaced among sports collectors, particularly when numerous official league autographed baseball examples, signed with the pen, began to bleed into the surface. Collectors migrated away from the Sharpie for use on highly porous surfaces, but solidified its presence in the collectibles market by using it for most other occasions.

A good, quality fine-tipped ink remains the best choice when autographing a baseball. Many collectors also began avoiding the marker because of its large strokes, which impair character definition. However, for all non-porous surfaces, especially when the item's characteristics are ideal for a large signature, the Sharpie remains a practical solution.

Several types of pens and ink were introduced during the last 15 years, from gold and silver markers, to "hot" colored pens and metallic inks. For many of these materials, it is far too early to determine what types of deterioration characteristics they will exhibit.

For collectors who are serious about preservation and safety, "material safety data sheets," or MSDSs, are available from every manufacturer. Each sheet describes the ink's ingredients and any potential safety hazards that may be exposed.

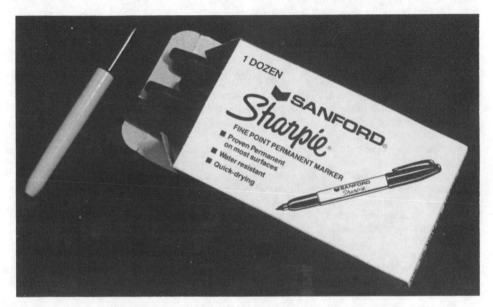

"Sharpie" markers are generally used on 8x10 photos.

Pen and ink identification

Pen and ink are just a few of the elements that a collector has at his disposal to help identify or authenticate an autographed item. Although more complex than simple dating methods, pen and ink identification can provide collectors with additional information.

Since writing instruments have evolved over time, pen identification is an obvious adjunct to dating. From steel and fountain pens, to the ballpoint and felt tip pens, each employs a distinctive stylographic variety. Using many common and inexpensive tools, collectors can carefully analyze signatures. Under magnification and with a good light source, beginning and ending strokes can immediately be associated with a particular writing instrument. A "Pen Identification" chart has been provided here to help simplify the task.

Ink also has a value in determining the age of writing. From iron gall ink varieties to nigrosine inks, each has specific properties that can be identified by a sample's reaction to chemical reagents. To determine if a document was prepared with different pens, an authenticator can study the chemical composition of the ink.

A typical nondestructive approach for ink comparisons uses a device called a microspectrophotometer. This device studies the amount of certain lights absorbed by the ink. Additionally, a method called thin-layer chromatography separates dyes that make up certain inks, such as those used in a ballpoint pen.

Many other advanced methods also exist that can remove a small amount of the ink from the writing surface for analysis. Many federal agencies have a complete library of commercial inks, and the unique dye patterns, or "ink fingerprints," they exhibit. From these patterns, a specific writing device can be determined and the ink can be identified by year.

Perhaps one day these advanced methods will be so simple and cost effective that the risk of acquiring a forged signature will be dramatically reduced.

Being able to identify an ink helps determine when something was signed.

Pen Identification Chart

Origin date	Writing device	Characteristics/Comments
Early 1950s	Porous tip pens	Porous material tips, in a variety of shapes and sizes. Relatively uniform line width, lack "nib tracks" or roller marks. Ending strokes often appear dry. "Sharpie" popular in mid-1970s, although available in late 1960s. Some permanent markers will evidence bleeding. Early felt-tip markers badly fade.
Mid-1940s	Ballpoint pen	Distinctive line appearance due to ink and ball combination. Produces line of even width. Early samples will exhibit blotting, skipping and fading. Recent pen varieties produce more free-flowing ink.
1884 *	Fountain pen	Continuous ink flow. Contrast between up-strokes and heavier downstrokes.
1870s	Stylographic pen	Continuous ink flow. Uniform width on up-strokes and downstrokes.
1858 **	Steel pen	Nib tracks evident, indentation may be possible. Dip pen writing characteristics. Stub pen; more shaded strokes, distinguishable on tops of rounded letters. Dip pen writing characteristics. Double line pen; dual line effect. Dip pen writing characteristics.

Notes:
** = Esterbrook, U.S. manufactured.
* = Waterman manufactured.

| Chapter 5 |

How To Acquire
Sports Autographs

A direct approach may yield you an autograph from Eric Davis.

Your goal in collecting sports autographs determines how you acquire items for your collection. For example, collectors who specialize in autographed team basketballs from NBA champions realize their task requires tremendous dedication and financing, especially compared to more general forms of collecting.

The dedication may mean spending hours outside of Chicago Stadium in hopes of adding a few key signatures to an incomplete team basketball, while the alternative is spending a few hundred dollars to purchase the completed item. Whatever method you choose, it should meet your collecting goal.

For most collectors, successful acquisition of sports autographs requires a combination of indirect and direct methods. There are seven major ways to acquire sports autographs:

* Direct method

1) In-person request.

* Indirect methods

2) Correspondence with the individual, usually by mail.
3) Acquiring through a friend, relative or team personnel.
4) Purchasing items from dealers, promoters, memorabilia outlets, catalogs, shopping networks, etc..
5) Purchasing at an auction.
6) Trading.
7) Autographed sports trading card inserts.

Baseball card shows provide opportunities for getting autographs.

In-person requests

Acquiring a signature in person is still the most preferred and enjoyable way to collect sports autographs. Not only does a collector get to meet a sports celebrity, he also receives a visual confirmation of the signature's authenticity.

Timing, or being in the right place at the right time, is usually the critical factor in successful acquisitions. But most collectors don't know where that place is or when to be there. Say, for example, you're taking a trip to Boston to watch the Bruins play the Nordiques.

You're staying at a hotel within walking distance of the Boston Garden, so you have plenty of time to pursue autographs. The first two questions you ask are:

Where, in or around the Boston Garden, should I go?

When should I arrive there?

These are difficult questions to answer, particularly if you are not familiar with the facility.

The biggest mistake a novice collector makes is thinking that the only chance for success is at the very beginning or ending of a game, where the event occurred.

Most successful collectors never even buy a ticket. Instead, they become totally familiar with daily routines of their subjects, so they can choose specific times and places for all their autograph requests. This may mean arriving at the rink four hours before the game to stand near the facility's player entrance. Or, it may mean stopping by a premier gourmet restaurant known to be frequented by certain players after the game.

It's ridiculous to wait for hours, pushing and shoving, at the ballpark for two signatures when you can get 10 times that amount in minutes somewhere else, at a different time.

Included as part of this chapter is a chart entitled "Sports Autograph Collector Team Fact Sheet." To be successful at acquiring autographs in person, you should prepare a familiar sheet for each of your local professional teams. With this sheet you can cost-effectively plan your autograph strategy.

Sports Autograph Collector Team Fact Sheet

Team: Syracuse Chiefs   **Address:** MacArthur Stadium
Syracuse, N.Y. 13208
(315) 474-7833

League: International League
Level: AAA

Affiliation: Toronto Blue Jays
Player Accommodations: Various local apartment complexes; families live together, most players room with teammates.

Primary Hotel of Visiting Team: Sheraton Inn, 7th N. Street, Liverpool, N.Y.
Phone: (315) 457-1122

Daily home schedule:

Noon-1 p.m.	Managers and coaches arrive at ballpark, locker and weight room available to players.
1-2:30 p.m.	Early player arrivals, most for early batting practice.
2:30-3:30 p.m.	Early batting practice, additional player arrivals.
3:30 p.m.	Practice begins.
7:00 p.m.	Game time.

Player Access: Excellent   **Player Entrance:** Accessible, unguarded.

Player Parking: Accessible, unguarded.

Player Appearances: Numerous - ballpark (picnic area), baseball card shows, car dealers, etc.

Designated Autograph Area at Ballpark: Yes.

Mail Response: Very good.

Stadium Notes: All club dignitaries, scouts, player relatives and friends sit in a box seat section directly behind home plate. The souvenir shop at stadium does not sell any autographed team memorabilia.

Primary Local Shopping Mall: Carousel Center - less than one mile from the ballpark.

Frequented Player & Coach Establishments:

* Bleachers - Sports Bar & Restaurant, 602 Old Liverpool Road, Liverpool, N.Y.
* Change of Pace - Sports Bar, 1802 Grant Blvd., Syracuse, N.Y.
* Liverpool Country Club - Public Golf Course, Morgan Road, Liverpool, N.Y.
* Club Chameleon - Night Club, Bear Street, Syracuse, N.Y.

Additional Notes: The baseball club does donate autographed and unautographed memorabilia, including game-used equipment, to certain local charities.

Eric Karros and Brett Butler take time to sign autographs for their fans.

Every serious collector should spend one afternoon outside the major sports facilities in their town or city, especially when there is a home game scheduled. The first two areas you should locate are the "Player Entrance" and "Player Parking Lot."

Public access to these areas, especially if they are unguarded, allows for direct player contact. Familiarize yourself with the player's car and when he usually arrives at the facility. If you know the home team's players' vehicles, you can determine who has already arrived and who has not.

The visiting team generally arrives to the facility by bus, van or taxi, about three hours before the game. Since most of the visiting team's players stay at the same hotel, they usually arrive at the park in groups, making it hectic for collectors to stop each player individually.

The best approach in this situation is to team up with three other collectors and predetermine which collector is going to stop which player. A group of four collectors, each stopping a different player, is particularly useful for players arriving in vans or cabs.

Inside the sports facility, familiarize yourself with areas that offer the greatest opportunity for direct player contact. Accessible areas between the clubhouse or locker room exit and the area of play usually provide the best autograph opportunities.

Monitor the accessibility to team bench or dugout areas. These areas are often guarded or have ushers who keep autograph seekers away. Sometimes, however, a player will begin signing near one area of the bench, causing autograph seekers to flood the seating aisles nearest that point.

This distraction usually leaves other aisles near the bench unguarded, providing a perfect opportunity to walk unnoticed to the front row of that section. It is the patient and subtle sports autograph seeker who is the most successful.

MacArthur Stadium in Syracuse has a specific area for autograph seekers.

When you finally find the right autographing position inside the sports facility, act like you belong there. Don't be conspicuous; instead, adapt to the crowd around you. If you're holding six hockey sticks and have three pairs of skates wrapped around your neck, you'll probably be treated like an autograph collector.

If you bring any items to be autographed, they should not be directly visible. Don't walk around the ballpark with four pens in your hand and a binder filled with trading cards.

It is not unusual for a player to make several appearances for local vendors or sponsors. If you know Reggie White is appearing at a local car dealership, make the effort to be there for a free autograph. If you are unaware of any local player appearances, consult your local newspaper, especially the ads in the sports section. Or, contact the team's public relations office for a detailed listing.

The most often overlooked in-person source for acquiring autographs is at local businesses, especially restaurants, night clubs and shopping malls. After a game, most players will join their family, friends or teammates for a nice dinner at a local restaurant.

It's not unusual for professional athletes to frequent local establishments with a sports theme. For example, after a Buffalo Bills home game, many players dine at the "Sports City Grill," owned by quarterback Jim Kelly.

Ironically, most fans don't recognize an athlete outside his element or without a uniform on. Because I have the luxury of owning a sports bar and restaurant, I have witnessed this anomaly several times. I remember talking to Blue Jay fans who had driven from Toronto to watch an exhibition game between the team and its Triple A affiliate, the Syracuse Chiefs.

After the game they stopped by my restaurant and indicated they collect autographed sports memorabilia. They showed me four autographed cards they fought to have signed at the ballpark.

What they didn't realize was that there were four players seated at the table next to them. I, like most owners of these types of establishments, respect a player's right to privacy and would never acknowledge his presence in the facility without his permission.

What I have seen, however, is that players are more than happy to autograph items for their fans, especially away from the ballpark, as long as the requests are made congenially and not while the player is in the middle of eating his meal. Nothing upsets a professional athlete more than having an autograph collector completely disrespect his right of privacy.

Where To Meet Professional Athletes

* **Shopping Malls** - The primary shopping mall in any city is always an excellent place to meet professional athletes. Always position yourself at the central point of the mall, never at a specific exit. If the mall has multiple floors, stay on the main level. During the season players will shop between 11 a.m. to 2 p.m. - if there is a night game scheduled. If a day game is scheduled, they will shop or possibly attend a movie after the game. Many malls include movie theaters.

* **Sports Bars or Restaurants** - A great place to meet professional athletes, primarily after the game. Choose the top two sports bars in any city or town, close to the facility, and you probably won't be disappointed with who is there. Players will normally arrive about one hour after the game.

You might find Yogi Berra, Al Kaline or Joe DiMaggio on the golf course.

* **Local Public Golf Course** - Most professional athletes love to play golf, especially on off days, when no game is scheduled. Position yourself outside the pro shop and be aware that golfers start on either the first or ninth hole, depending upon how crowded the course is.

* **Hotels** - A hotel lobby can be an excellent place for acquiring sports autographs. Some teams publish in their media guides where they stay while in different cities. Members of the media can also be an excellent source for finding out this information. Keep in mind that many athletes, such as Cal Ripken Jr., do not register under their own names. Thus, calling the hotel operator to find out if he is staying there will be fruitless. Professional sports teams will usually stay in the same hotel, making it easier for accounting purposes and usually less expensive.

The trick I always use is to request to be put in contact with the team's trainer. If the trainer is at the hotel, so are the players. I have never heard of a team trainer registering into a hotel under an assumed name. Hotels employ their own security force and many strangers are questioned as to their purpose there. While in the lobby, be inconspicuous; this is usually best achieved by sitting in a chair and reading the local newspaper.

* **Airports** - Most professional level teams charter their own planes for transportation. It depends on the specific team's travel expenses and its destination. A visiting team will leave from its hotel and travel by bus to the airport. A home team may meet at the stadium, allowing players to leave their cars at the sports facilities lot - reducing expenses - so they can take a bus to the airport. The airport's access and which airline is handling the flight determines if the bus stops at the main terminal to unload the passengers or is allowed to drive out onto the airport's tarmac and right up to the plane.

I have taken a few commercial flights with professional sports teams, purely by coincidence. If the team utilizes commercial flights, then the airport can provide an excellent autograph opportunity. Airport personnel, especially luggage carriers, are a good source for this information.

* **Night Clubs** - Every city has its share of nightly hot spots, or night clubs that flourish on certain days of the week. If the New York Yankees are playing the Red Sox in Boston, you will probably find some of the "Bronx Bombers" at the hottest night spots in "Bean Town." You will usually find more members of the visiting team at a night club than home team players. The reason is simple; when players are at home they want to spend as much time as possible with their families. Also, expense money is normally only allocated for road trips.

* **Other Places** - Don't overlook health clubs, museums, zoos, video stores and even delicatessens.

Correspondence with an individual, usually by mail

Most collectors add to their collections by sending autograph requests directly or indirectly to the athlete through the mail. But this method of obtaining a signature has an unpredictable success rate.

Not only do many requests go unanswered, but they are often lost or misplaced. The increased popularity of collecting autographs has inundated athletes with mail requests for their signatures.

Because collecting sports autographs is now a business to many, most professional athletes are skeptical of the sincerity associated with a mail request. Add to that the many invitations the athlete receives to attend sports trading card shows as an autograph guest, and you can understand why many requests are not answered.

There are certain individuals who do respond to autograph mail requests, particularly if they are perceived as sincere, brief and include a self-addressed, stamped envelope. A short list of athletes with good response rates is included in Chapters 10 and 11 of this book.

This doesn't mean they are the only ones who respond, or that a response is guaranteed. The list is intended to indicate a player's tendency for this type of request.

Christian Laettner offers collectors a chance to join his fan club.

Putting together a direct mailing of autograph requests can be a costly undertaking. The hidden expenses of such a project are included in a cost breakdown of mailing 100 baseball requests through the U.S. Postal Service. There obviously are variables involved in any cost breakdown. However, the point to be made is the initial expense, with no guarantee for success.

Direct Mailing

Cost breakdown for mailing 100 baseball autograph requests

Item	Cost	Comments
* 100 ruled index cards	.97	- for SASE
* 100 4 1/8x9 1/2 envelopes	$3.00	xxx
* one ballpoint pen	.59	xxx
* 200 29-cent postage stamps	$58.00	- two for each letter *
* one 1993 World Almanac	$7.95	- used for address reference
* 15 packs of Topps baseball cards	$12.67 **	- 79 cents a pack; needed 15 packs to get 100 different players.

Total: $83.87
Cost per single baseball autograph request: 84 cents ***

Note: * one stamp for request, one stamp for SASE included; assumes no international (Canada) mailing.
** purchased at 79 cents per pack retail price; includes New York state sales tax.
*** assumes only one baseball card included per request.

Most major league teams send out schedules and sometimes collectibles.

Acquiring through a friend, relative or team personnel

As expected, this method of obtaining signatures is usually very successful. The greater your access to the subject, the increased chance of obtaining his autograph.

As a collector, you should make a sincere effort to get to know anyone affiliated with your local professional team, from ushers to ticket takers. Knowing team personnel increases your success rate. Also, don't forget about the media, especially newspaper reporters; they have a tremendous access to professional athletes and are usually very willing to discuss the particular subject they are writing about.

If you see a reporter in a restricted area at a sports facility, watch him closely; he is usually waiting for an accessible athlete to interview. Reporters typically work under strict deadlines; when they arrive at the facility they waste little time in pursuing their subjects.

Getting to know a player's family or relatives can be a bit more difficult, but can be accomplished with a gradual, sincere approach. Athletes are generally allowed complimentary tickets for each game. These tickets are generally for a specific box seat area, usually close to the team bench.

Obviously, this depends on the facility and whether the player is a visiting athlete or from the home team. An astute collector will recognize this area by the concentration of women and small children.

This task is easier to accomplish at a small minor league facility than at Madison Square Garden, but can still be accomplished. By arriving early, you will can enhance your efforts in finding this area and identifying player friends or family.

An athlete will often greet friends and relatives before the game begins, usually during practice. Watch who he approaches and where that individual sits after the conversation.

Also, monitor who walks in and out of the "Players Entrance" after the game. It won't take long to recognize family members, even by name.

It's also advantageous to have a media guide available, indicating alongside an athlete's photograph the names of his friends and family. Once you've identified these people, it's just a matter of polite conversation, at an appropriate time, to develop a level of trust.

Always respect an individual's right to privacy. Use discretion when approaching for an autograph request. If a player has had a bad game, he won't be thrilled with a deluge of autograph requests after leaving the locker room. Nor will he be very accommodating.

Purchasing items from dealers, promoters, catalogs, shopping networks, etc.

An entire book could be written on this subject, but simply put, "Let the buyer beware." Purchasing items from an established dealer with a good reputation for quality, service, price and availability is paramount.

An established dealer often offers a variety of autographed material at a fair market price. When you purchase autographed sports memorabilia, each item should have an unconditional guarantee of authenticity, based not only on a printed certificate of authenticity, but also upon the dealer's willingness to accept a returned item due to authenticity concerns.

An established dealer should provide a reasonable return policy, typically 14 days from time of purchase. If a collector is unsatisfied with a purchase, he should promptly return it in the same condition. If the item is unique or costly, ask the dealer about its origin or provenance. This method is often used by collectors of rare historical documents.

Another benefit of an established dealer is his knowledge base, not only in authenticating a specific item, but in how to acquire certain autographed collectibles. Developing a good relationship with a variety of established dealers only adds to your collecting satisfaction.

Once a dealer realizes your commitment toward your goal, he can usually offer you access to some of his purchasing sources. A serious collector should always have a comprehensive want list of desired items.

This list should indicate price range, condition, and time frame for acquisition. Many quality autographed sports items never reach dealer advertisements. Instead, they are acquired by known collectors who specialize in a certain field.

Billy Herman actually signed some baseballs for Rollie Fingers.

Always ask to be added to a dealer's mailing list for future catalogs or sale notifications. Most dealers will comply, but catalogs can be very expensive to produce and distribute. Therefore, staying on a dealer's mailing list will probably require either a purchase or a catalog fee.

On average, a good collector receives three to five catalogs each week. An excellent source of comparison shopping, they provide new insights into the hobby, knowledge of recent acquisitions, and an understanding of each dealer's specialties. Occasional contact with established dealers is necessary so you don't miss a key acquisition; after all, a catalog only represents a small amount of a dealer's available inventory.

It won't take long to realize that dealer prices for similar and identical items can vary significantly. Dealers primarily price their items based on their local appeal or demand and the availability or scarcity of the item. There are, however, times when a dealer may develop an emotional attachment to a piece.

For example, a Florida dealer was pricing an autographed Dan Marino football at what I thought was twice the market value. I later realized the ball belonged to his father, who had recently died. Thus, the price was higher.

To illustrate the concept of market variability, a chart is included to compare prices of single-signature baseballs advertised by four different dealers. Assuming the dealers are of equal integrity, offer the same return policy and an identical product, you can see that by purchasing a Joe DiMaggio autographed baseball from dealer "C" you can save yourself a quick $111.

Although the point is clear that comparison shopping can save you money, you must also remember the integrity of the dealer and his assurance that the product is indeed genuine. As is often the case, if the deal sounds too good to be true, it probably is.

Autographed Single-Signature Baseballs

Dealer Pricing Variances

Player Name	A	B	C	D
Joe DiMaggio	$350	$275	$239	$295
Ted Williams	125	99	99	145
Willie Mays	45	40	29	35
Hank Aaron	45	35	-	-
Stan Musial	50	40	-	35
Johnny Bench	35	35	-	-
Steve Carlton	30	28	-	25
Brooks Robinson	25	20	-	-
Lou Brock	30	25	-	-

Note: Prices do not include postage and handling; - = not available. All prices quoted from advertisements in March 18, 1994, issue of *Sports Collectors Digest*.

Team-issued catalogs and programs are perfect for autographing.

Purchasing from satellite shopping networks and gift catalogs is an interesting dichotomy. Although they offer every collector instant access to a variety of autographed memorabilia, they do so at what many consider to be extravagant price levels.

The companies claim there are substantial costs in marketing products this way; that is the justification for the pricing. While I agree totally that there are significant costs involved in printing catalogs and renting satellite time, I do not believe an Eric Karros or Pat Listach (each a 1992 Rookie of the Year) autographed baseball is worthy of a $39.95 price tag.

Listach and Karros are fine young prospects, but they are just starting their careers. Remember that since the inception of independent league Rookie of the Year awards in 1949, only eight out of the 92 chosen have made it into the Baseball Hall of Fame.

I am not implying that all products offered through these sources are high priced; they are not. Nor am I implying that you can't find an outstanding limited-edition sports collectible at a great price; you can. Just be realistic in your purchases and keep your collecting goal in mind.

In time (especially following the Dec. 13, 1993, decision by New York City's Consumer Affairs Department to charge Hall of Famer Johnny Bench with 10 civil violations and fine him $5,000 for making false claims and guarantees while appearing on the Home Shopping Network), this method of acquiring autographed collectibles will prove to be very worthwhile for collectors.

Hall of Famer Al Lopez signs during an Induction Day ceremony.

Another source for obtaining sports autographs is to attend a major collectibles show where professional athletes are signing for a fee.

Athletes at these shows are guaranteed a fee for their services, so you in essence are purchasing your autographs from the promoter. The advantages to this method are clear - guaranteed authentic signatures on the items of your choice, plus a brief encounter with a professional athlete.

The disadvantages are the long waiting lines, and other inconveniences associated with attending a public event, and the cost. Included in this chapter is a chart entitled "Attending a Major Collectibles Show," which puts into perspective the associated costs of attending a show.

This method of acquiring autographs varies in cost, depending upon the show's location, athletes in attendance and the show's promoter. Remember, the more pieces you have signed, the lower the defrayed costs of attending the show.

Attending a Major Collectibles Show

Cost Breakdown

Travel Costs

* 400 miles (round trip) x $.24 per mile * = $96.00

Show Costs

* Parking = $5.00 (Note: Unable to take advantage of limited free parking)
* Show admission = $5.00 (Note: A weekend pass was available for $8.00)

Autograph Costs

Guest: Willie Mays (Baseball)

- Cost of material to have autographed: **	
- 12 official league baseballs	$70.20
- shipping & handling	$5.00
	$75.20
- Autograph fee per baseball - $35.00	$420.00
Subtotal -	$495.20

Guest: Emmitt Smith (Football)

- Cost of material to have autographed: **	
- 10 unofficial league footballs	$500.00
- (purchased locally)	
	$500.00
- Autograph fee per football *** - $75.00	$750.00
Subtotal -	$1,250.00

Guest: Mike Bossy (Hockey)

- Cost of material to have autographed. **	
- 10 official logo pucks	$80.50
- shipping & handling	$5.00
	$85.50
- Autograph fee per puck - $12.00	$120.00
Subtotal -	$205.50

Note: * Figure based on average corporation expense analysis.
** Purchased prior to show.

Summary

Travel costs -$96.00 *
Show costs -$10.00 **
Autograph costs $1,950.70 ***

Total - $2,056.70

Note: * Does not include food and beverage (optional).
** Assumes no free parking.
*** The number of pieces to be signed was predetermined by the collector.

Analysis

Total pieces signed = 32

Cost per item - prior to travel and show costs:

- A single-signed Willie Mays baseball	$41.26
- A single-signed Emmitt Smith football	$125.00
- A single-signed Mike Bossy puck	$20.55

Cost per item - after adding travel and show costs: *

- A single-signed Willie Mays baseball	$44.57
- A single-signed Emmitt Smith football	$128.31
- A single-signed Mike Bossy puck	$23.86

Note: * To defray travel and show costs, add $3.31 per item signed. The more pieces signed the lower the defrayed cost.

Purchasing at an auction

Auction catalogs are useful for their research value.

As the hobby has matured, many major auction houses have increased participation. These auctions have become a platform for the sale of the hobby's finest examples of sports autographs, from Larry Bird's autographed warmup jacket to a rarely-seen autographed 8x10 photograph of "Shoeless Joe" Jackson.

These major auction houses are unearthing some of the finest pieces available in the market, while attracting some very prominent buyers. In addition to discovering key collectibles, these auction houses are also gauging market demand and keeping collectors current on what is attracting buyers. Although shrewd buyers may find bargains, the excitement of the event usually lends itself to overpriced acquisitions.

The greatest advantage these auction houses bring to the average collector is their catalogs, most of which provide detailed descriptions and photographs. They are generally available for public purchase weeks before the event.

Serious collectors, who for some reason can't attend the auctions, should still purchase these catalogs for the research value they offer or to submit mail bid forms on items that interest them. Before participating, however, collectors should be aware of all the terms and conditions of sale.

Trading

Trading with fellow collectors is another option available to the autograph collector. Many veteran collectors have built a wonderful network of individuals to trade with across the country.

This method of acquiring autographs is particularly gratifying because you often receive items to fill your needs, while helping a fellow collector toward his hobby goals. Choose who you trade with the same way you would choose a local dealer to purchase from.

Find a dealer who specializes in the same material you collect. Before you make or approve any trade, be sure that all items involved in the transaction are clearly identified, especially with regard to condition.

Should you receive any material in a trade that does not meet your satisfaction, immediately return it. Collectors vary in their interpretations of an item's condition, or grading, as well as their knowledge level of signature variations.

Do not be surprised if a collector rejects a trade item because of either factor. Also, don't take it personally; the returned items are strictly based on one collector's interpretation.

Finding someone to trade with is simply a matter of contacting those individuals whose names appear in many of the advertisements in trade periodicals, such as *Sports Collectors Digest, Sports Cards* and the *Sports Card Price Guide*.

Also, many collectors who have computers can access the computer networks, submitting and receiving electronic mail. Many even offer autographed sports memorabilia for sale.

Autographed sports trading card inserts

Although not usually cost effective and certainly not predictable, this is another method of acquiring autographs. There is a great deal of excitement involved when you are searching through packs of sports trading cards, hoping to find an autographed insert. As a collector area of specialization, however, it is restricted to those few who have less concern for cost and greater interest in production or availability.

The result of this marketing approach is that it has lured many trading card collectors into the field of autographs. What began as a buying incentive from card manufacturers has now created a whole new hobby niche of collectors.

While many trading card dealers continue to complain about new card issues, they praise the increased use of autographed inserts. Most collectors welcome the change, saying it has increased their interest in the hobby.

The public's acceptance has resulted in the birth of many new companies, including Signature Rookies of Factoryville, Pa. In 1994, the company is marketing 12,500 boxes of trading cards that feature top rookies and prospects.

Each box contains 36 packs, six cards per pack, with a guarantee of one autographed card per pack. I purchased box #02632 from a local sports trading card dealer for $180. An analysis of the contents of that box is provided here for your reference.

Signature Rookies

Card collation analysis of one box

Box #02632
Total box production: 12,500

Card #	No.	Card #	No.	Card #	No.
1	3	21	5	41	4
2	2	22	5	42	4
3	4	23	3	43	4
4	5	24	3	44	4
5	5	25	5	45	4
6	5	26	5	46	5
7	4	27	4	47	4
8	4	28	5	48	5
9	5	29	3	49	4
10	4	30	5	50	3
11	5	31	4		
12	4	32	5		
13	3	33	5	5 - Hottest Prospect cards (A)	
14	5	34	5	5 - Cliff Floyd cards (B)*	
15	5	35	2	Hottest Rookie	
16	3	36	4	* - 1 autographed (22/225)	
17	4	37	4	2 - signature vouchers for:	
18	5	38	5	— Michael Tucker	
19	5	39	5	— Ricky Bottalico	
20	5	40	5	27 - Hottest Prospect mail-in	
				cards	

Autographed cards (No. includes these cards)

Brian Bevil, Garret Anderson, Rod Henderson, Keith Heberling, Brook Fordyce, Orlando Miller, Todd Hollandsworth, Tyrone Hill, Paul Sporljaric, Herbert Perry, Alex Ochoa, Mike Neill, John Burke, Alan Benes, Robbie Beckett, Justin Thompson, Joey Hamilton, Rickey Greene, Wayne Gomes, Matthew Drews, Jeff D'Amico, Bryn Kosko, Brooks Kieschnick, Jason Kendall, Mike Kelly, Jay Powell, Kurt Miller, Chad McConnell, Sean Lowe, Dan Smith, Calvin Reese, James Wright, John Wasdin

Subtotal - 33 cards: two signature vouchers, one Cliff Floyd autographed card
Total - 36 autographs (one per pack)

Retail cost: $180 ** Cost breakdown: $5 per signature **
** = prices may vary

Upper Deck Authenticated offers genuine autographs of several star players.

Autographed Insert Cards

Manufacturer Overview

Baseball

Year	Set	Value	Comments
1990	Upper Deck (UD) Reggie Jackson Heroes	$450	xxx
1991	Donruss Elite Ryne Sandberg	$400	xxx
1991	Score Mickey Mantle	$500	xxx
1991	UD Hank Aaron Heroes	$400	xxx
1991	UD Hall of Fame Heroes	$120	Killebrew, Perry, Jenkins (3,000)
1991	UD Nolan Ryan Heroes	$600	xxx
1992	Donruss Elite Cal Ripken Jr.	$400	xxx
1992	Fleer Roger Clemens	$165	random inserts in packs
1992	Fleer Ultra Tony Gwynn	$140	xxx
1992	Score Joe DiMaggio	$600	xxx
1992	Score Chuck Knoblauch	$80	xxx
1992	Score The Franchise	$250	Stan Musial
1992	Score The Franchise	$500	Mickey Mantle
1992	Score The Franchise	$200	Carl Yastrzemski
1992	Score The Franchise	$1,500	Mantle, Musial, Yastrzemski
1992	Topps Gold Brien Taylor	$60	12,000 (one per factory set)
1992	UD Johnny Bench/Joe Morgan Heroes	$300	xxx
1992	UD Ted Williams Heroes	$450	xxx
1993	Fleer Tom Glavine	$100	random inserts in both series packs
1993	Fleer Ultra Dennis Eckersley	$140	xxx
1993	Donruss Elite Will Clark	$325	5,000 autographed inserts
1993	Donruss Elite Dominators Juan Gonzalez	$350	xxx
1993	Donruss Elite Dominators Don Mattingly	$300	xxx
1993	Donruss Elite Dominators Paul Molitor	$200	xxx
1993	Donruss Elite Dominators Nolan Ryan	$400	xxx
1993	Leaf Update Frank Thomas	$400	xxx
1994	Fleer Tim Salmon	$125	xxx
1994	Classic Minor League Dave Justice	TBD	xxx

Football

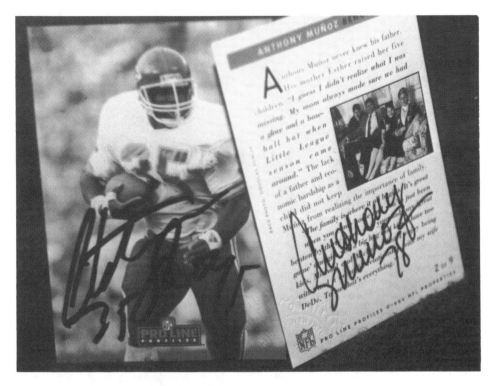

ProLine Profiles cards have had 35 football players sign cards.

1991	Pro Set Erik Kramer	$30	card #824
1991	Pro Set Ozzie Newsome	$35	card #699
1991	Pro Set Lawrence Taylor	$275	card #336, #394
1991	UD Heroes Joe Montana	$325	random inserts in Series I (Low)
1991	UD Heroes Joe Namath	$285	random inserts in Series II (High)
1992	Action Packed (AP) Barry Sanders	$365	random inserts in foil packs
1992	All World Tim Brown	$135	A2
1992	All World Desmond Howard	$65	A1
1992	All World Joe Namath	$150	A3
1992	Collector's Edge (CE) John Elway	$115	xxx
1992	Collector's Edge Ronnie Lott	$85	xxx
1992	Collector's Edge Ken O'Brien	$25	xxx
1992	Fleer Mark Rypien	$40	random pack inserts
1992	Fleer Ultra Chris Miller	$65	random inserts in foil packs
1992	Fleer Ultra Reggie White	$110	random inserts in foil packs
1992	Pacific Steve Largent	$125	xxx
1992	Pacific Bob Griese	$125	xxx
1992	ProLine Profiles cards	varies	nine-card sets
1992	Pro Set Erik Kramer	$35	1,000 autographed inserts
1992	Pro Set Emmitt Smith	$225	1,000 autographed inserts
1992	SkyBox Impact Jim Kelly	$100	xxx
1992	SkyBox Impact Jim Kelly/Magic Johnson	$450	xxx
1993	Collector's Edge John Elway	$95	xxx
1993	Fleer Steve Young	$150	random inserts in packs

1993	Pinnacle Franco Harris	$25	3,000 autographed inserts
1993	ProLine Live autograph sets	$1,500	common signatures $15-$20
			Montana $275, Aikman $200,
			Favre $160, Foster $100
			35 different players
1993	Score Dick Butkus	$35	3,000 autographed inserts
1993	SkyBox Jim Kelly/Magic Johnson header card	$125	xxx
1993	Fleer Ultra Michael Irvin	$150	random inserts in packs

Basketball **

1991	UD certified Jerry West Heroes	$150	random inserts in High Series packs
1991	Fleer Dikembe Mutombo	$80	random inserts in Series II
1991	Fleer Dominique Wilkens	$125	random inserts in Series II
1992	Fleer Darryl Dawkins	$45	SD300
1992	Fleer Larry Johnson	$200	random inserts in Series I
1992	Fleer Shawn Kemp	$150	SD266
1992	Fleer Kenny Walker	$15	SD277
1992	NBA Hoops Patrick Ewing	$125	xxx
1992	NBA Hoops Magic Johnson	$250	xxx
1992	NBA Hoops John Stockton	$115	xxx
1992	SkyBox Admiral/David Robinson	$200	AU1
1992	SkyBox Magic Johnson	$300	AU2
1992	Fleer Ultra Stacey Augmon	$50	JS215
1992	Fleer Ultra Duane Causwell	$10	JS212
1992	Fleer Ultra Pervis Ellison	$30	JS207
1992	Fleer Ultra certificate Scottie Pippen	$160	random inserts in Series I packs
1993	Classic Gold Shaquille O'Neal	$350	xxx
1993	Fleer Clyde Drexler	$125	random inserts in all Series I packs
1993	Fleer Ultra Karl Malone	$175	random inserts in all Series I packs
1993	NBA Hoops David Robinson voucher	$150	random inserts in all Series II packs
1993	NBA Hoops Magic Johnson/	$400	random inserts in all Series II packs
	Larry Bird voucher		

Hockey

1991	Pro Set Patrick Roy	$275	card #125, 599
1991	Score Bobby Orr	$250	xxx
1991	UD Heroes Brett Hull	$300	xxx
1992	Fleer Ultra Jeremy Roenick	$200	xxx
1992	Score Canadian Olympic Maurice Richard	$200	random inserts in foil packs
1993	Leaf Mario Lemieux card	$375	random inserts in foil packs
1993	Pinnacle Alexandre Daigle	$185	xxx
1993	Fleer Ultra Adam Oates	$145	xxx
1994	Classic pro hockey prospects	$60-$110	10,000 randomly-inserted players:
			Yashin, Juneau, Freisen,
			Bonsignore, Kovalev, Rheaume,
			Whitten, Bonk, Pronger

* Note: Values taken from *Sports Card Price Guide* data, March 1994
** Note: Star Pics was the first card company (1990) to insert autographed cards into a set. Since that time every major card manufacturer licensed by the NBA has followed, except Topps.

Acquiring In-person Autographs

Collector Hints

* Be prepared - Often you will only have ONE autograph opportunity, so be prepared. Have both a new "Sharpie" and ballpoint pen immediately accessible. Know what you're going to have signed by each player and have it also at your fingertips.

* Be timely with your request - The timing of an autograph request is the key element that will determine its success. Try to put yourself in the athlete's position. For example, a hockey team wins during overtime on a key goal. Who is more likely to be obliging to an autograph request following the game, the goalie who gave up the goal or the player who scored it?

* Don't be conspicuous - Blend into your surroundings as much as possible. Act like you belong in your environment. Wearing recognizable media clothing, such as NBC Sports, or ESPN, can help you in all professional-level facilities. Always look and act professional.

* Conceal all the material you are going to have signed - Keep all of the material you are going to have signed concealed until the last possible minute.

If you can stop your target from moving, his signature will be much nicer.

* You must stop the subject from moving - Do not allow the subject to walk while he is signing his autograph. As he walks he is decreasing his available signing space, causing other collectors to loose an autograph opportunity. Additionally, by walking he is not concentrating on the items to be signed, usually resulting in a very poor autograph. Always approach the subject directly, allowing as little space as possible to move around you. Placing the storage bag, concealing the material you are having signed, directly in front of him will help the task.

* Block all accessible paths between you and the subject - Using other collectors, you can strategically place yourself so that there is no clear path between the subject and his destination. Similar to electricity, the subject is going to always choose the path of least resistance or, in this case, the trail that has the least amount of autograph seekers. Your placement along an autograph path is also critical. If you recognize a player's friend, spouse or relative who is also waiting for the player, stand near that person. Standing near the most attractive member of the opposite sex will also increase your chances of being recognized.

Try to get a player to sign his signature on a flat surface.

* Always have flat items placed on a clipboard - Flat items are cumbersome to sign if a similar surface area is not available. Placing the items gently underneath the clip allows for the much needed support. Additionally, trading card collectors can place more than a single item, side by side, underneath the clip, possibly allowing for a quick, additional signature.

* The subject's hand must be available for a signature - It is not unusual for your subject to be carrying an equipment bag, locker room bag, etc.. If you see that a subject has both hands occupied, you are going to have to find a way to free-up one of them so that he can autograph your items. The easiest way is to offer to hold the item for him while he signs your material.

* Learn a few basic phrases of common languages - Not everyone who plays professional sports in this country is fluent in English. Learning some basic phrases in Spanish, French and even Russian will prove to be particularly helpful in many instances.

* Be courteous, yet firm, with your request - Always be courteous to your subject: "May I please have your autograph, Mr. Montana?" "Thank you very much. I really appreciate it." Respect your subject, but do not be timid with an autograph request. You must be aggressive, but not overbearing. For a professional athlete, complying with an autograph request is not an obligation. Thus, the more appealing you make the situation, the better the chance you'll get a positive response.

* Exercise perseverance - Not everyone will comply with your request. In fact, some athletes will just choose to ignore your solicitations. These situations can be difficult, possibly requiring a different approach to a request, or repeated solicitations. Whatever the alternative, be patient and don't give up!

* Know your subject - Doing a little biographical research on a subject can also be helpful. Knowing an athlete's hometown, his hobbies or even his alma mater can lead a subject into conversation with you, which can end with an autograph request.

Hints for acquiring autographs through the mail

* Always include a self-addressed, stamped envelope (SASE) for convenient response. Please be sure the enclosed envelope is of proper size to house the returned material, and that the proper postage is affixed.

* Be brief, personal and sincere with your request. Exhibit in a few sentences your genuine interest in, and knowledge of, a player's career. Courtesy is paramount.

* Avoid form letters. In addition to being impersonal and unflattering, the letters typically have a low response rate.

* To avoid confusion and disappointing responses, requests should be succinct and specific. If personalization is desired, please clearly indicate it in your request.

* Be conscious of a player's time by including no more than one or two items to be autographed.

* Be reasonable with your expectations. Some players receive hundreds of requests a day; they have little time to read a request, let alone respond to it.

* Don't risk sending expensive items through the mail. Although I am astounded by the accuracy and promptness exhibited by the U.S. Postal Service, most collectors are not in position to replace lost merchandise.

* Be creative with your request. Before sending out a letter, collectors should ask these questions: What is unique about my request that will make a player respond? Will my request stand out among the hundreds of others he receives? What would be my reaction to such a request?

Common mail bid auction rules

* Postage and insurance are typically added to the invoice.

* Most auctions do not allow "buy" or unlimited bids. A buy is when the auctioneer is told by a bidder to buy the lot for a reasonable cost mutually determined, commonly 10 percent above the previous bid.

* Lots are commonly not to be broken into individual items. Therefore, bidders are requested to bid by the lot.

* The highest bid should represent the maximum selling price of the lot; no additional charges beyond postage and handling should be added to the total.

* Invoicing by the seller should commence within 10 days after the closing date of the sale. Payment upon receipt of invoice is expected promptly. Included with the invoice, and provided by the seller, should be an SASE as a courtesy to the highest bidder.

* Mail bid sales commonly close two weeks from the date of auction publication, unless otherwise stated by the seller.

* As a guarantee that the highest bidder will honor his bid, the seller may require a deposit. This deposit is typically not returned if the high bidder fails to honor his bids. It shall, however, be applied as partial payment against the bid made by the highest bidder. Any deposit requested by

the seller must be clearly stated in the catalog or advertisement. Any deposits being held by the seller from unsuccessful bidders must be returned promptly following the close of the auction.

* Any item not properly described - conditioning or grading, year, manufacturer - by the seller may be returned to the highest bidder. All items should be guaranteed authentic by the seller.

* A seller should allow a grace period of up to two weeks upon receipt of buyer for returns from highest bidder.

* A seller has the right to reject a bid for any reason whatsoever.

* A bidder is obligated to honor any and all bids submitted.

* Any unusual exception to common mail bid rules for an auction must be clearly stated by the seller in the auction catalog or advertisement.

* A pre-registration procedure may be requested to simplify bidding procedure on the final day of the auction.

* A seller should be accessible during specific times during the auction's duration to answer questions from bidders.

* A seller may request minimum bid increases over previous bid.

Hints for purchasing items at a sports memorabilia show

Comparison shop first before you make an impulsive purchase.

* Get there early - There's a lot to be said in the old adage "The early bird gets the worm." The best selection of autographed sports memorabilia is generally at the beginning of the show.

* Allocate plenty of time - You can not make clear, concise decisions if you are rushed.

Concentrate on the task at hand; try not to get distracted.

* Know what you are looking for - Know why you are attending the show. Always bring a compact, updated list that is readily accessible.

* Know what you are willing to pay - Before the show, know what you will pay for the items you want. Consult a price guide if necessary; bring it to the show.

* Stay within your budget - Know how much money you can spend at the show to stay within your collecting goals.

* Never buy an item on your initial pass - Review the entire show before purchasing an item. Comparison shopping can save a collector considerable cash.

* Write down asking prices - During your initial review of the show, write down the prices each dealer is charging for the items you are interested in.

* Never pay full price - The autographed sports memorabilia market is very volatile and dealer pricing is often very subjective. A dealer, keeping in mind profitability, prices his material to cover his initial cost and any added expenses for attending the show. Different dealers have different sources, thereby accounting for many of the pricing variances of identical items. Don't get taken, yet realize that the dealer is in business to make money.

* Thoroughly examine your purchase before leaving the dealer's table - Know the condition of your items when you purchase them. If you are purchasing autographs, always bring a magnifying glass for examination purposes. While examining something, remove its protective enclosures. Protective surfaces can disguise flaws or alterations.

* Know from whom you are purchasing - Always request a business card, or name, address and phone number of any dealer from whom you have made a purchase. If you have any future concerns about your purchase, you will know where to contact that dealer. Also, if you enjoy purchasing from him, you will want to know where to send him a copy of your want list.

* Know a dealer's area of expertise - An autograph dealer generally scrutinizes his purchased signatures in greater detail than a sports trading card collector might in a similar situation. If you know the autograph dealer you are purchasing from only purchases in-person autographs and is extremely knowledgeable in the field, then your concerns for authenticity are diminished.

* If you are uncomfortable with an aspect of an item, don't buy it - It is better to be safe than sorry in the field of autographed sports memorabilia. I have seen many collectors fall prey to their emotions; they purchased questionable items, only to find out later that the piece is not authentic.

* Be there late - In addition to being at the show when it opens, be there at the end. Dealers will often lower prices so they don't have to repack something to take home. Also, you can ask the dealer if he made any interesting purchases at the show and if he's willing to sell any of the items.

* Be sure your purchase is packaged properly - Many dealers attending shows are what collectors call "weekend warriors;" they are more concerned with getting to the show, setting up, selling the items and then leaving, than making sure your purchase is packaged to avoid damage in transport.

* Don't leave your purchases unguarded - Once you have purchased an item, you own it. Therefore, if it's lost or misplaced, then you are responsible. More than once I have seen collectors accidentally leave purchases at another dealer's table because they set the items down to examine a different piece.

* Have fun! - Enjoy yourself. Isn't that your primary goal in collecting? Also, always find out when and where the promoter's next show is before you leave.

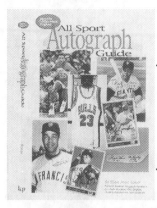

Chapter 6

Autograph Variations

Sometimes a player will note a significant event with his signature.

As a collector of sports autographs, the element of the hobby that you will find most fascinating, yet perplexing, is the variations in an athlete's signature. These anomalies or deviations are typical departures from the usual way that the athlete signs his or her name. Autograph variations can be a result of many factors, such as an athlete's mood, health, age (not a factor with active players), environment, popularity, writing instrument and the item the signature is placed upon. Variations can be either subtle or dramatic, depending upon the individual.

The task of tracking signature variations is arduous, time-consuming and often expensive. The alternative, however, is mistaking a genuine signature for a forgery because the collector was unfamiliar with a signature variation. Tracking signature variations is typically done through direct or indirect autograph requests. Responses from autograph requests, authentic or facsimile, are compared and noted for any unusual changes.

When comparing indirect autograph responses, collectors always use samples that are known to be authentic, most of which come from in-person requests. Because some variations are subtle and occur over a long period of time, collectors are advised to acquire samples of their subject's signature on a periodic basis.

Any time an athlete's signature appears in print, I remove it from its source, date it and place it in my files for future reference. I also monitor periodicals that serve the hobby, such as *Sports Collectors Digest* and *Sports Cards*, for any articles that may address the subject of autograph variations.

For years, Dave Miedema has been writing a column in *Sports Collectors Digest* called "Up Autograph Alley." This column, a wonderful source for information on the topic of signature variations, has also educated collectors on the many issues influencing the hobby. Every serious sports autographs collector has benefited from Miedema's work; as a hobby we owe him a great deal of gratitude.

Collector groups and organizations can also be a useful forum for information on signature variations. Many collectors specialize in certain individuals, teams or sports, and are usually more than happy to discuss their recent acquisitions.

Many autograph variations are the result of the collector choosing the wrong time to make an autograph request. Timing is of paramount importance, not only for a successful response, but for an excellent-looking autograph.

I once saw Bo Jackson during spring training mobbed by autograph seekers, trying to make it from the players' locker room to his car parked just a short distance away. Jackson, who does not like autograph requests to begin with, was trying to oblige to as many requests as possible, without having to stop walking - a typical autograph avoidance technique. When the incident finally concluded, I looked at some of the signatures obtained by the autograph seekers. Because of the circumstances there were several variations to the many illegible Jackson autographs.

A collector can't control an athlete's mood, health or popularity prior to an autograph request. But he can control the proper timing of a request, the item signed and the device used to sign that item. As a collector, your use of good timing will usually reduce many common autograph variations.

Common autograph variations

Every autograph is made up of strokes or marks made by a writing instrument. A writing instrument has characteristics such as ease of use, ink adherence and drying qualities and stroke thickness. The characteristics of a writing instrument can vary depending upon the surface it is in contact with. The person using the writing instrument has control over the amount of strokes he chooses to use in his signature. He also controls its size, its angle or slant, and its legibility and flamboyance that is indicative of the character formations that make up his name.

To better understand these autograph variations, let's examine the signature of Pittsburgh Penguin hockey star Mario Lemieux.

Mario Lemieux is a perfect example for noting autograph variations.

Autograph Variations

Subject: Mario Lemieux

• Strokes or signature breaks

Lemieux varies significantly in the number of strokes he uses to make up his signature. Included here are three samples, all obtained in person, and each exhibiting different signature breaks. His single-stroke signature is typically used when he's surrounded by autograph seekers. He does take greater care in signing more expensive items, such as jerseys; the autographed jersey has four signature breaks.

• Signature size

Lemieux will vary the size of his signature to fit the item being signed. For example, he'll reduce his signature to fit on a hockey puck. The large "L" in Lemieux, which resembles a "C," is typically the largest letter in his signature.

• Signature slant or angle

Lemieux's signature commonly slants right. It is a consistent slant with little degree of fluctuation, regardless of its placement on an item.

Mario Lemieux's signature is quite flamboyant.

• Character formation

The character formations in Lemieux's signature vary considerably. His signature, which often appears as "MiCel" or "MuCel," is very illegible due to the lack of character formation in the non-capitalized letters. I have seen a few early examples of his signature where the "ar" and "o" could be identified. When the "a" in Mario is left open, which is usually the case, it can resemble an "i." The "M" in Mario has always been fairly consistent in character formation, with the second loop often three to 10 times larger in height. The "ux," like so many other lowercase letters in his name, is often dropped or unrecognizable. The flamboyance of his signature will vary a bit with his mood, but is usually clearly evident in the longer strokes.

Signature variations are common in the evolution of an individual's autograph. Every serious collector of sports autographs should study the variations in the signatures of the athletes he collects. Unless you have access to a tremendous amount of material, your familiarity with a subject will usually be limited.

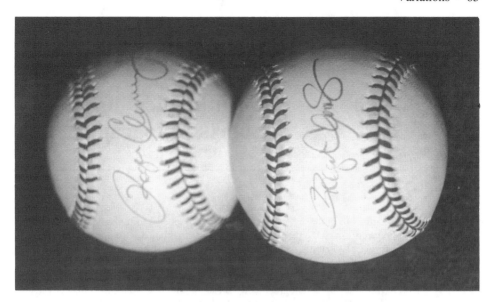

Set aside time to study the variations in a player's signature.

Take advantage of every opportunity to view an athlete's signature, whether it's spending an hour in a memorabilia store, or cutting out samples that appear in Sports Collectors Digest advertisements. Don't be afraid to contact other collectors, who may even provide you with photocopies of some of their in-person autographs. Also, the purchase of quality reference materials is always a wise decision.

More often than not, signature variations are immediately dismissed as forgeries. A well-educated collector who is aware of these transitions is then in a better position to make a good purchase.

Current Trends In Signatures

The Evolution of Celebrity Sports Autographs

• Decreased number of strokes	Example: Ryne Sandberg (1)
• Using the first initial instead of a first name (Barry Foster)	Example: B. Foster
• Dropping an entire first or last name	Example: Isiah or Shaq
• Dropping insignificant letters from a name (Frank Thomas)	Example: "Fk Th"
• Increased flamboyance	Example: Emmitt Smith

Chapter 7

Authenticating Sports Autographs

From "ghost" signatures to autopens and facsimiles, autographed sports memorabilia collectors face an increasing concern for authenticity. These elements, combined with a marked increase in the purchase of forged signatures, some even accompanied by a counterfeit "Letter of Authenticity," complicate the role of the sports autograph collector.

In addition to being a diligent, patient and prepared collector, he must also have some authentication skills. But the sports autograph collector is not alone; anyone who collects valuable material faces the threat of forgery. From sports cards to uniforms, the collector's role as an authenticator is expanding, and with it so is his knowledge base.

During the last five years, I have seen increased concern about authenticity, not only by collectors, but by corporations, user groups and the media. The initial rapid growth of the hobby, combined with the lack of accurate reference sources, made it easy for unauthentic items to enter the hobby.

Unscrupulous dealers went easily undetected by a strong purchasing base of new and inexperienced collectors. Now, primarily due to the accessibility of new resources, collectors have access to the many examples of authentic signatures, making it easier to detect a forgery. The hobby, far less naive, is more willing to take action against those who wish to tarnish its reputation.

Despite the available resources, every collector, regardless of which facet of the hobby he participates in, must spend time educating himself on current authentication techniques in order to reinforce his purchasing decisions.

In the long run, your ability to educate yourself will save you time and money. There are only a handful of experts in this business; they are predominately private collectors who spend an inordinate amount of time and money dedicating themselves to the task of authentication.

Fortunately for the majority of collectors, an expert's opinion will not be required for your purchases because you, too, have committed yourself to the task of authentication. Just by purchasing this book you will learn most of what you will need to make sound decisions.

There are experts in the area of signature authentication, many of whom have had formal studies in the field of forensic science. Forensic science, in its broadest definition, is the application of science to law. A forensic scientist combines his general knowledge with the technology of science for the enforcement of certain laws.

One area of specialization in forensic science is document analysis, which involves the examination of handwriting and typewriting to ascertain the source or authenticity of a questioned document. Document examiners do not possess some type of mystical powers; their success is predetermined on applying the knowledge they have gathered through experience and formal education to comparisons between questioned samples and known authentic writings.

The key element of their determination is based on their ability to gather authentic samples of known authorship or origin. Collecting these samples can often be an arduous and expensive task. That is one of the main objectives of this book - to simplify this task.

Like fingerprints, an individual's handwriting is unique, so there are definitive characteristics that make up each of our signatures. Although no two individuals write exactly alike, there can be marked resemblances. Just ask baseball autograph collectors about the unusual similarities between the signatures of Mr. and Mrs. Lou Gehrig.

An autographed sports memorabilia collector is usually a dedicated sports fan, usually having an in-depth understanding of how the various games are played and who the individual personalities of each sport are. He may recognize when the most opportune time is to acquire the signatures of certain individuals, what items that person will or won't sign, and even how much care that athlete takes with each autograph.

Being aware of the signature habits of various athletes can be useful in authentication. For example, if you a dealer is offering a Joe DiMaggio autographed bat for sale that he claims to have acquired recently, while the "Yankee Clipper" was strolling through LaGuardia Airport, it may be beneficial to understand how reluctant the subject is to signing autographs in general, especially baseball bats.

Every basketball autograph collector knows how hard it is to obtain a Bill Russell signature. You, too, must be equally as knowledgeable with your subjects.

This genuine Steve Carlton game ball refers to his 3,000th strikeout.

As a collector, you'll need to acquire a knowledge of the correct methods of comparing handwriting signatures and the impact factors, such as ink, paper, signature surface and even a signer's health, have on an autograph. These combined factors will most often determine authenticity.

Not any one element alone is conclusive proof that an item is indeed genuine. I have seen a few collectors mistake an authentic autograph for a forgery, due to just a variance in one of these factors.

In many cases, the uncharacteristic quality of a signature can be attributed to an extreme or unusual circumstance that happened before or during the signing. The excitement of a moment, such as reaching a career milestone, or the devastating effects following a heart attack, can contribute greatly to signature variations.

Collectors should also remember there are many unusual autographed sports items. I have seen authentic signatures of Babe Ruth and Reggie Jackson on the same baseball, signatures on lawn furniture, on baby strollers and even on airplanes.

Having unusual items signed causes skepticism among future potential buyers; it's a good practice to avoid. To a serious collector, the type of material that was signed and the ink that was used can provide clues to an item's authenticity.

If the autographed material was manufactured after a player's lifetime, then the item is clearly a forgery. For example, at one show I ran across an autographed Babe Ruth 8x10 black-and-white photograph. Because I have a strong background in printing, I knew the photograph was a halftone created by a popular laser scanner.

The scanner was not available during Ruth's lifetime, so the item was a forgery. Although I would have concluded the same thing after a careful analysis of the signature, it was unnecessary because the item's authenticity was already determined.

Tools

Forensic scientists have sophisticated computer-based image processing systems in their laboratories. These systems utilize the latest technology in laser scanning to lift signatures, by creating a duplicate image, directly off a variety of surfaces, including photographs, footballs and hockey sticks.

Once scanned, the images can be manipulated in various ways for comparison. Signatures can actually be reconstructed and merged with other samples to determine authenticity. Although these systems are too expensive to the average collector, if prices continue to decrease it won't be long before they can be purchased reasonably. Most collectors, however, do not need such sophisticated tools, but it is important to realize that this technology exists.

The microscope is a practical tool for most collectors. Through the lens of a microscope the authenticator can examine specific characteristics of letter formation, pen stroke and line weight.

Various light sources, such as ultraviolet or infrared, can also detect the existence of materials, such as pencil, erasure fragments, assorted ink types and various chemicals. Also, by changing the direction of a light source you can make many abberations more apparent. As your confidence in authentication grows, you might consider purchasing a variety of lighting.

The most affordable and useful tool to collectors is the magnifying glass, which is used to study characteristics such as ink accumulations and line thickness. A magnifying glass, ruler and protractor are an excellent starter "authenticity kit" for a new collector.

Handwriting and signature characteristics and comparisons

The writing style that is acquired by someone learning to write is that which is fashionable or appropriate to that particular era. As children, we were taught predominantly two methods, either Palmer or Zane-Blosser, which were introduced in the 1880s.

Today, these methods, in slightly modified forms, are still taught in elementary schools. The writing styles of children are very similar because they have not yet grown comfortable with the standard letter forms.

As a child matures, the act of writing becomes a subconscious act, and he is more willing to express himself with its form. We all have several habitual shapes and patterns that are characteristic to our signatures. These identification points are precisely what collectors are going to have to identify in key sports signatures.

The forger's goal is the impossible task of consciously duplicating an unconscious task of an individual. Signing an autograph is an unconscious task, requiring little effort mechanically, physically and mentally to be associated with its completion.

A forger, however, exerts tremendous effort in trying to duplicate his subject's signature. His effort alone is a deterrent to success, because he must think about what he is doing.

Variations in letter and word spacing, slant, speed, pressure, size, flamboyance and connecting strokes are only a few of the items an authenticator looks for. Where a signer places his autograph on the paper, if he dots the "i"s and crosses his "t"s - these are personal writing habits.

Authentication begins with a selection of examples that are known to be genuine. If authentic examples are cost prohibitive, the reproductions of these samples can be used. Be advised that some characteristics, such as pen pressure and ink accumulations, can be masked with reproductions.

Every autographed sports memorabilia collector should develop a "clip" file. These are copies of signatures that are known to be genuine. I usually cut the autographs from the copies so they fit onto 3x5 index cards. Then I put them in a file box. Remember to date and source each signature before you store it.

These files can be particularly helpful in tracking signature variations. An individual's signature may change dramatically over time, so periodically update your files.

If politely asked, most dealers and some private collectors will exchange reproductions of original material, because they, too, want to keep up with changes in signature styles. It is hoped the samples in this book will get your reference library off to a great start.

Normal handwriting, as most of us know, is produced with very smooth strokes, consistent in strength and noticeably careless in detail. The only exceptions are often the writing of ill or aged individuals.

Forgers tend to add detail to their subject's signatures. This is usually a definitive character formation, such as a letter which is often unrecognizable in an original signature. A good forger can duplicate smooth strokes, but it is usually at the cost of having inconsistent pen pressure.

The forger becomes so caught up in producing a smooth stroke that he doesn't realize his writing instrument has left the surface of the piece. Complicating the task of collecting sports autographed material is that many of us choose to collect non-flat items.

Signature variations are common when a subject is signing his name to a variety of surfaces. Also, irregular or textured surfaces, such as footballs and basketballs, require a porous tip pen. While these pens allow for a bolder signature, they are extremely difficult to authenticate because of the lack of detail in character formation - the pen is too thick, and the irregular surface does not lend itself to smooth strokes. Simply stated, autographed footballs and basketballs are a forger's dream because they mask detail.

Observant collectors find that certain characteristics are common to many forged signatures and are fairly easy to detect. They include unusual or uncommon breaks in a signature; an unusual change in stroke thickness as a result of stiff starts or ends instead of flying starts or endings; or unusual roughness in upward or downward strokes, indicative of slow careful reproduction.

Roughness in the strokes is not enough to certify a fake. As mentioned previously, tremors in the writing of an individual can result from age or ill health, as witnessed by comparing early examples of a player's signature to those later in his life.

As some autographed baseball collectors have found, you should be more speculative of a smooth signature that was obtained later in the life of a Frankie Frisch, Charlie Gehringer or Luke Appling, than a rough example.

The most common mistake made by beginning collectors is the failure to recognize authentic autographed material from earlier in a player's career. Signatures evolve and may change considerably over the individual's lifetime. Notable examples are Joe Montana, Mickey Mantle, Magic Johnson and Joe DiMaggio.

The material that the autograph adorns can readily unmask a fake, as was the case with the Babe Ruth photograph mentioned earlier. When you are authenticating any item, your examination starts with the signature and ends with the material that was signed.

Although it can be difficult, try to monitor the manufacturers of equipment used by professional teams. Teams and manufacturers often attach tags to their equipment for identification purposes.

For example, the 1983 "home," or white jerseys, of the San Diego Padres were manufactured by Wilson. The company's manufacturer tag is sewn on the inside back of the uniform and includes the player's size.

There is also a team identification tag located at the bottom left corner of the jersey. This 1x2 piece of the same material, sewn to the outside of the jersey, indicates the player's number, such as 16, followed by the last two digits of the year, "83." Note any changes in labeling or tagging; a company will often change styles every season.

For collectors of "game-worn" autographed equipment, this is an absolute necessity, as there is little reference material available on the topic. It is also not unusual for a forger to falsely age material, especially paper. Remember, the aging of any material should reflect natural, not extreme, characteristics. Your area of expertise determines where you should focus your research efforts.

Studying writing devices and the characteristics of the inks they use is also helpful in determining an item's authenticity. There are sophisticated testing techniques to determine the age of inks, but most are too expensive for the average collector. Therefore, you should examine the deterioration characteristics of various inks, such as fading. This, accompanied by a strong understanding of writing devices, will help you determine the age of an autographed item.

Pencil, as a writing device, is a completely different scenario. Pencils were, and are still, rarely used for letters or documents, but they were traditionally given to fans who purchased a scorecard. This is why so many early baseball programs are autographed in pencil.

A forged pencil signature is the most difficult to detect, because it can easily be retouched. The graphite in pencil is applied, whereas ink is absorbed. The direction of pencil strokes is difficult to determine, usually requiring an expert to examine paper fibers under a microscope. Collectors, especially beginners, should shy away from purchasing pencil autographs.

The traced signature is a common forgery technique. This simple method involves placing a signature on top of a lit surface, then tracing over it with some form of writing device. Porous tip pens are avoided because the absorption characteristics of the ink are reciprocal to the signing time.

The longer a signer takes to write, the more ink is absorbed by the application surface or applied by the writing device. In some cases, pencil is first used to trace a signature, then ink is applied over the graphite. Once the ink is dry, the forger erases the graphite, leaving only the later signature.

These signatures are easy to detect due to the lack of smooth strokes and spontaneous curves. Careful examination through a magnifying glass or a microscope will also expose indentations or erasure marks. Facsimile signatures are often printed, photographed or stamped, and are easily identified by their lack of natural writing characteristics.

"Ghost" and secretarial signatures are also common forms of unauthentic signatures that you may encounter. "Ghost" signatures are unauthentic samples, often created with the subject's knowledge. They are usually condoned because the athlete's popularity overwhelms his ability to respond to each request.

Babe Ruth had clubhouse personnel respond to many requests for his signature. Secretarial signatures are mostly associated with sports executives. Often, a busy travel schedule prevents an executive from responding directly to his mail, so he authorizes his secretary to do so. Many secretarial signatures have a set of small initials at the end of the signature, identifying it as such.

Machine-rendered signatures, commonly done by devices called "autopens," mechanically reproduce a person's signature. For years these devices were predominantly used by politicians, but are now being used by athletes, too. Some notable athletes, such as Joe Montana, have allegedly turned to this alternative.

Since no one can sign his name exactly alike twice in a row, superimposing the signatures over a light source and having them match identically is a common way to identifying an autopen signature. Occasionally, an item will move while the machine is reproducing a signature, causing a slight variation. However, if a majority of the characters and strokes matched previously-obtained samples, you have an autopen autograph.

The key complicating factor is when multiple patterns are being used by the machine to duplicate signatures. During his administration, President Kennedy had seven different patterns, noted by autograph expert Charles Hamilton. Worth noting is that these devices can also store salutations, sentences and even paragraphs.

A technique that has grown in popularity with forgers is adding fake signatures to items, such as basketballs or baseballs, that already have a few authentic autographs adorning them. One year during a Baseball Hall of Fame induction in Cooperstown, N.Y., I was trying to obtain as many signatures as I could on a baseball.

A small crowd of us on the front steps of the inductees' hotel were doing our best to stop as many baseball celebrities as we could. I struck up a conversation with a photographer who, in addition to taking pictures, was also having a few baseballs signed.

We were interrupted when an inductee came from the hotel and a mass of autograph seekers flocked to his side. Most of us got his signature, except for the photographer. When I went to console him, he said, "No problem. I'll just add his name to the ball. It's for my grandson anyway, and he'll never know the difference."

Before I could stop him, he did exactly that. Believe me, there was no malicious intent involved with the task, but just think about the confusion that will surround that baseball if it's ever offered for sale.

Some forgers will also add signatures to old, naturally-aged paper. If ink is used, the result will be a feathering, or an abnormal absorption pattern created on the paper. This technique is typically used on items that already have a few genuine examples, to help mask authenticity concerns.

The forged signatures are most often added at the edge or bottom of the material, so as to not conflict with any of the authentic signatures. The forger does this so that if an item is detected as a forgery, he can still clip out the original signatures and recycle them back into the market.

Mistaken identity can also add to the confusion of identifying a signature - that's Cal Ripken Sr. not Cal Ripken Jr., Claude Lemieux not Mario, and Larry Johnson, not Vinnie, Marques, Kevin, or Magic!

A skilled forger using his freehand skills and having a strong knowledge of writing materials and his subjects' signing habits can achieve a certain amount of similarity. Fortunately, experts agree that perfect forgeries, if you excuse the term, are rare, if not impossible.

Understanding the characteristics of forgery is the first step toward authentication. What to look for in a signature is the next step. I have included a useful chart for these purposes.

Common signs of forgery

What should you look for?

• Incorrect material

Make sure the type of material signed can be dated to the subject's lifetime. As an example, while attending a baseball card show I discovered a single-signature baseball of Hall of Famer Lloyd Waner. The first thing I noticed was that it was signed on an "Official American League" baseball, but I knew Waner had only played in the National League.

This is not an uncommon occurrence, but most collectors prefer a player's signature on a proper league ball. The perplexing point was that the league president's facsimile signature on the baseball was Bobby Brown's. Brown did not assume that office until a year-and-a-half after Waner's death.

• Incorrect writing materials

The knowledge of writing instruments and materials enhances a collector's chance of obtaining an authentic signature. A Boston Bruins memorabilia collector once sent me an autographed team sheet to help authenticate. After determining that it was from the 1938-39 season, the year they were Stanley Cup Champions, I noticed some peculiarities with the signatures. Most of them were in fountain pen, but a few were written in ballpoint pen.

Since ballpoint pens were not available at that time, I concluded that they were probably added later. We also researched the backgrounds of the players who signed in ballpoint pen to confirm that they had not died before the pen's invention. This example shows why understanding writing instruments and knowing when they were introduced to the public can be helpful.

• Off-scale writing

Forgers often unconsciously reduce the size of their subject's signature. As a sports autograph collector, you will be amazed at the variations in size of an athlete's signature.

A perfect example is Emmitt Smith's signature. I have an 8x10 color photograph of Smith that has an autograph that measures 5.5x6.5. Now that's a big signature!

Shifts in popularity can also impact a player's signature. When Don Mattingly was an emerging rookie, his signature was much smaller and dramatically less flamboyant. As his popularity grew, so did the size of his signature.

• Uncommon form

Any unusual variation of a subject's typical form of handwriting should immediately elicit authenticity concerns. Signature breaks, character definitions, slant and beginning and ending strokes should all be consistent with known examples.

This is not to say that subtle shifts don't take place in a player's signature; they do. Just be aware of any dramatic variations. It's better to wait and confirm that a variation has occurred in an athlete's signature than to own a questionable example.

• Tremulous writing

Tremulous writing is a characteristic of old age, illness, illiteracy and forgery. Irregular pen pressure and a quivering line quality are indications of a slowly-drawn forgery.

Typically, signatures are smooth and confident, with little pen pressure variation. Ascending and descending loops are excellent checkpoints for tremulous signature examination. Irregular surfaces, such as footballs, basketballs and gloves, only complicate the task of identifying tremulous writing.

• Tracing

Tracing, a very common form of forgery, is easily recognizable. Traced signatures are filled with unnatural characteristics, such as slowly drawn lines that lack any natural variations or spontaneity. Also, indentations, erasures and pencil marks are usually noticeable under magnification.

Forgers usually trace many items at a time. Because these items are often traced from the same example, they will generally superimpose at many points in the signature.

• Stroke irregularity and retouching

Quick, carefree strokes of consistent pen pressure are indications of normal handwriting. However, forged signatures are often slowly drawn with too much emphasis placed on detail.

Irregular pen lifts, or areas that indicate that a writing device has ceased, paused and then continued writing, also indicate a forgery. They are particularly easy to spot on glossy photographs where the subject has used a porous tip pen. Pen lifts are the dark spots at the ends of each stroke.

Retouching, although often a sign of forgery, does occur. My favorite retouch story is one involving an autographed baseball from broadcasting great Mel Allen. While Allen was signing, a journalist began asking him questions.

I knew Allen liked to talk, but did not realize he took his time when signing autographs. After each question, Allen would stop in the middle of a writing stroke, respond, then return to that spot and retouch it so that it appeared continuous. Then he'd go on to the next letter.

The result after 20 minutes of waiting was a signature that has about five noticeable points where retouching has taken place, and a reference library's worth of delightful baseball stories.

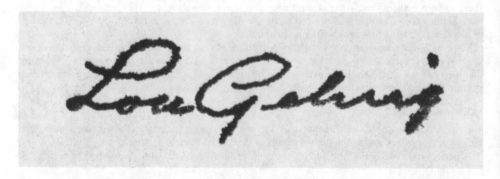

This fake Lou Gehrig signature illustrates a feathering pattern.

• Writing applied to old material

A common technique used by forgers is to add signatures to old material, such as programs, scorecards, media guides, tickets, yearbooks, or just about anything that can be dated or shows some form of natural aging.

Often, these signatures are in pencil or ballpoint pen, because forgers realize that the ink from porous tip pens will make a feathering pattern when applied to older paper-based materials.

Signature Comparison Characteristics

The two main writing characteristics used by most experts for signature comparison are:

1) Line quality

Which includes:

❑ Pen position (where a line or signature begins and ends)

❑ Pen pressure (consistent or inconsistent; most noticeable in upward and downward strokes)

❑ Writing speed, rhythm, or tremor (any slowly-drawn line indicators?)

❑ Signature breaks (are the breaks between characters in a first or last name, if any, consistent with known examples?)

2) Form

Which includes:

❑ Proportions (capitalization versus lowercase)

❑ Slant (right or left)

❑ Beginning and ending strokes (location and flamboyance)

❑ Character formation (particularly capitalization, and the letters e, a and o, the crossing of the t's and the dotting of the i's, and a character descender)

❑ Character spacing

❑ Style (flamboyance)

❑ Legibility

These three Joe Montana autographs are fakes.

Wayne Gretzky - signature comparison characteristics

The "Great One" has won nine Art Ross trophies (NHL top scorer), nine Hart trophies (NHL MVP), three Lady Byng Memorial trophies (sportsmanlike play) and is the NHL career leader in points and assists. During the 1993-94 season he surpassed Gordie Howe's, his idol, mark of 801 goals.

Gretzky's signature is fairly accessible in the market, as are numerous forgeries. The two main writing characteristics used by experts to determine authenticity are line quality and form. Using these characteristics, four Gretzky forgeries will be compared to his authentic signature, so that you can understand some of the finer points of signature analysis.

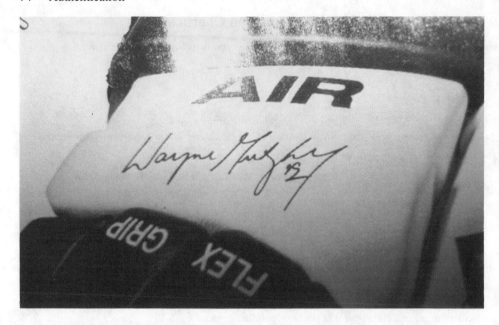

Genuine Wayne Gretzky autographs like this one are often forged.

Signature comparison characteristics

• Line quality

❑ Pen position - The beginning stroke of the "G" in Gretzky is noticeably closer to the signature's baseline in three out of four forgery samples. The "r" in Gretzky intersects the "G" in every sample. While I have seen exceptions, particularly on hockey pucks, Gretzky commonly does not intersect these two strokes to the degree that is shown in the forged examples.

❑ Pen pressure - This is difficult to determine without viewing the samples in person. Although the pen pressure is consistent in the forgeries, it is also to a greater degree than is typical of an authentic Gretzky signature.

❑ Writing speed - Again, difficult to determine without viewing the samples in person. However, a careful analysis indicates a larger quantity of ink was dispersed by the writing instrument than is normally seen in examples of this form. This indicates a slower than usual writing speed and is a sign of forgery.

❑ Signature breaks - There are two major and three minor signature breaks that are indicative of an authentic Gretzky autograph. A major break is a common occurrence in a signature; any variance from is usually a forgery. The two major breaks in Gretzky's signature fall between the "W" and "a" in Wayne and between the "G" and "r" in Gretzky. Minor breaks are often inconsistent in use, typically altered due to signature speed or writing surface, and not in themselves a clear indication of a forgery.

The three minor breaks I have witnessed in Gretzky's signature are between the "y" and the "n" in Wayne (uncommon and usually on hockey stick blades or other large surfaces), between the stem of the "t" and the crossing of the "t" in Gretzky (uncommon in earlier signatures, very common in recent examples), and between the "z" and the "k" in Gretzky (uncommon in earlier signatures, somewhat uncommon in later examples, especially on hockey pucks and with signatures obtained under accelerated signing conditions).

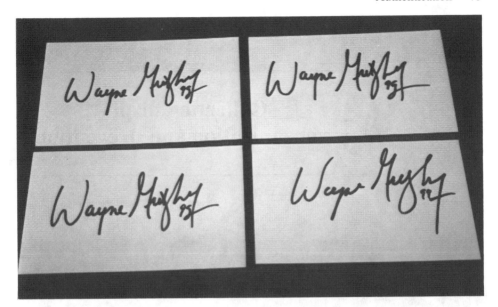

Each of these Wayne Gretzky signatures is a forgery.

• Form

Analyzing the form of Gretzky forgeries is where the signatures are really unmasked due to inconsistencies.

❏ Proportions - The lowercase lettering in the forgeries is too big when compared to authentic examples.

❏ Slant - An authentic Gretzky signature has a greater degree of right slant than indicated in the forgeries. Typically, the smaller the item Gretzky signs, the greater degree of right slant in his autograph. The slant of the ascending stroke used to connect the "z" to the "k" is often close to being parallel with the descending stroke of the "y" in Gretzky - none of the forgeries exhibit this characteristic.

❏ Beginning and ending strokes - Slightly more flamboyance indicated in the descending stroke of the "z" in Gretzky. The loop created by the stroke is larger and slightly more rounded when compared to an authentic signature.

❏ Character formation - The "a" in Wayne is closed in nearly all original samples I have seen of his signature. None of the forgeries exhibit this tendency. While the character formation of the "G" in Gretzky is similar to an original, the forger has missed a key element of the letter. With the exception of one signed poster I have seen, every authentic signature of Gretzky has had the second peak of the letter "G" higher in height than the first peak in the letter. Also, a greater degree of character formation is indicated in the letter "k" when comparing to original examples.

❏ Character spacing - In all but one of the forgeries, the "e" in Wayne is too close to the "n." A major flaw in every one of the forgeries is the space between the upward stroke of the "z" and the stem of the "k" in Gretzky. An original Gretzky example will leave little (very uncommon), if any, space between these letters.

❏ Style - No overt flamboyant variations, but the increased descending loop of the "z" is noticeably larger in one forgery.

❏ Legibility - As with most forgeries, they are more legible than authentic examples.

Conclusion

There is no question that the four examples pictured are indeed forgeries. They all exhibit an extraordinary number of inconsistencies when compared to an original signature.

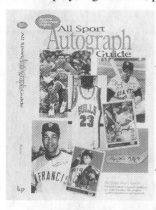

Chapter 8

Collection display, organization and prevention

This display is featured in Bleacher's Sports Bar in Liverpool, N.Y.

Display

A serious collector takes pride in displaying his collection of autographed sports memorabilia. After all, it is the fruits of his efforts. It is hard to believe that anyone would wait two hours in an autograph line, pay a $25 signing fee, then take the item home and leave it in a place where it can be lost or damaged.

It is in each collector's best interest to properly display, store and organize his collectibles. Not only is it a way to track the cost effectiveness of his purchases, but it ensures the collector that those items he has collected have been preserved and have not been duplicated by an additional purchase.

For example, a friend placed an autographed picture of Red Grange in an inexpensive standard-size store-bought frame. He hung it in his downstairs playroom. A year went by before he realized that the Grange signature had faded significantly and part of the photograph had become discolored. Because he worked during the day, he never realized that the afternoon sunlight had direct exposure to his photograph through a downstairs window. The sunlight faded the signature, and the cardboard mat from the frame chemically reacted to his photograph, staining both of the contact surfaces.

Any autographed sports item, if it can not be properly displayed, should be properly stored. During the past few years the hobby has been fortunate enough to have companies manufacture many new storage products specifically aimed at providing safe and aesthetically appealing displays for autographed sports memorabilia. Collectors can now purchase Lucite display cases that conveniently exhibit autographed baseball bats, hockey pucks, basketballs, footballs and even hockey sticks. Prices vary by manufacturer, with most offering a quantity discount.

Nowhere is the word "display" better understood than inside the walls of the Baseball, Basketball, Football and Hockey Hall of Fame museums. Each exhibit does more than just commemorate a specific person or moment; it reaches out to educate the viewer by taking him back in time. The exhibits are designed to compliment the architecture of each of the specific museums. Items or artifacts are assembled and reassembled until the proper grouping of images lends itself to the exhibit. While it is the goal of the exhibit to educate, it is the role of the curator to preserve. Painstaking care is taken to assure that each item is properly adhered, framed or placed into its appropriate position.

When creating an effective display, it is important to put yourself in the viewer's shoes. Be sure to clearly identify each item and its significance to the exhibit. Nothing is more frustrating to a viewer than seeing an item in an exhibit and not understanding its relevance. Most displays are chronological or theme-related to avoid viewer confusion.

This display is featured in Bleacher's Sports Bar in Liverpool, N.Y.

Framing

The most popular form of displaying autographed sports collectibles is by having them framed. Because collectors are now having everything framed, not just flat items, the term framing is becoming synonymous with having an exhibit case constructed. For our use here, however, we will concentrate on framing paper-based collectibles such as photographs, letters and documents. Your

Pittsburgh Penguins star Mario Lemieux warrants his own display.

concern for the quality of preservation used in framing will determine the materials used, where it will be done and the cost.

Foremost to remember is that nothing in the way of tapes or adhesives should be attached to the document for mounting on mat board. This is not an extreme caution; instead, it is one more technique in avoiding paper damage. I have seen many pieces damaged when documents or photographs that were adhered to mat boards were improperly removed from frames. There are certain adhesives that archivists use in framing. However, they are out of the average collector's realm.

Assuming you are framing a piece that is surrounded by a mat board which encapsulates sensitive documents, placing it between two pieces of high grade Mylar or using Mylar corners for photographs are typical archival techniques. Many very sensitive documents require deacidification, especially if they are printed on acidic paper or have an incorporation of a high alkaline paper within the document.

Collectors should contact a local archivist before determining whether a specific item should be encapsulated. If an archivist determines that this technique is appropriate, be sure that the item is not entirely encapsulated, allowing several places for the document to breathe. Always use acid-free double-stick tape to adhere both sheets of Mylar together.

Mat boards come in all shapes and sizes. Whatever your preference is, however, make sure the mat is 100 percent cotton rag content. Unlike paper mats, rag mats do not yellow over time. How many times have you seen severely stained or yellow mats at antique shows?

Ultraviolet light is the number one nemesis of every sports autograph collector; it is the primary source for the deterioration and fading of a signature. The type of glass or Plexiglas you choose for your frame should provide the maximum protection against ultraviolet radiation. Be sure the masking paper which covers the acrylic surface states ultraviolet filtering characteristics or UF-3. Also, be sure that no part of the glass or acrylic is in direct contact with the framed item. Occasionally, subtle forms of condensation can appear on the inside of the frame and can damage the surfaces it touches.

Once an item is properly framed, your final step in its preservation is to be sure it is hung in a place that avoids direct sunlight. Properly lighting a framed piece or a display can be difficult. Fluorescent lighting is common, but like any form of light, if it's not properly filtered of its harmful rays, it may damage a piece over a prolonged period of time.

If built-in display lighting is an option, collectors should realize that the heat generated by the light will affect the humidity in the case and possibly the items inside. Silica gel tablets or beads are recommended in areas or environments where a high humidity point could damage the collectible. External, indirect lighting, properly filtered, and not focused right on the display, is most common.

Organization

As a collection grows, organization increases in importance to the collector. Although collectors differ in their approaches to documenting their collections, they all try to choose an approach that is flexible to their needs, yet specific in terms of acquisition information. Many collectors with access to personal computers choose a database software package that best fits their needs. Those without that option may simply choose to use an index card file system.

Whatever approach you take, make sure you detail the following information: name or description of the item, place of acquisition and date, condition, purchase price, seller information (name, address, phone number) and return policy. If the autographed sports item you acquired has several signatures, list each name that appears on the piece. Also, if the item was acquired at a sports memorabilia show it is useful to record the show promoter's name, address and phone number.

For example:

Acquisition - 1993-94 Orlando Magic team basketball

Date of acquisition - 5/2/94

Purchase price - $650

Condition - Excellent

Place of acquisition - Sports World, 226 East Main St., Orlando, Fla. 32801

Return policy - 30-day unconditional money-back guarantee.

Comments - Basketball contains 12 signatures: Dennis Scott, Anthony Bowie, Anfernee Hardaway, Scott Skiles, Nick Anderson, Litterial Green, Donald Royal, Todd Lichti, Anthony Cook, Keith Tower, Shaquille O'Neal and Jeff Turner. The Turner and O'Neal signatures difficult to identify. Skiles' signature is slightly smeared.

Storage

The Baseball Hall of Fame has storage areas for bats and jerseys.

What form of autographed sports memorabilia you collect will partially determine the most cost-effective method of storage. Collectors often choose to store their most treasured signatures in local bank safe-deposit boxes. This, however, might not be a viable option for those who collect items such as autographed team hockey sticks. A safe, climate-controlled environment, where items can be stored easily and compactly, and risk-free from contact with foreign surfaces, is ideal. Fireproof cabinets and safes are also cost-effective alternatives for storage.

Naturally, if you are going to spend a substantial amount of time and money on your collection, ensuring its safety should be of paramount importance. Those who choose to store a collection at home might want to install a quality home security system or have a comprehensive insurance policy covering the collectibles.

One habit that is particularly helpful, and a requirement of most insurance policies, is photographing your collection. Additionally, photographs can prevent unneeded handling of a collectible, while providing an instant compact reference to the item.

Preservation, Display and Storage

Autographed Sports Memorabilia

Baseballs, basketballs, footballs and hockey pucks

Plastic holders or display cases are aesthetically pleasing, but only really serve to keep the items clean. Unless the material has a filter built into it, it is not protecting the signature from harmful ultraviolet radiation. The best way to preserve these items is to wrap them in a non-acidic material and place them in a light-free, climate-controlled environment. Signature deterioration is also enhanced by the type of ink used in the writing device and the material it is applied to. There is nothing you can apply to signatures on these items to better preserve them.

Baseball, basketball, football and hockey jerseys

Many autographed sports jersey collectors believe that framing a jersey is the most effective method of protecting it. This is incorrect, because whenever pressure is applied to the fabric it is going to deteriorate. Most archivists agree that the best way to display a jersey is on a padded hanger. Although modern day jerseys are manufactured with man-made fabrics that are extremely durable, older woolen uniforms are not, so they require greater sensitivity.

A common mistake made by collectors is framing a jersey against natural felt. Only polyester felt should be used because natural felt, while it deteriorates, can chemically react and harm the jersey. Flat storage in an acid-free box is the recommended method for storing jerseys.

Never alter a jersey in any way, especially by adding or removing tags or patches. Tags and patches are critical to the authentication process and are placed on the jersey for a reason. Jerseys can also be authenticated through stitching and thread identification. Never try to reapply a broken stitch without first consulting an expert in jersey restoration. A final word of caution is to be careful when laundering a jersey. Many of the new highly concentrated detergents can stain certain fabrics if they are directly applied.

Baseball bats and hockey sticks

If a bat or hockey stick is broken, a protective finish can be added to reduce splinters. The main reason in storing each item in individual containers, such as bat tubes, is to prevent surface damage when it is moved. Since finished wood is not very porous, a signature has minimal absorption into the surface. Some players opt for unfinished bats or sticks, but if these items are autographed with porous tip pens you will be able to witness the ink spreading into the wood grain.

Bats with colored surfaces, such as the black commemorative bats that Hillerich & Bradsby has produced over the years, should be stored in tubes that use the hard plastic end caps. I have witnessed my own autographed Billy Martin black bat have its finished removed where it was in contact with a soft vinyl end cap.

Bleacher's Sports Bar features this bat rack display.

Helmets, hats, gloves, cleats, skates and shoes

Helmets are extremely durable and are not considered a high risk item to conservators. However, I have seen the finish on some old football helmets begin to deteriorate and chip after being exposed to light for a prolonged period of time.

Old hat visors can become brittle and break, especially if they are exposed to sunlight. Since some early hats were made of woolen fibers, like jerseys, they should avoid any applied pressure.

Gloves, cleats, skates and shoes, if made of leather, should annually be treated with a conditioner so that they don't become brittle and crack. If any of these items are autographed, take considerable care in avoiding contact with the signature and all of its surrounding area.

Baseball, basketball, football and hockey cards

Storing your autographed sports trading cards in an 800-count box, although inexpensive, does little to protect the item. Individual sleeves or semirigid holders help ensure the cards remain in good condition, but are not necessarily the best alternative for prolonged storage.

Since cards are made of cardboard, like most papers today, they are made of ground wood pulp. Characteristic of this paper is short weak fibers that include lignin, which is a chemical that deteriorates into acid. The acid produced breaks down the fibers of the paper and makes your cards brittle.

This acid can also severely discolor the card. The amount of acid in paper is determined by a "pi" test. Modern cards indicate a level 3.0 and below, which is a substantial amount of acid. There are expensive ways to neutralize the acid, but most are very costly and not easily accessible to the average collector.

Always store your autographed sports trading cards in an environment of constant temperature (65-70 degrees) and humidity (50 percent), that does not have excessive, or be prone to, condensation. Always avoid contact with direct sunlight and try to keep the collection in total darkness if it's being stored over a prolonged period of time.

If your autographed cards are in long-term storage, you may want to put them in non-vinyl sheets (polyethylene, polypropylene or mylar), one per slip and placed in a D-ring binder that will lay flat on a shelf. Do not use vinyl sheets - polyvinylchoride (PVC) - which emit hydrochloric acid. If boxes are preferred, use only acid-free cardboard boxes.

Preservation

Preservation is mainly mentioned regarding paper-based collectibles. But it is also a critical, important factor for all forms of autographed sports memorabilia. Most forms of sports collectibles deteriorate from many of the same factors that effect paper. These factors include the collector himself, environmental elements, such as light temperature and humidity, and the material's own characteristics. A checklist of hints and suggestions has been provided here.

Preservation Checklist

The Collector

❑ Each month inspect your collection for signs of deterioration.

❑ If any item needs immediate attention, due to deterioration, contact a professional conservator.

❑ Do not excessively handle an item.

❑ Storage should be designed to accommodate the size, weight, and environmental concerns of your collection.

❑ Never alter an item's original condition, such as removing tags, retracing a line, etc..

Carl Yastrzemski has a display in the Baseball Hall of Fame.

The Environment

❑ Never display an item in direct sunlight.

❑ Properly screen all light sources from ultraviolet radiation - sunlight, fluorescent light.

❑ Monitor all heat sources, including incandescent bulbs. Incandescent light bulbs do not emit ultraviolet radiation. The suggested lighting, using a 100-watt bulb of this type, would be indirectly focused at a distance no closer than three feet.

❑ Storage and display conditions should be maintained at 65-70 degrees Fahrenheit and at a relative humidity of 50 percent.

❑ Keep your collection dry and well ventilated. All ventilation filters should be cleaned periodically.

❑ Avoid smoking, eating or drinking near your collectibles.

❑ Use only acid-free or recommended archival storage supplies.

The Item

❑ Avoid contact with any alien surfaces. When one type of material touches another, a chemical reaction occurs.

❏ Never attempt to preserve an autograph by adding a substance to its surface.
❏ Use professional grade collectibles; avoid inexpensive alternatives.
❏ Use only high-grade inks that are applicable to the surface they will adorn.
❏ Inspect an item's condition prior to having it autographed, to notice any flaws.
❏ Do not remove autographed items from protective enclosures unless absolutely necessary.

Maybe one day your item will end up in the Baseball Hall of Fame.

The fate of your collection is in your own hands. Budgeting a percentage of your purchasing money toward preservation is a wise investment. Many outstanding autographed collectibles have been ruined out of carelessness by the collector. Museums such as sports Hall of Fames are non-profit organizations that survive on the public's support for not only funding, but for the items that are on display. The number of autographed sports items that are privately owned far exceed those owned by any of the four major sports museums. That is why it is our duty to preserve these items for the generations that will follow. Someday, it may be your autographed UCLA college jersey of Troy Aikman that will find its way to Canton, Ohio!

Archival Storage Materials & Conservation Supplies

Cost estimates of selected products

Item	Price range *
• Acid-free magazine file	$11.50
• Archival document case	$3.90-$5.30 (3 min., size varies)
• Newspaper storage boxes	$10.60 (2 min.)
• Costume storage boxes	$28.75 (for uniforms)
• Cloth labeling tape	$11.65 (per roll, uniform labels)
• Preservation kit	$70.15 (Starter, assorted materials)
• Card file boxes	$3.00 (3x5 cards)
• Buffered acid-free wrapping tissue	$92.25 (500-foot roll, 40" wide)
• "Pigma" fade-proof pens	$2 (acid-free black or red ink)
• Archival mounting corners	$4.20 (box of 500)
• Wei T'o deacidification spray	$21.45 (spray)
• Permalife bond paper	$8.45 (package of 500 sheets)

* = Prices will vary on quanity and are subject to change.

All prices quoted from Gaylord Brothers Archival and Storage Materials & Conservation Supplies 1994 Catalog No. 4.

Gaylord Brothers offers some of the finest archival, storage and preservation materials. For a copy of a catalog, or to order merchandise, call 1-800-448-6160, from 8 a.m. to 7 p.m., or write to Gaylord Brothers, P.O. Box 4901, Syracuse, N.Y. 13221-4901.

Chapter 9

Sports Autograph Values

Where there's a demand for a Cy Young ball, there's a market.

Finding out how much your autographed Emmitt Smith photograph is worth usually means turning to a page in a price guide, but understanding just how that value was determined requires a greater understanding of the hobby. The key factors influencing the value of autographed sports memorabilia are condition, supply, demand, form and source. For those whose business is buying and selling autographed sports memorabilia, understanding these factors is essential to their success. To a novice or casual collector they are important, but far less significant.

A brief history of sports autograph values

Because there is a demand for sports autographs, there is a market. Where there is a market, there is a need by the buyer and the seller to understand value. Most of us started collecting out of our love for sports and the opportunity to share in the achievements of the athletes we cherished. To preserve those moments, and as an assurance that the memory wouldn't fade, we often asked an athlete for his autograph. It was proof, too, that we really did meet the athlete.

A Mickey Mantle autographed baseball can bring $90.

During the 1950s, sports autograph collectors weren't interested in values; the autographs were obtained in person, so the value was in the moment, not on the paper. Although there was radio, it took television to bring our sports heroes to life, allowing us to finally see the faces of DiMaggio, Chamberlain, Gifford and Howe.

As television evolved, we were treated to more games from a variety of sports. Although the attendance of some sports waned during the 1960s, it would flourish again in the 1970s. The word "athlete" was slowly being replaced by the term "sports personality" or "sports celebrity."

The growing interest in professional athletics sparked an increase in collectibles, especially sports trading cards and autographs. Companies, wondering about what new products they could sell in this market, were also interested in the appeal of the sports celebrity who would be selling those products. We knew "Broadway Joe" Namath could throw a football, but could he convince those men watching television to buy a brand of shaving cream?

The competitive cable market, new and affordable satellite equipment, and what seemed to be a never-ending appetite for sports all paved the way for many new sports networks, including ESPN. Increased competition meant higher fees for the rights to broadcast professional sports. And, of course, there was the "athlete," who felt that he too, was entitled to his share of the revenues.

Lucrative multi-million dollar contracts soon became necessary to assure that a team's "sports celebrities" would remain in town for another season. Soon our athletes-turned-celebrities were appearing in magazine advertisements, syndicated television shows, commercials and even movies.

The growth in sports trading cards, specifically baseball, generated additional sports trading card shows, which soon expanded to include autograph guests to boost revenues and attendance. The added cost of having a sports celebrity appear at a show often meant the promoter was forced to charge a fee for an autograph. With greater exposure came an increase in autograph requests and the need for finding out where and how to contact the person.

Major League Baseball was the first of the four major sports to combine all the necessary ingredients to entice autograph collectors. For a market to be viable collectors need: access to their subjects - at the ballpark or at home (*Baseball Address List*); a cost-effective acquisition method - through dealers, in person or by mail; a price guide - to validate an autograph's value (several exist); a way to confirm a signature's authenticity (*The Baseball Autograph Handbook, No. 2*); and a way to monitor the market (*Sports Collectors Digest*).

As the market matures, in-person access to many major players has been reduced, but indirect sources, such as satellite shopping networks and product catalogs, have expanded. You may not be able to obtain a free Cal Ripken Jr. signature at the ballpark, but at least you can still obtain an autograph, despite the purchase price.

Although the cost of sending an autograph request through the mail has doubled since 1980, many players still respond; it's a cost-effective solution to acquiring sports signatures. It's also fortunate for collectors that sports autograph values, for the most part, have kept pace with the market (see chart below). At least this way you know that the time and effort you put into acquiring a signature will probably prove to be worthwhile.

Another refreshing factor is that the issue of authenticity is constantly being addressed in the market. Never before have so many facsimile signatures been available to collectors for comparison purposes to confirm an item's authenticity.

Baseball Autograph Value Comparison
1983-1993

Player	1983			1993		
	Cut	Photo	Ball	Cut	Photo	Ball
Ted Williams	$3.50	$12	$27	$20	$65	$145
Mickey Mantle	$6	$13	$40	$20	$60	$90
Whitey Ford	$1	$3	$11	$4	$15	$25
Al Kaline	.75	$3.50	$10	$3	$14	$20
Stan Musial	.75	$3.50	$11	$8	$25	$50

Note: All prices courtesy of *Sports Collectors Digest*. Prices were averaged from randomly selected advertisements appearing in issues from the specific time period.

The definition of value

Value has two different meanings to collectors. To many the word means "that quality of a thing which makes it more or less desirable, having an intrinsic or inherent worth." It is this definition which I hear most from many satisfied customers, collectors who can't put a value on their collection, because there is no monetary equivalent to the satisfaction they have received from acquiring sports autographs.

The other definition some collectors use is "estimated worth." These collectors, or should I say businessmen, can readily estimate the fair market value for every item in their collections. If you view your collection with very little emotional attachment - if there is little or no remorse in the sale of your Wayne Gretzky autographed photograph - then your definition of value is "estimated worth." Whether you like it or not, your definition of value is going to effect how you collect autographed sports memorabilia.

The collector who is concerned with an item's "estimated value" can't wait for next month's price guide to come out so he can track the appreciation in his collection. The interest level he finds in his subject is at "face value." There is no concern for the human emotion involved in an athletic triumph, only a dollar level attached to its achievement. This is the collector who "turns the stomach" of many professional athletes, for it is this opportunist who is the first to run to the nearest sports trading card store to dispose of his recently-acquired sports autographs.

A friend of mine recently told me why Mario Lemieux has been so reluctant about signing trading cards. Apparently, Lemieux witnessed a young child who, upon receiving a signature from the star at rink side, immediately turned to his nearby friend and asked $10 for the autographed hockey card. It still amazes me how it only takes one careless collector to ruin a wonderful situation or moment for so many others. Unfortunately, this type of collector is part of the hobby and is unavoidable.

The collector who defines value as "that quality of a thing which makes it more or less desirable, having an intrinsic or inherent worth" seldom reviews a price guide. When he reluctantly does, it is usually to determine a price level for his collection as a requirement for his insurance policy.

For this collector, there is no price that he can put on his Montreal Canadiens program autographed by Patrick Roy. This collector drove four hours to Montreal to watch the team he has loved since childhood play the Boston Bruins. He owns every single sports trading card of Patrick Roy, a man he respects as the best goaltender in the NHL. He waited for two hours for the chance to ask Roy for his signature; when the goalie complied, an irreplaceable smile which would last a lifetime came to the collector's face. He can't attach a value to the autograph he received because he can't replace the moment.

Unfortunately, professional athletes are unable, in most cases, to identify which collector is approaching them. We need to emphasize the later form of collecting. Perhaps this simple scenario would help: "Excuse me, Mr. Roy. Would you mind signing an autograph for me? I drove four hours to watch you play. My name is Tom, and if you don't mind, it would mean an awful lot if you personalized it 'To Tom.' Thank you very much."

The factors that influence value

Not all collectors are fortunate enough to have a professional sports team in the city where they live. These collectors are forced to acquire many autographs indirectly, such as through dealers. But to do this efficiently, it is necessary to understand value; knowing the key factors that influence value will help prevent you from being overcharged for an item.

There are five key factors that determine an autograph's value - condition, scarcity or supply, demand, form or what you have signed, and source or from whom you purchased.

Condition

The condition of the signature and the condition of the material that was signed are considered by most dealers to be the paramount factor effecting an item's value. The signature should be bold, clear and unobstructed by any portion of the material that was signed or by any other signatures that appear with it. The material that was signed should reflect, as much as possible, the original state of that object.

The only exception would be game-worn equipment, which would naturally show some indications of wear. But severe damage to the item, such as uniform tears or large pieces missing from a hockey stick, can negatively detract from the value of the autographed item.

It is not unusual for some autographed items to reflect certain aging characteristics. Collectors are probably most familiar with the aging characteristics of paper-based collectibles, such as light stains, discoloration due to fading or inconsistent wear due to folding. Hockey sticks and baseball bats will typically exhibit discoloration due to the aging of the finish applied to them during the final stages of production. Jerseys will exhibit loose threads and some fading.

Collectors anticipate certain aging characteristics which, therefore, have little or no effect on value. But any flaw that is not part of the normal aging process will have a negative impact on the value. For example, the value is less for autographed baseballs, basketballs or footballs that have been excessively worn because of mishandling.

The type of ink and the writing device used for an autograph can effect an item's condition, thus impacting its value. All material has a level of porosity, or a degree to which fluids, air or light can pass through or into them. The higher the level of porosity, the greater the chance of deterioration occurring.

Unfinished hockey sticks, jerseys and official league baseballs are very porous, so when certain inks are applied to them they spread into the surface. This is why so many autographed baseball collectors prefer ballpoint ink signatures over those produced by other porous tip markers. Many inks react negatively to the surfaces they are touching, causing dramatic discoloration over a short period.

Scarcity or supply

The scarcity or supply of a form of autographed sports memorabilia will typically have a reciprocal effect on the demand for the piece. This is particularly true with the signatures of deceased individuals and many of the pioneers of the four major sports. In baseball, Babe Ruth's autograph has always been in great demand. Even though Ruth signed frequently, the supply continues to be insufficient to meet the demand. Although "Shoeless Joe" Jackson is not a member of the Baseball Hall of Fame, his signature is highly sought after, not only for the mystique created by the movies that have recently depicted him, but because he was considered an illiterate for many years. It wasn't until late in his life that he learned to sign his name.

Joe Jackson essentially drew his signature.

The Jacksons owned a liquor store in Greenville, S.C.. When accompanied by his wife, Jackson would never sign anything. Or, if forced, he would sign an "X." When he was left alone, his wife would leave a piece of paper with his name written on it, just in case he needed to sign for merchandise or possibly an autograph. Jackson would essentially draw his autograph, sometimes taking close to a minute to complete.

Today, "Shoeless Joe" Jackson's autograph is considered the most valuable sports autograph in history. The first Jackson clipped signature that entered the market was sold for $23,000. More recently, an 8x10 photograph of Jackson sold for $28,000 in a sale held by Odyssey Auctions of Corona, Calif.

Scarcity can often be difficult to determine; many times the market will move based on a rumor. A player's signature will immediately skyrocket in value, even though there has been no confirmation that the information is indeed true. A few years ago a collector I knew bought Stan Musial autographed baseballs at twice the current market price because he heard a rumor that Musial wasn't going to sign baseballs anymore. The rumor was incorrect; the collector foolishly spent an awful lot of money.

Fluctuations in supply are often temporary, as is the case with most athletes who are actively involved in their sport. The demand for the signatures of the game's biggest stars builds during the regular season, but is typically met during the off-season when many attend sports memorabilia shows. Many players sign during the regular season, but with less frequency.

There are also times when a dealer, after purchasing a large amount of autographed checks or documents from an estate, has offered them for resale to the market. This flood of material fills current demand, driving values down for that type of autographed item. Thus, it may take many years for the market to replenish the demand and drive values up again.

Demand

The demand for many sports autographs has been so strong that athletes have resorted to stamped facsimile, secretarial, or machine-signed autographs, or occasionally even complete disregard. The massive correspondence to players such as Wayne Gretzky, Michael Jordan, Barry Bonds and Emmitt Smith, if attended to personally, would leave them little time for their own everyday needs. To reduce the response time to requests made by mail, some players, including Mugsy Bogues and Alonzo Mourning, only sign one item per person. This helps meet current market demand without frustrating collectors, or resorting to unauthentic responses which only confuse the public.

Some clubs, such as the Philadelphia Flyers, hamper demand by sending out 4x6 color postcards - compliments of JC Penny stores and Lee in the Delaware Valley - that bear facsimile signatures on the front. Although collectors are grateful that their requests are at least acknowledged, this method only increases demand.

Significant achievements, such as reaching a career milestone or induction into a sports Hall of Fame, can immediately effect demand. An example of this, Phil Rizzuto, has been accessible to collectors for many years through the mail and by attending several baseball card shows. However, it wasn't until his induction in 1994 that anyone saw a noticeable increase in the demand for his signature. This increase will remain until all public demand has been met.

Changes in a player's popularity, for whatever reason, also effect demand. Usually they are triggered by a poor athletic performance, or career-threatening injuries, but they can happen after an event that the public may consider distasteful. Early in 1994, the demand for autographs from players such as Mark Rypien, Brett Hull, Christian Laettner and Jose Canseco has been reduced because they haven't met the public's performance expectations.

These demand changes are often cyclical. As you can see by examples listed, any of these athletes can put together a tremendous year, so now is the best time to buy these athletes' signatures; they are probably at the lowest possible prices.

The signatures of recently deceased players, especially former or current stars, are always in demand, often commanding two or three times what an average autograph from this individual would have commanded prior to his death. If an unpredictable circumstance claims a player's life, demand can be enormous, as exemplified by the reaction of collectors after the deaths of Roberto Clemente and Thurman Munson.

Form

The type of material the collector has signed and its relevance to the subject impacts the item's value. This is why a Teemu Selanne autographed hockey puck is worth more than his signature on a hockey card. This is not to say that you can't be creative, like having a baseball signed by Deion Sanders, Bo Jackson and Michael Jordan. You can, but restrict yourself from having foolish or unrelated items autographed.

How many times have we seen unprepared fans flock to request the signature of a sports personality on a napkin? I have never met someone who collects napkins, either the dinner or the cocktail varieties. If you collect autographed sports memorabilia, choose a form which is at least appealing and accepted by the majority of the participants in the hobby.

Although popular forms of collecting may be less creative, they offer greater range of acquisition possibilities. Adding to an autographed sports trading card, baseball, hockey stick or football helmet collection is easier than more bizarre forms of collectibles, such as clocks, furniture and glassware.

Baseball collectors believe in having only official league baseballs autographed, primarily because they are dateable and subject to less authentication scrutiny. Also, official league baseballs are identical to those used by the professionals. Because this has become an accepted form of collecting, official league autographed baseballs have greater value than other types. Whenever a collectible can be dated, it reduces a collector's concern for authenticity and increases the item's value.

Autographed baseball collectors also prefer single-signature baseballs, or balls with only one autograph on the sweet spot (the side opposite the name of the league's president), over multiple-signed balls. This is why a single-signature baseball of Lou Gehrig is worth more than an equivalent signature on a baseball accompanied by the names of Johnny Allen, Frank Crosetti, Bill Dickey and Doc Farrell. In this case, less is more in terms of value.

Autographed letters containing great, or extremely relevant or even controversial content, are a highly-sought form by collectors. A letter from Pete Maravich discussing his style of basketball play is far more intriguing than a simple note thanking someone for an autograph request. Admittedly, professional athletes are not known for their letter writing prowess, but if you pick this form to collect, remember that value is a function of content.

Source

When mentioning sports autograph values in my other books, I have been reluctant to acknowledge that the source or where the item was acquired could have any impact on the value of a piece. Increasing market concerns for authenticity have forced me to reconsider its absence. Although the source of a signature can impact an autograph's value, it has a lesser effect than any of the factors listed previously.

Because it is getting extremely difficult for the average collector to authenticate the sports autographs he is buying, he is not afraid to spend the extra money to purchase an autographed Roger Staubach football directly from the Dallas Cowboys for $129.99. Yes, he could have saved himself as much as $40 by choosing an alternative source, but his level of purchasing confidence would have been reduced. In this case, his lack of experience in authentication determined his purchasing source.

What scares me about saying the source has an impact on value is that I have seen many larger companies intimidate smaller collectors into purchasing their products by using a "forgery fear" in their marketing tactics. Let me state it clearly that the signature you receive in person, be it at a show, or in the arena, is of equal, if not greater value, than a purchase you make from a major autograph memorabilia supplier.

"Letter of Authenticity" or not, if a major company or dealer files for bankruptcy, what do you honestly think it's going to take, in terms of time and finances, to redeem your autographed Reggie Jackson baseball (for which you paid $79.95) after you have authenticity concerns?

A final word on value

Remember, it is not the dealer, player or promoter who determines value. It is the collector. Your willingness, justifiable or not, to pay a certain price for an autographed sports item has an impact on value. While there is little doubt in my mind that an autographed Joe Montana football will eventually increase in value, there is a point at which the collector refuses to purchase an item. You, the collector, make that decision.

These major dealers and companies are in business to make money, or they won't be around for long. If they can't get the price they are seeking for an autographed sports item, there is only one alternative - lower it. Stagnant inventory doesn't pay bills or impress investors, but sales do.

My father once told me, "An item is only worth what someone is willing to pay for it."

Sports Autograph Values

What factors influence the value of autographed sports memorabilia?

• Condition

The condition of any collectible is considered the premier factor in determining its value. With autographed sports memorabilia it is often not only the condition of the signature that is important, but also the state of the item it adorns. Any item that a collector chooses to have signed should be in the best possible condition, which usually represents the original state of the object. Additionally, there should be no alterations to, or variations from, the item's original state.

The type of ink and writing device used for an autograph can effect an item's condition, so it therefore has an effect on value. Many autographed baseball collectors prefer not to invest in autographs written with porous tip pens, such as Sanford's "Sharpie," for fear that the signature will bleed into the baseball over a prolonged period of time.

• Scarcity/supply

The scarcity or supply of any autographed sports item has a direct impact on its value. Typically speaking, the lower the supply, the greater the demand for the piece. Obviously, the death of any prominent athlete has an immediate effect on the value of his signature. The degree to which it effects the value depends upon the known writing habits of the individual and the current market demand.

When the supply of a signature has not been met, a short-term scarcity can occur in the market. With a professional athlete this is often attributed to a recent achievement.

• Demand

The demand for a particular sports autograph can be attributed to a known lack of supply, or it can simply be based on the athlete's popularity at a given time. If an athlete achieves a specific milestone it often increases the demand for his signature. On the contrary, should he incur a career-ending injury, or be having a terrible season, the value of his signature will typically decline.

Also remember that the popularity of certain forms of autographed sports memorabilia can effect the demand or value. More individuals collect autographed baseballs than signed caps. Just because an item has a higher price tag doesn't mean it is in greater demand.

• Form

The type of material the athlete signed and the relevance of that item impacts its value. This is why an autograph from Charles Barkley on a basketball is worth more than his signature on a 3x5 index card. Items that can be dated, such as Official League baseballs and government postcards, are also desired by collectors. An item that can be associated with a particular period or date is beneficial for authentication purposes, and therefore can command greater value than a similar undated piece. Autographed letters are valued by content, or the relevance of the material written by the athlete. Collectors of autographed sports books prefer signed first editions over later editions, another case where form impacts value.

• Source

The increased demand for autographed sports memorabilia has spawned new concerns for authenticity. Collectors who are unsure of their expertise with determining the authenticity of a certain player's signature don't mind paying a higher autograph price if they have a greater level of comfort with its source. Although the source of a signature can impact an autographs value, it has a lesser effect than those factors listed above.

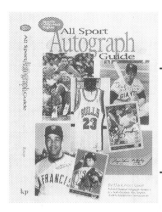

Chapter 10

The Top 100

Aikman, Troy

Considered one of the hottest properties in the National Football League, Aikman once again led the Dallas Cowboys to the Super Bowl in 1994. He threw for 3,100 yards and 15 touchdowns during the regular season. His completion rating of 69.1 percent was tops among qualified quarterbacks in the National Football Conference. The tough competitor is regarded as a team leader.

Aikman has done private signings and shows, but as his popularity grows, his accessibility will decrease. He is considered by many major corporations to be the next superstar in terms of endorsements. If you have little luck by mail or in person, you can always order the following items from the official Dallas Cowboys Catalog: a personally-autographed Aikman photograph on a plaque ($79.99), a QB Club autographed football ($129.99), an autographed authentic NFL jersey ($199.99), or an official game helmet ($319.99).

Aikman's four-stroke signature varies in character formation, particularly the "ro" in Troy and the "man" in Aikman. Capitalization size usually depends upon what he is signing. On a photograph, the largest letter is often the "A" in Aikman; on a football, the "T" in Troy usually dominates. He sometimes puts his number, 8, over the "man" in Aikman.

Football: $115 Photograph: $31

Address: c/o Dallas Cowboys, Cowboys Center, 1 Cowboys Parkway, Irving, Texas 75063-4727

Marcus Allen

Allen, Marcus

Allen finished seventh in rushing in the American Football Conference with 764 yards in 1993. In showing everyone that after 11 seasons with the Raiders he is still one of the finest running backs around, as a Kansas City Chief Allen led the league with 12 rushing TDs. The MVP of Super Bowl XVIII and the 1981 winner of the Heisman Trophy, Allen moved into the top 10 for lifetime rushing yards in 1993.

Allen's bitter feud with Raiders' boss Al Davis effected his popularity, causing the demand for his signature to fall. But Allen showed that, despite the adversities he faced while in Los Angeles, he remained committed to his goals and was willing to prove it in Kansas City. Allen is truly one of the game's greatest running backs.

As Allen turned his career around in Kansas City, he became more obliging to in-person autograph requests, but traditionally does not respond to mail autograph requests. His five-stroke signature is very flamboyant. The "M" in Marcus resembles a star or asterisk. By the time the stroke reaches the "llen" in Allen the characters are indiscernible.

Football: $70 Photograph: $17

Address: c/o Kansas City Chiefs, One Arrowhead Drive, Kansas City, Mo. 64129

---

* You must stop the subject from moving - Do not allow the subject to walk while he is signing his autograph. As he walks he is decreasing his available signing space, causing other collectors to loose an autograph opportunity.

Alomar, Roberto

One of the finest all-around players in the game today, this four-time All-Star hit .326 in 1993, while driving in 93 runs. He continues to astound everyone with his defensive prowess and quickness. Alomar can also be a threat on the base paths; he's averaged more than 50 stolen bases during the past three years. He enters the 1994 season with 1,054 hits; that's not bad for someone 26 years old.

Alomar does sign in person, but mail requests are often inconsistent. His eight-stroke signature has five breaks that can vary. His signature can be a bit difficult to interpret; many of the character formations are often unrecognizable.

Baseball: $30 Photograph: $16

Address: c/o Toronto Blue Jays, The SkyDome, 300 Bremner Blvd., Suite 3200, Toronto, Ontario, Canada M5V 3B3

Avery, Steve

Avery already has 50 career wins and 466 strikeouts; that's not bad for a kid who just turned 24. After making his first All-Star appearance in 1993, he finished the year 18-6, with a 2.94 ERA. Although he may give up a hit per inning, he averages almost three times as many strikeouts than walks, which is one of the finest ratios among National League starters.

Avery, always an accessible signer, does many private signings during the off-season. His signature has changed dramatically since he was acquired as a first-round draft pick in June of 1988. His four-stroke signature has two common breaks, between the "t" and the "eve" in Steve, and between the "A" and the "v" in Avery. Avery crosses his "t" typically with the beginning of his second signature stroke and does the same with his fourth stroke that bisects the letter "A" in Avery. The character formations of the "ev" in Steve are often the only undefinable letters in his signature.

Many collectors mistake his earlier signatures for forgeries because of the dramatic differences. A sample of both signature types has been provided here.

Baseball: $25 Photograph: $18
Address: c/o Atlanta Braves, P.O. Box 4064, Atlanta, Ga. 30302

Barkley, Charles

The Most Valuable Player in 1992-93, "Sir" Charles placed fifth in scoring and sixth in rebounding for the season. He ranks fourth in the NBA in scoring the last six years, behind only Michael Jordan, Karl Malone and Dominique Wilkins. His career field goal percentage is fourth all-time and first among active players. Barkley's brash style of play is his trademark.

Barkley has taken over as the NBA's endorsement king, now that Jordan has left the game of basketball. He can be a very circumstantial signer; if there is a crowd and television cameras around, your chances of getting an autograph improve.

Barkley's large three-stroke signature can vary in character formation. The "es" in Charles and the "k" in Barkley often have little if any recognizable formation. The two-stroke "B" in Barkley often resembles a "13" in its formation. He occasionally places his number, 34, underneath his signature, with the stem of the "4" made from the descending stroke of the "y" in Barkley.

Basketball: $145 Photograph: $24

Address: c/o Phoenix Suns, 201 E. Jefferson, P.O. Box 1369, Phoenix, Ariz. 85001

Hints for acquiring autographs through the mail

* Avoid form letters. In addition to being impersonal and unflattering, the letters typically have a low response rate.

* To avoid confusion and disappointing responses, requests should be succinct and specific. If personalization is desired, please clearly indicate it in your request.

* Be conscious of a player's time by including no more than one or two items to be autographed.

Belfour, Ed

After only six seasons, Belfour has already notched 23 shutouts. In 1993-94, he finished among the top five NHL goaltenders in four categories: shutouts, games played, goals-against average and wins. The two-time Vezina Trophy winner (as best goalkeeper) is just the fifth goalie in history to record a pair of 40-win seasons.

Belfour can be an evasive signer at times; mail autograph requests have unpredictable results.

Belfour's large two-stroke signature exhibits no signature breaks. The trademarks of his signature are the large "E" in Ed, which is often the largest letter in his name, and the "lf" letter combination that resembles a large "y." The letter spacing in his signature is very large and he often writes his uniform number, 30, underneath his last name.

Puck: $36 Photograph: $17

Address: c/o Chicago Blackhawks, Chicago Stadium, 1800 W. Madison St., Chicago, Ill. 60612

Hints for acquiring autographs through the mail

* Always include a self-addressed, stamped envelope (SASE) for convenient response through the mail. Please be sure the enclosed envelope is of proper size to house the returned material, and that the proper postage is affixed.

* Be brief, personal and sincere with your request. Exhibit in a few sentences your genuine interest in, and knowledge of, a player's career. Courtesy is paramount.

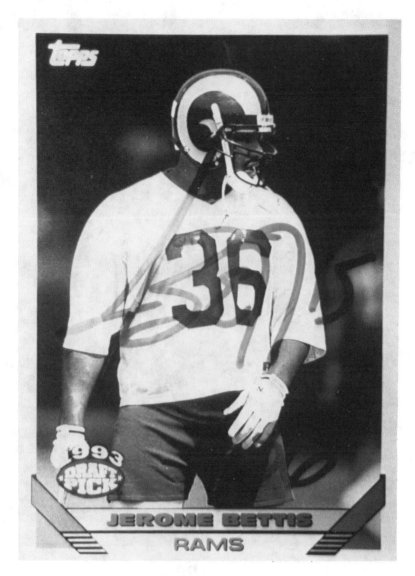

Bettis, Jerome

The powerful and quick former Notre Dame star showed everyone in the NFL that he is going to be a force in the future. In his first year with the Los Angeles Rams, Bettis rushed for 1,429 yards and seven TDs, losing the NFC rushing title to Emmitt Smith by only 57 yards.

Bettis is a gracious signer in person and through autograph mail requests. Combine his winning attitude with his on-field statistics and you have the recipe for a popular superstar.

His seven-stroke signature is almost printed in its style. The large "J" resembles the number "4," while the "B," which connects to the "J" to form its stem, resembles the number "3." The "tt" configuration appears like "77." Bettis often places his uniform number, 36, underneath his last name.

Football: $85 Photograph: $25
Address: c/o Los Angeles Rams, 2327 W. Lincoln Ave., Anaheim, Calif. 92801

Bledsoe, Drew

The former Washington State star impressed many New Englanders in his rookie season with the Patriots, passing for 2,494 yards and 15 TDs, while displaying his tremendous potential.

Bledsoe has been an obliging signer thus far, but as his popularity increases, so will his mail.

Bledsoe's four-stroke signature has two common breaks, between the "D" and the "r" in Drew, and between the "B" and the "l" in Bledsoe. His first name seems to have been condensed to "Dw," as the "re" character combination is indistinguishable. The "e" and the "soe" are also difficult to recognize in Bledsoe. The hallmark of his signature is the large "D," which comes to a point at the pinnacle of its character height, and the left slant. The point in between both loops of the "B" typically does not intersect the letter's stem. His entire signature resembles "DwBW" in appearance. Bledsoe often includes his uniform number, 11, after his name.

Football: $65 Photograph: $21

Address: c/o New England Patriots, Foxboro Stadium, Route One, Foxboro, Mass. 02035

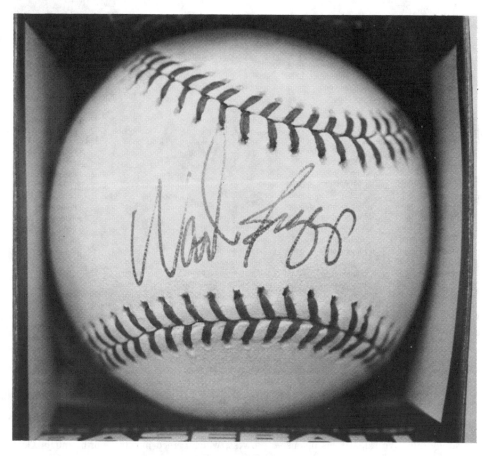

Boggs, Wade

A five-time batting champion, Boggs started the 1994 season with 2,267 hits and a lifetime batting average of .335. After falling to a career-low average of .259, Boggs bounced back by batting .302 in 1993. A solid contact hitter who walks more than he strikes out, he can hurt opposing teams with his on base percentage.

Although a lot of his popularity waned because of his poor 1992 season, but the move to New York, along with another .300 plus season, should bring him back into the collectors' spotlight.

His superstitious behavior adds to many unpredictable autograph responses. He has a tendency to always visit the same restaurants, so picking up on where he dines might be your best bet in grabbing an in-person signature. One collector I know, after being ignored by Boggs during a request for his signature, told Boggs that he went 3-for-4 after the last game when he autographed one of his cards. Boggs heard the response and complied with the request.

The third baseman has an expedient three-stroke signature with only one common break, between the "W" and "a" in Wade. His signature has shown only slight changes in letter size over the past few years. He typically never closes a character and the "e" in Wade is often unrecognizable.

Baseball: $28 Photograph: $17

Address: c/o New York Yankees, Yankee Stadium, Bronx, N.Y. 10451

Bonds, Barry

Considered by many to be the finest all-around player in the game today, Bonds has won the National League Most Valuable Player Award three times in the last four years. Complementing his strong offensive skills is his defensive prowess, which earned him his fourth straight Gold Glove award in 1993. He is considered the definition of a franchise player, making the Giants the hottest ticket in San Francisco in 1993. He reached career peaks in every department during the 1993 season. Many believe it is just a matter of time before he becomes the National League's first Triple Crown winner since 1937.

Commonly criticized for his personality, Bonds can be an elusive signer. For a long time he wouldn't sign any autographed baseballs on the sweet spot, but this is changing. He may sign mail requests sent to the team, but they will not be prompt responses. Going into the 1994 season, Bonds still had four unanswered mail bins from the prior season awaiting his response.

Bonds graduated from Serra High School in San Mateo, Calif., which is located only 20 miles from Candlestick Park. He occasionally visits the school. Since he's a 10-handicap golfer, it is not unusual to find him at some of the Bay area's finest country clubs. He's also an aspiring actor, a member of the Screen Actors Guild. He loves making television show appearances and belongs to many other industry-related groups. The outfielder has donated autographed balls and bats to many charities, including the United Way.

His signature can include eight separate strokes, with character formation in the lowercase letters often variable. Both the capitalized "B"s are typically two strokes, but can vary in slant and flamboyance. The character combination of the "ds" in Bonds often resembles an 8.

Baseball: $40 Photograph: $21

Address: c/o San Francisco Giants, Candlestick Park, San Francisco, Calif. 94124

Bourque, Ray

A four-time James Norris Trophy winner as the league's best defender and a 12-time All-Star, Bourque concluded the 1993-94 season with 1,188 career points as a defenseman. Bourque, the team's first choice in the 1979 draft, eighth overall, showed his appreciation to the organization by winning the Calder (most proficient rookie) Memorial Trophy the following year.

Bourque is an average signer. Mail autograph requests remain unpredictable.

His four-stroke signature has two common breaks, between the "R" and "a" in Ray, and between the "B" and the "o" in Bourque. The flamboyant formations of both capitalized letters is nearly identical, with the exception being the looped final stroke to finish the "B." The "ur" and "ue" in Bourque are often indistinguishable or dropped entirely from his name. Two looped strokes are added underneath the loop of the "q" to form "77" - his uniform number.

Puck: $27 Photograph: $15

Address: c/o Boston Bruins, Boston Garden, 150 Causeway St., Boston, Mass. 02114

Hints for attending card shows

* Get there early - There's a lot to be said in the old adage "The early bird gets the worm." The best selection of autographed sports memorabilia is generally at the beginning of the show.

* Allocate plenty of time - You can not make clear, concise decisions if you are rushed. Concentrate on the task at hand; try not to get distracted.

Bure, Pavel

Bure was the Soviet National League's Rookie-of-the-Year in 1989, the year he was drafted by Vancouver. In his first NHL season in 1992-93, he scored 110 points, earning the Calder (most proficient rookie) Memorial Trophy. He finished sixth in scoring in 1993-94, adding 107 points to his totals.

Bure has so far been an above average signer, but autograph mail requests are still unpredictable.

His four-stroke signature has two breaks, between the "B" and "u" and between the "r" and the "e" in Bure. His typical "P. Bure" signature resembles "P.Pl2" in its formation. The character formations, size and slant of both the "B" and the "P" are nearly identical.

Puck: $28 Photograph: $15

Address: c/o Vancouver Cannucks, Pacific Coliseum, 100 N. Renfrew St., Vancouver, British Columbia, Canada V5K 3N7

---

* Don't be conspicuous - Blend into your surroundings as much as possible. Act like you belong in your environment. Wearing recognizable media clothing, such as NBC Sports, or ESPN, can help you in all professional-level facilities. Always look and act professional.

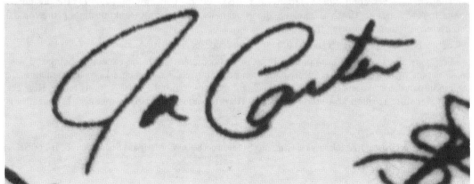

Carter, Joe

During his 11-year career in the majors, Carter has established himself as a solid run producer with excellent power. Yes, he will always be remembered for the home run he hit to win the 1993 World Series, but it is Carter's leadership that has brought a lot more to the Toronto Blue Jays. He enters the 1994 season with 1,523 hits - 275 are home runs.

Carter is not a frequenter of baseball card shows, and he can be elusive to autograph seekers. Requests made in person can be successful, but will depend upon Carter's mood. When his spirits are high, he can be very gracious to autograph requests.

His four-stroke signature has increased in flamboyance over the years. Most of the character formations are distinguishable, with his trademark being the large capital "J" in Joe and "C" in Carter.

Baseball: $38 Photograph: $23

Address: c/o Toronto Blue Jays, The SkyDome, 300 Bremner Blvd., Suite 3200, Toronto, Ontario, Canada M5V 3B3

Chelios, Chris

Chelios added a second Norris Trophy to his collection of awards in 1992-93. He posted 73 points in 84 games to finish second on the Blackhawks in scoring, ranking among the top 10 defensemen in the NHL during the season.

Chelios is an obliging signer, but mail autograph requests can be unpredictable.

Chelios' two-stroke signature commonly exhibits no breaks. With the exception being the "os" combination, nearly every letter of his name can be identified. The trademarks of his signature are the rabbit-eared formations of the "h"s and "l" and the large capitalized "C"s in his name. His very upright signature is often at a 90-degree slant. He often adds his uniform number, 7, beneath his last name.

Puck: $25 Photograph: $13

Address: c/o Chicago Blackhawks, Chicago Stadium, 1800 W. Madison St., Chicago, Ill. 60612

---

* The subject's hand must be available for a signature - It is not unusual for your subject to be carrying an equipment bag, locker room bag, etc.. If you see that a subject has both hands occupied, you are going to have to find a way to free-up one of them so that he can autograph your items. The easiest way is to offer to hold the item for him while he signs your material.* Learn a few basic phrases of common languages - Not everyone who plays professional sports in this country is fluent in English. Learning some basic phrases in Spanish, French and even Russian will prove to be particularly helpful in many instances.* Be courteous, yet firm, with your request - Always be courteous to your subject: "May I please have your autograph, Mr. Montana?" "Thank you very much. I really appreciate it." Respect your subject, but do not be timid with an autograph request. You must be aggressive, but not overbearing.

Clemens, Roger

On the road back from a very disappointing 1993 season, Clemens had one of his finest springs in years. The three-time Cy Young Award winner enters 1994 with 2,033 strikeouts and a career ERA of 2.94. Only Clemens and Hall of Famer Grover Cleveland Alexander have ever led a league in ERA and shutouts in three consecutive years.

Clemens can be an elusive and temperamental signer. He has done some private signings over the years, which has accounted for many of the baseballs that are in the market. But his appearances are still relatively few compared to some of his peers.

Clemens' signature has varied in size and character formation during the last decade. His three- or four-stroke signature can exhibit breaks between the "R" and the "o" in Roger, and between the "C" and the "l" and occasionally the "n" and the "s" in Clemens. Trademarks of his signature are the unique character formation of the "R" in Roger, the beginning stroke of the "l" in Clemens, which starts way below the signature's baseline, and the "s" at the end of his last name that resembles an "8."

Baseball: $38 Photograph: $27

Address: c/o Boston Red Sox, Fenway Park, Boston, Mass. 02215

Hints for acquiring autographs through the mail

* Be creative with your request. Before sending out a letter, collectors should ask these questions: What is unique about my request that will make a player respond? Will my request stand out among the hundreds of others he receives? What would be my reaction to such a request?

Coffey, Paul

The 11-time All-Star finished the 1993-94 season with more than 1,200 career total points. The two-time James Norris (best defenseman) Memorial Trophy winner now brings his leadership and athletic prowess to the Detroit Red Wings.

Coffey has been an obliging signer over the years; his signature should prove to be easy acquisition.

Coffey's unique five-stroke signature exhibits three breaks - between the "P" and the "u" in Paul, between the "f" and "f," and between the "f" and "e" in Coffey. His last name can be illegible at times, often resembling a "y7R" in its appearance. He often places a 77, his uniform number, in between the descenders of the second "f" and "y" in Coffey.

Puck: $26 Photograph: $14

Address: c/o Detroit Red Wings, Joe Louis Sports Arena, 600 Civic Center Drive, Detroit, Mich. 48226

---

* Conceal all the material you are going to have signed - Keep all of the material you are going to have signed concealed until the last possible minute.

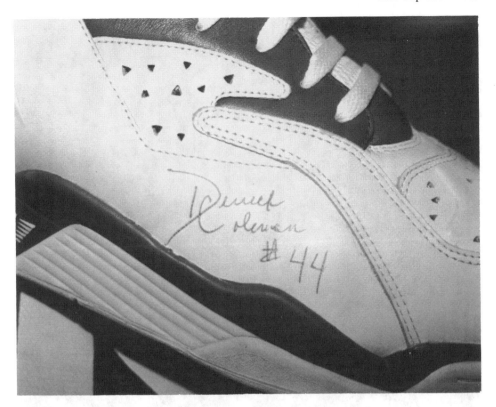

Coleman, Derrick

Although he still receives more criticism than respect, "DC" was one of only four NBA forwards to average 20 points and 10 rebounds per game during the 1992-93 season. He finished the year with 1,572 points and 852 rebounds. "DC" was voted to his first All-Star team in 1993-94 and matched his statistics from the previous season.

Coleman is an evasive signer in person. Mail autograph requests usually remain unanswered. He will sign autographs for friends or team personnel, but often reluctantly.

Coleman's four- or five-stroke signature has common breaks between the "D" and the "e" in Derrick and between the "C" and the "o" in Coleman. Both the "D" and the "k" in Derrick can be either a single- or two-stroke character formation. The "C" in Coleman often intersects the "D" in Derrick to represent "DC" - his trademark. The capitalized characters in his name are often six to eight times larger than the lowercase letters. He often puts his uniform number, "#44," beneath his last name.

Basketball: $85 Photograph: $19

Address: c/o New Jersey Nets, Brendan Byrne Arena, East Rutherford, N.J. 07073

Hints for acquiring autographs through auctions

* Any auction item not properly described - conditioning or grading, year, manufacturer - by the seller may be returned to the highest bidder. All items should be guaranteed authentic by the seller.

Craig, Roger

Although it wasn't a banner year for Craig, his 8,189 career yards after the 1993 season ranks him 13th all-time in rushing. He's a fine receiver, too; the running back led the league in receptions in 1985 as a San Francisco 49er.

Craig has been an elusive signer at times, but appears to be improving with age. Mail autograph requests sent to him still remain unpredictable.

Craig's four-stroke signature has varied little over time; most of it occurs in the character formation and flamboyance of the "aig" in Craig. The letter spacing in his signature is very large, possibly due to the few characters in his name.

Football: $40 Photograph: $10

Address: c/o Minnesota Vikings, 9520 Viking Drive, Eden Prairie, Minn. 55344

---

* Shopping malls - The primary shopping mall in any city is always an excellent place to meet professional athletes. Always position yourself at the central point of the mall, never at a specific exit. If the mall has multiple floors, stay on the main level. During the season players will shop between 11 a.m. to 2 p.m. - if there is a night game scheduled. If a day game is scheduled, they will shop or possibly attend a movie after the game. Many malls include movie theaters.

Cunningham, Randall

Cunningham remains injury prone, but few can forget that 1990 season when he threw 30 TD passes and ran for 942 yards. He still has considerable drive and tremendous athletic ability. Cunningham's popularity has diminished very little with fans.

Cunningham can be an elusive signer; mail autograph requests are often unanswered. Fortunately, he does make several public appearances, so in person autograph requests are often successful.

The Eagles quarterback's two- or four-stroke signature has two occasional breaks - between the "R" and "a" in Randall and between the "C" and the "u" in Cunningham. The character formation of the "R" is very compact and may resemble a "V." A good authentication point is to compare the slant of the "d" and that of the first "l" in Randall; they should be similar. The slant of the last "l" typically varies from its predecessor's.

The "g" in Cunningham often varies in size and flamboyance. The "h" often resembles an "l," because it does not contain the loop of the letter. The "am" in his last name is often dropped. Cunningham often puts his uniform number, 12, underneath his last name.

Football: $65 Photograph: $22

Address: c/o Philadelphia Eagles, Broad Street and Pattison Avenue, Philadelphia, Pa. 19148

Dawson, Andre

"The Hawk" entered the 1994 season with 2,630 hits, including 412 home runs. An eight-time All-Star, he has resigned himself to the role of designated hitter at the age of 40. Dawson, who strung together eight consecutive seasons of 20 home runs, has a career batting average of .281.

Dawson is an obliging signer. Like Eddie Murray, Dawson has been overshadowed by many of the popular younger players. He is at a very critical time of his career; a few more seasons can make the difference in his Hall of Fame chances.

Unlike his career, Dawson's signature has gone through many dramatic changes. To quote one person's observation of his signature, "it's bizarre." His four-stroke signature has a break between the loop and the stem of the "A" in Andre and between the "D" and the "a" in Dawson. The notable trademarks of his signature include the large loop of the capitalized "A" that resembles a "C," a capitalized "D" that resembles a "c," and what appears to be his entire last name shifted a full lowercase character size, below the baseline of his first name.

Baseball: $24 Photograph: $14

Address: c/o Boston Red Sox, Fenway Park, Boston, Mass. 02215

Hints for acquiring autographs through the mail

* Don't risk sending expensive items through the mail. Although I am astounded by the accuracy and promptness exhibited by the U.S. Postal Service, most collectors are not in position to replace lost merchandise.

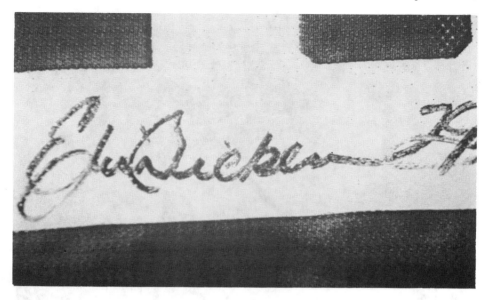

Dickerson, Eric

Dickerson reached the 10,000-yard plateau faster than any player in league history, but he hasn't had a 1,000-yard season rushing since 1989. Due to an injury he added only 91 yards to his total in 1993. Still, Dickerson trails only Walter Payton on the NFL's all-time rushing list.

Dickerson's signing status has been like his game - unpredictable. His popularity has slipped considerably, as has the demand for his signature.

Dickerson's three- or four-stroke signature has varied in size and character formation over the years. Typical signature breaks fall between the "E" and the "r" in Eric, and between the "D" and the "i" in Dickerson. The trademarks of his signature are the large double-looped "E" of Eric, the connection of the "c" in Eric to the "D" in Dickerson, and varying size and shapes of the capitalized "D."

Football: $50 Photograph: $17

Address: c/o Atlanta Falcons, Suwannee Road at I-85, Suwannee, Ga., 30174

Hints for acquiring autographs through the mail

* Be conscious of a player's time by including no more than one or two items to be autographed.

* Avoid form letters. In addition to being impersonal and unflattering, the letters typically have a low response rate.

* Be reasonable with your expectations. Some players receive hundreds of requests a day; they have little time to read a request, let alone respond to it.

Drexler, Clyde

Drexler, another member of the U.S. Olympic "Dream Team," concluded the 1993-94 season with 17,136 career points. During his years in Portland, "Clyde the Glide" has averaged 20.7 points per game and is one of only eight NBA players ever to reach the 1,600 steals plateau.

Drexler can be an evasive signer. Mail requests for his signature are often unanswered. An autograph collector's best bet is to catch him at a public appearance or track him down at a visiting team's hotel in a city that you are a familiar with.

Drexler's six-stroke signature has three common breaks - between the "C" and the "l," between the "y" and the "d" in Clyde, and between the "D" and the "r" in Drexler. His signature can vary in character formation, particularly with the "ler" letter combination in Drexler. The "D" in Drexler can vary in size, flamboyance and character formation. The "D," typically the largest character in his signature, may occasionally resemble a "J" or "V." The "e" and "er" in Drexler are often indistinguishable. Drexler crosses the "x" in his last name with a separate, long, descending stroke. The often flamboyant ending stroke of his name will usually curve upward and descend to create a loop.

A consistent element, and a good authentication point in his signature, has been the right slant of the "l" and "d" in Clyde and the "D" in Drexler. The slant of these characters should be very similar. Drexler, with often a very expedient stroke, adds his uniform number, "#22," beneath his last name. To minimize signing time, this is typically done with only three strokes and often resembles a "=hu" configuration.

Basketball: $80 Photograph: $20

Address: c/o Portland Trailblazers, 700 NE Multnomah St., Suite 950, Lloyd Building, Portland, Ore. 97232

Hints for acquiring autographs through the auctions

* Any unusual exception to common mail bid rules for an auction must be clearly stated by the seller in the auction catalog or advertisement.

Elway, John

The "Comeback Kid" came back in 1993 to lead the league in nearly every passing category. Elway passed for 4,030 yards, 25 TDs and finished with an efficiency rating of 92.8. His 63.2 percent completion percentage led the league.

Don't send your autograph requests to the "Comeback Kid;" they probably won't come back. Your best bet is to catch him in person, in a visiting team's town.

Elway's signature has been as consistent as his right arm, showing only minor variations over the past few years. His three-stroke signature has one break that falls between the "w" and the "a" in Elway. The "J" in John will vary slightly in size and slant, with the "o" enclosed in the letter.

Football: $90 Photograph: $27

Address: c/o Denver Broncos, 13655 E. Dove Valley Parkway, Englewood, Colo. 80112

Hints for acquiring autographs through the auctions

* A seller has the right to reject an auction bid for any reason whatsoever.

* A bidder is obligated to honor any and all bids submitted.

Esiason, Boomer

Esiason finished the 1993 season with the fourth highest rating of all quarterbacks in the AFC, passing for 3,421 yards and 16 TDs. He still impresses Jets fans as he climbs the list of leading lifetime passers.

Fortunately for collectors, Esiason makes several public appearances and is obliging to in-person autograph requests. Autograph mail requests, however, are often unpredictable.

Esiason, who typically signs just "Boomer," may or may not have a signature break between the "B" and the "o." Over the years his character formation has deteriorated only slightly by becoming more rounded in its appearance. The large "B" in Boomer is typically four times the size of his lowercase letters. He usually underlines Boomer with a separate stroke or by doubling back his finishing stroke upon completion of the "r." Boomer often adds his uniform number, 7, or "#7," underneath his large (3x6 signature on an 8x10 photograph) signature.

Football: $70 Photograph: $20

Address: c/o New York Jets, 1000 Fulton Ave., Hempstead, N.Y. 11550

---

* Be timely with your request - The timing of an autograph request is the key element that will determine its success. Try to put yourself in the athlete's position. For example, a hockey team wins during overtime on a key goal. Who is more likely to be obliging to an autograph request following the game, the goalie who gave up the goal or the player who scored it?

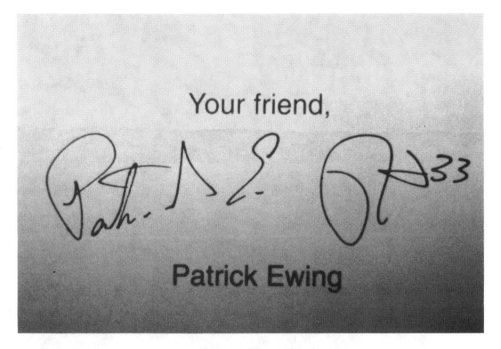

Ewing, Patrick

Ewing posted his usual numbers in 1993-94 - 24.5 points per game, adding 11.2 rebounds and 2.74 blocks per game, too. The center surpassed Walt Frazier during the season to become the Knicks' all-time leading scorer. He also made his seventh All-Star game appearance. He's considered the New York Knicks' franchise player.

Despite his often nasty image on the court, Ewing can be a real gentleman once he steps off. Active in numerous charities, he has been a real inspiration to many children in the tri-state area. He never forgets about his Georgetown days and often visits Madison Square Garden during the "Big East" tournament in March each year.

Ewing will sign in person. Many collectors have been successful by meeting him during practice sessions held at SUNY Purchase in Westchester County. Other attempts at acquiring his signature, especially inside "The Garden," have been very difficult. Mail is answered with a form letter and assorted Knicks collectibles. If you send cards to be autographed they will not be returned.

Ewing's often seven-stroke signature can vary significantly in size and character formation. The "t" in Patrick is usually quite large, while the "k" in Patrick resembles an upside down "V." Of all the characters that make up his last name, only the "E" is usually identifiable. His signature will prove to be a very difficult signature to authenticate because of all the anomalies.

Basketball: $130 Photograph: $36

Address: c/o New York Knicks, Madison Square Garden, Two Pennsylvania Plaza, New York, N.Y. 10001

---

* Be prepared - Often you will only have ONE autograph opportunity, so be prepared. Have both a new "Sharpie" and ballpoint pen immediately accessible. Know what you're going to have signed by each player and have it also at your fingertips.

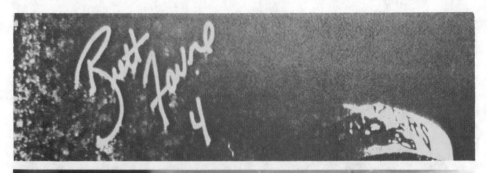

Favre, Brett

One of the NFL's hottest young quarterbacks, Favre made the Pro Bowl in his first season as a starter in 1993. In 1992 he passed for 3,227 yards and 18 TDs, despite not starting until the fourth game of the season. Favre had a nearly identical performance the next year, passing for 3,303 yards and 19 TDs.

Favre is an obliging signer in person, but mail autograph requests can be unpredictable.

His seven-stroke signature has three common breaks - between the "B" and the "r" in Brett, between the "F" and the "a," and between the "v" and the "r" in Favre. The large two-stroke "B," which can resemble an "R," is the hallmark of his signature and typically the largest letter in his name. The "e" in Favre can vary in size, but is typically larger than the other lowercase characters. Favre places his uniform number, 4, underneath his last name.

Football: $80 Photograph: $17

Address: c/o Green Bay Packers, 1265 Lombardi Ave., Green Bay, Wis. 54304

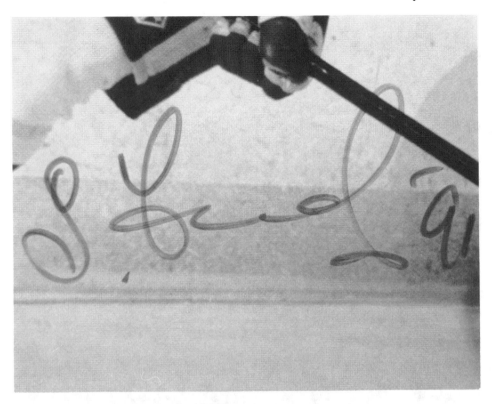

Fedorov, Sergei

Fedorov, a two-time All-Star in only in his fourth NHL season, continues to impress everyone. The Red Wings had the league's only pair of 50-goal scorers on the same team in 1993-94 - Ray Sheppard and Fedorov. At 24 years of age, he has already topped 300 total points.

Fedorov can be obliging to in-person autograph requests. Mail requests have been unpredictable so far, but collectors say that he does respond.

Fedorov's two-stroke signature has no common breaks. He typically signs only "S. Fedorov," and his autograph can vary in size, character formation and flamboyance. The "S" often resembles a flamboyant "J." Only the "F" and the "d" are distinguishable characters in his last name. He typically adds his uniform number, 91, at the end of his name.

Puck: $22 Photograph: $14

Address: c/o Detroit Red Wings, Joe Louis Arena, 600 Civic Center Drive, Detroit, Mich. 48226

---

* Block all accessible paths between you and the subject - Using other collectors, you can strategically place yourself so that there is no clear path between the subject and his destination. Similar to electricity, the subject is going to always choose the path of least resistance or, in this case, the trail that has the least amount of autograph seekers.

Fielder, Cecil

Although he resembles a defensive lineman rather than a first baseman, Fielder represents the best run-producer in baseball over the last four years. The only player to hit the 50 homer level since 1977, he doesn't hesitate to include a few tape measure blasts each season. Fielder is especially dangerous with runners in scoring position.

Fielder's flamboyance is also exemplified in his signature. His five-stroke signature has two main breaks, between the "C" and "e" in Cecil and between the "F" and "i" in Fielder. His trademarks are the large "C" in Cecil which descends below and underneath most of his first name and the large looped "F" in Fielder that resembles a "Z." The character formations of the "ec" in Cecil and the "el" in Fielder are nonexistent in most signature samples. The "r" at the end of his last name often resembles the number 8.

Fielder does respond to mail requests for his autograph, but limits each letter to one item.

Baseball: $31 Photograph: $16

Address: c/o Detroit Tigers, 2121 Trumball Ave., Detroit, Mich. 48216

Foster, Barry

An ankle injury caused Barry Foster to miss the last seven games of the 1993 season. In 1992, Foster lost the league's rushing title to Emmitt Smith by only 23 yards. During that season he broke five Steeler offensive records, and his NFL record-tying 12 100-yard games shattered the previous record of seven held by Franco Harris.

Foster, a very gracious signer, is accessible to fans. He traditionally answers mail requests for autographs. If his performance in 1994 equals that of 1992 and he continues to oblige autograph requests made by collectors, his popularity will soar.

He typically signs "B. Foster." His signature can vary in character formation. The "er" in Foster is usually dropped from his signature. The third stroke of his signature intersects the "F" in Foster to form the middle of the letter.

Football: $45 Photograph: $12

Address: c/o Pittsburgh Steelers, Three Rivers Stadium, 300 Stadium Circle, Pittsburgh, Pa. 15212

George, Jeff

Following a season that limited him to only 10 games, George passed for 2,526 yards and eight TDs. He had the ninth highest rating among AFC quarterbacks, which is not too bad if you're familiar with the Colts' offensive line.

George is a gracious signer in person and through mail autograph requests. He may also include a Colts trading card in response to mail requests.

His three-stroke signature contains a consistent signature break between the "G" and the "e" in George. The hallmark of his signature is the large (five to six times that of his lowercase letters), rounded "G" in George, which is very distinct in its formation, often resembling the number 9. The "o" in George is usually the only unrecognizable letter in his name. Worth noting is the lack of similarity between the "f"s in Jeff. The letters differ in size and formation. George typically places his uniform number, "#11," underneath his signature.

Football: $55 Photograph: $18

Address: c/o Indianapolis Colts, 7001 W. 56th St., Indianapolis, Ind. 46224

Hints for acquiring autographs through the mail

* Always include a self-addressed, stamped envelope (SASE) for convenient response through the mail. Please be sure the enclosed envelope is of proper size to house the returned material, and that the proper postage is affixed.

* Be brief, personal and sincere with your request. Exhibit in a few sentences your genuine interest in, and knowledge of, a player's career. Courtesy is paramount.

Gilmour, Doug

Gilmour, who is an outstanding defensive forward, helped the Maple Leafs reduce their team goals-against total from 294 in 1991, to 241 during the 1992-93 season. He also set a team record for most points in one season and was the NHL's Frank J. Selke (defensive prowess) Trophy winner in 1992.

Gilmour can be evasive at times as a signer and is unpredictable through mail autograph requests.

His one- or two-stroke signature can vary significantly in size and character formation. Like Joe Montana's signature, following the completed loop of the "l" in Gilmour, he begins a whole new baseline above the original. Gilmour often signs "D. Gilmour;" his signature resembles "DGl" in its appearance. The "oug" in Doug and the "i" and "mour" in Gilmour are often indistinguishable or dropped from his signature. The loop of the unclosed "D" in Doug will be nearly identical in size, slant and formation to the "l" in Gilmour. He often adds "93" beneath his last name.

Puck: $27 Photograph: $15

Address: c/o Toronto Maple Leafs, Maple Leaf Gardens, 60 Carlton St., Toronto, Ontario, Canada M5B 1L1

Gonzalez, Juan

Back-to-back 40 home run seasons combined with three straight years of 100+ RBI is worth noting, especially when the player is only 24 years old. The scary part about Gonzalez is he's just beginning to refine his swing, having reduced his strikeout ratio dramatically in 1993. His towering home run blasts are known for frequency and distance; ask anyone who saw him win the 1993 All-Star Game home run hitting contest.

During the off-season Gonzalez spends most of his time at his home in Puerto Rico. He has done a few private signings, but the demand for his signature has yet to be met. For a time Gonzalez would respond to autograph seekers by mail with a facsimile-autographed black-and-white team-issued photograph, accompanied by a "Thanks, but I'm too busy to sign" letter.

The often six-stroke expedient signature of Gonzalez can vary in size, character formation and slant. Signature breaks are found most often between the "u" and "a" in Juan and between the "G" and the "o" and the "l" and the "e" in Gonzalez. His signature breaks will vary; characters are often dropped to increase his autograph time. During recent signings he has eliminated half of the "G" and the "e" in Gonzalez.

Baseball: $32 Photograph: $18
Address: c/o Texas Rangers, P.O. Box 90111, Arlington, Texas 76004

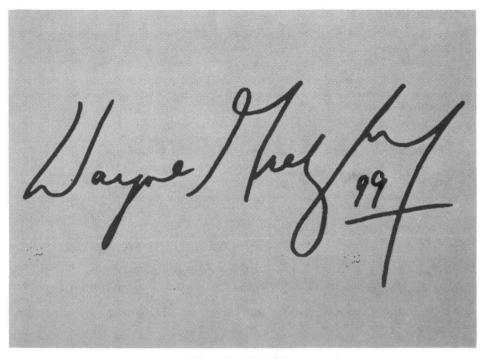

Gretzky, Wayne

"The Great One," considered by most to be hockey's greatest player, has broken nearly every existing offensive record. He concluded the 1993-94 season with 2,458 points, 803 of which are goals. The 13-time All-Star has won nine Hart trophies, nine Art Ross trophies and five Lester B. Pearson awards.

Gretzky is an obliging signer in the proper circumstance. Screaming masses do little to positively influence his signing habits. Autograph mail requests are virtually ignored. He is totally aware of the marketing potential of his signature and will probably continue to sell autographed material through exclusive sources such as Upper Deck Authenticated.

The variations exhibited by his signature, and the demand for it, necessitate a character-by-character analysis.

Hints for attending card shows

* Know what you are looking for - Know why you are attending the show. Always bring a compact, updated list that is readily accessible.

* Know what you are willing to pay - Before the show, know what you will pay for the items you want. Consult a price guide if necessary; bring it to the show.

LetterVariations

W   A single-stroke letter with a right slant, it has varied in size over the years. Recently, the second loop formed by the downward stroke seems to have predominated in width over the first. The finishing height of the ascending stroke is usually higher than the origination point.

a   In recent examples, it is almost always a closed letter formation. In a hectic signing environment, however, he may drop the letter entirely.

y   In earlier examples, the descender of the letter is much shorter. The letter typically connects to the "n," but in larger forms (sticks) it may not.

n   The letter can vary in size and formation, and may even resemble a "v." In some rushed signatures, it is not unusual for him to drop the letter from his name entirely.

e   The "e" can vary in size and letter spacing. The ending of the stroke exhibits little flamboyance.

G   In earlier signatures, the "G" may connect to the "r," but over the last few years it is typically a single character formation. Over time the origin of the letter has also dipped further and further from the baseline. There is little, if any, loop found in the downward stroke of the letter. The loop created by the upward stroke, although typically lower in height, is larger and more pronounced than the loop in the downward stroke.

re   This letter combination has varied in size and legibility. It often resembles a "u" in recent signature examples.

t   Typically the last character of the second stroke in his last name. The letter can vary in height; it's smaller in early examples. The "t" is now crossed by the origin stroke of the "z," which is a diversion from earlier examples where the letter is not crossed at all.

z   The origin point of the stroke that forms this letter now crosses the "t" before descending and creating a loop that often varies in size. This loop is significantly smaller in earlier signatures.

ky   Formation One

In pre-1990 signature samples, the "ky" configuration is the continuation of the upward stroke of the "z." This stroke rises to the height of the "G" before forming a slightly curved stroke that reaches a pinnacle, before descending and either stopping, or making a sharp left 90-degree stroke that stops before reaching the "z"'s descender. If the stroke does stopprior to the 90-degree shift, Gretzky adds his uniform number, 99, between them to form a box-like formation.

ky   Formation Two

In recent samples, the "ky" configuration is also the continuation of the upward stroke of the "z," that rises to the same height as the example above. But the stroke descends much lower, to slightly above the baseline to actually include the formation of both the "k" and "y"'s loop. This w-like formation shows greater definition and a move away from the box-like formation of above. Gretzky still places the "99" between both descenders and underlines it. The character space between the "t" and the "k" is much larger in recent samples. He may even loop the second "9" in "99."

Gretzky's signature is often forged, but easier to authenticate than Joe Montana's autograph.

Puck: $75 Photograph: $42

Address: c/o Los Angeles Kings, Great Western Forum, 3900 W. Manchester Blvd., Box 17013, Inglewood, Calif. 90306

Griffey Jr., Ken

During the home run contest before the 1993 All-Star Game, Griffey became the first player to hit the Camden Yards warehouse. He also tied a major league record July 29, 1993, when he homered in his eighth straight game. Griffey, a four-time All-Star with 132 home runs and 453 RBI going into the 1994 campaign, will turn 24 in November.

Griffey Jr. has been extremely accessible to collectors through numerous private signings and card shows. He endorses several products and isn't afraid to spend a few off-season hours hawking his signature on a satellite shopping network.

Griffey's signature has been modified primarily in size and flamboyance over the last few years. His six-stroke signature has common breaks between the "K" and the "e" in Ken, and between the "G" and the "r" in Griffey. Over the past three years he has added a loop to the top of the first stroke in the "K," increased the size of the top loop of the "G," changed direction and size of the descender of the "y" and increased the size of the loop in "Jr." There is typically little to no character formation in the "en" of Ken and the "e" in Griffey.

Unlike Juan Gonzalez, there are plenty of Griffey Jr. autographed baseballs available in the market. The price has remained high primarily due to the public's unawareness of supply.

Baseball: $32 Photograph: $18

Address: c/o Seattle Mariners, P.O. Box 4100, Seattle, Wash. 98104

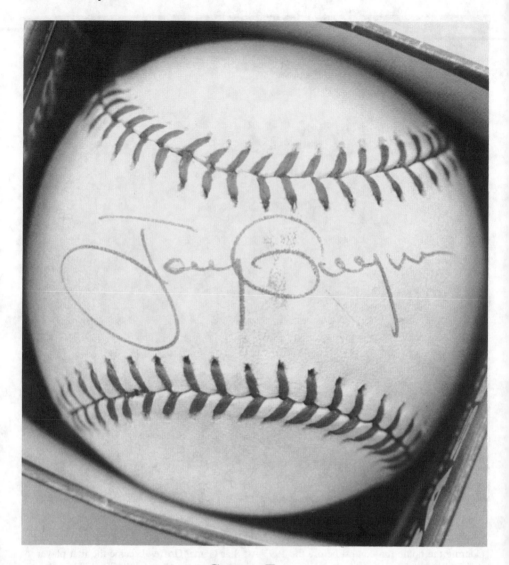

Gwynn, Tony

With four batting titles and five Gold Glove Awards to his credit, Gwynn began the 1994 season with 2,039 hits and a career average of .329. Only Stan Musial, Willie Keeler, Ty Cobb and Gwynn have had four five-hit games in a single season. He is not only a student of hitting, he is becoming a master at his craft, spending endless hours reviewing videotapes of his swing.

Gwynn is an extremely underrated baseball player with an undervalued signature. He has been accessible to collectors; his signature shouldn't prove to be difficult to add to a collection.

Gwynn's five-stroke signature typically exhibits three breaks. These signature breaks fall between the "T" and the "o" in Tony and between the "G" and the "w" and between the "y" and "n" in Gwynn. The trademarks of his signature are the large looped two-stroke "T" in Tony and the large rounded "G" in Gwynn. One interesting element, at least to an authenticator, is that the descenders of the lower case "y"s in his signature don't always slant in similar directions - uncommon in signature analysis.

Baseball: $26 Photograph: $15

Address: c/o San Diego Padres, P.O. Box 2000, San Diego, Calif. 92120

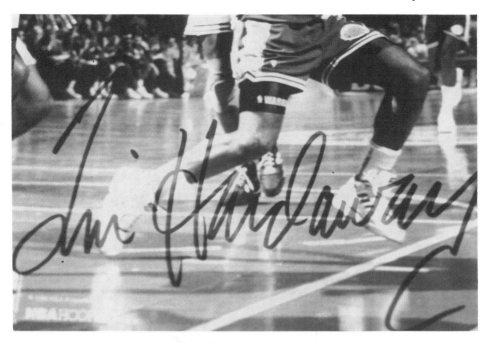

Hardaway, Tim

The only player in the NBA to average at least 20 points and 10 assists during the 1992-93 season, Hardaway finished second in the NBA in assists and 13th in scoring, averaging 21.5 points a game. The major playmaker on the Golden State Warriors, Hardaway hopes to rebound after missing the entire 1993-94 season with an injury.

Hardaway was traditionally a good signer, but has been a bit more unpredictable the last few years.

Hardaway's typically very large, five-stroke signature has varied primarily in flamboyance over time. Common signature breaks occur between the "H" and the "a," and between the "d" and "a" in Hardaway. The large "T" in Tim is typically the largest letter in his signature. The arm between the two stems of the "H" in Hardaway is created from a curling stroke that leads into the "a." All the letters that make up Hardaway's signature are usually discernible.

Basketball: $65 Photograph: $15

Address: c/o Golden State Warriors, Oakland Coliseum Arena, Nimitz Freeway and Hegenberger Road, Oakland, Calif. 94621

Hints for acquiring autographs through the mail

* Be conscious of a player's time by including no more than one or two items to be autographed.

* Avoid form letters. In addition to being impersonal and unflattering, the letters typically have a low response rate.

* Be reasonable with your expectations. Some players receive hundreds of requests a day; they have little time to read a request, let alone respond to it.

Hawerchuk, Dale

The four-time All-Star continues to be a great playmaker for the Buffalo Sabres. The 1985 Calder Memorial Trophy winner strung together five consecutive seasons of 100-plus total points with Winnipeg.

Hawerchuk is an excellent signer in person and by mail. Mail autograph requests with an SASE usually elicit a prompt response.

Hawerchuk's three- or four-stroke expedient signature often exhibits no breaks. The "D" in Dale and the "H," "r," "h" and "k" in Hawerchuk are typically the only recognizable letters in his signature.

Puck: $20 Photograph: $11

Address: c/o Buffalo Sabres, Memorial Auditorium, Buffalo, N.Y. 14202

Hull, Brett

A four-time All-Star, this St. Louis Blues right winger finished the 1993-94 season with 699 career points. After one of his best seasons in 1991, when he scored 86 goals and 45 assists, Hull was awarded the Hart Memorial Trophy and the Lester B. Pearson Award.

Hull is an extremely evasive signer; mail autograph requests often go unanswered. He should prove to be a challenging acquisition for any collector.

Hull's very large and simple four-stroke signature exhibits two common breaks, between the "B" and "r" in Brett and between the "H" and "u" in Hull. The second loop in his two-stroke "B" can sometimes resemble a figure 8. He uses a dual baseline signature technique that allows him to cross the "tt" in Brett with the beginning stroke of the "H" in Hull.

Puck: $50 Photograph: $28

Address: c/o St.Louis Blues, St.Louis Arena, 5700 Oakland Ave., St. Louis, Mo. 63110

Hints for acquiring autographs through the auctions

* A seller has the right to reject an auction bid for any reason whatsoever.

* A bidder is obligated to honor any and all bids submitted.

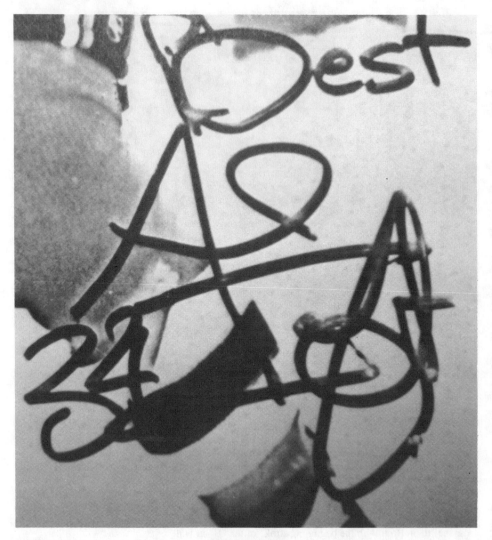

IaFrate, Al

IaFrate was Toronto's first choice in the 1984 draft. A three-time All-Star, the big defenseman was traded to Washington during the 1990-91 season. He put together his strongest season in 1992-93, scoring an impressive 66 points.

IaFrate is obliging to signature requests, but his mail can be somewhat unpredictable.

IaFrate's four- or five-stroke signature is a bit creative. He crosses the middle of the "A" in Al with the beginning stroke of the "I." He adds two intersecting strokes to the descending stroke of the "A" to form the "I." The "ra" and "e" of IaFrate are often dropped from his name. He typically adds his uniform number, 34, underneath the "A" in Al.

Puck: $22 Photograph: $12

Address: c/o Boston Bruins, Boston Garden, 150 Causeway St., Boston, Mass. 02114

---

* Know your subject - Doing a little biographical research on a subject can also be helpful. Knowing an athlete's hometown, his hobbies or even his alma mater can lead a subject into conversation with you, which can end with an autograph request.

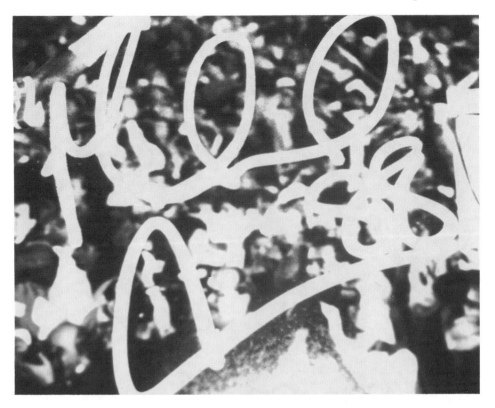

Irvin, Michael

Irvin caught 88 passes for 1,330 yards and seven TDs in 1993. A Pro Bowler for the third straight year, the wide receiver is a potent force in the Dallas offense.

Irvin is a flashy character on and off the field. Although he can be an evasive signer at the stadium, he is usually accommodating after the game, especially if he's away from the playing field.

Irvin's typical three-stroke signature can vary in size and character formation. The only common signature break appears between the "M" and the "i" in Michael. The "c" and "ae" in Michael, along with the "rvin" in Irvin, are usually indistinguishable. The formation of his last name resembles a triangle with a line extending to the right of its baseline. Irvin typically adds his "88" on top of the extended line which represents all the lowercase letters in his last name.

Football: $90 Photograph: $35

Address: c/o Dallas Cowboys, Cowboys Center, 1 Cowboys Parkway, Irving, Texas 75063

---

* Always have flat items placed on a clipboard - Flat items are cumbersome to sign if a similar surface area is not available. Placing the items gently underneath the clip allows for the much needed support. Additionally, trading card collectors can place more than a single item, side by side, underneath the clip, possibly allowing for a quick, additional signature.

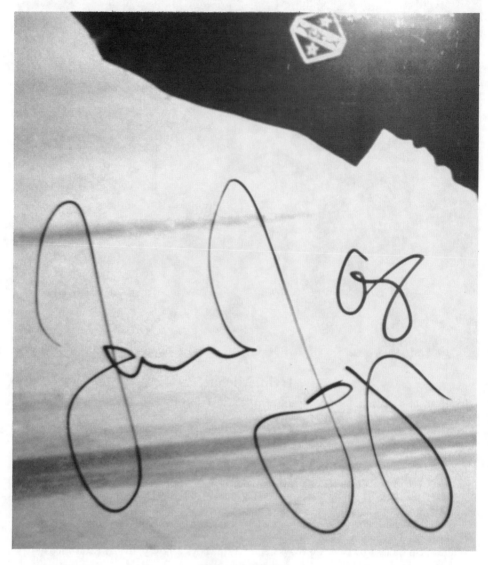

Jagr, Jaromir

The strong right wing was the Penguins' first choice in the 1990 draft. He topped his 94 points scored in 1992-93 with 99 in 1993-94. During the 1992-93 season he was named to the NHL All-Star team for the second consecutive year.

Jagr is an obliging signer in person. Mail autograph requests are answered promptly.

Jagr's two-stroke signature typically exhibits one break, between the "a" and "g" of his last name. The "om" in Jaromir is often indistinguishable. The "r" in Jagr often connects to the "J" in Jaromir. The "J"s in both names, although they can vary in character formation, are usually nearly identical in left slant. Jagr often places his uniform number, 68, just above the "gr" in Jagr.

Puck: $27 Photograph: $15

Address: c/o Pittsburgh Penguins, Civic Arena, Pittsburgh, Pa. 15219

Johnson, Kevin

"KJ" continues to be one of the game's elite point guards. The Phoenix Sun was hampered with injuries in 1992-93, but came back strong in 1993-94, finishing the season with 9,424 career points.

"KJ," a good signer in person, has finally stopped answering mail requests for his signature. Requests will return with the following letter: "Early in my career I took great pride in personally responding to all the mail I received from fans and friends throughout the country. Each year the volume of that mail has increased to such extremes that it has become impossible for me, as an individual, to personally satisfy the numerous requests that I receive each day. I have enclosed one of my current photos (B&W), along with my sincere apology for being unable to accommodate your request." signed KJ Suns.

Johnson typically signs just "KJ," which is a two-stroke configuration that has his uniform number, 7, bisecting both initials.

Basketball: $70 Photograph: $12

Address: c/o Phoenix Suns, 201 E. Jefferson, P.O. Box 1369, Phoenix, Ariz. 85001

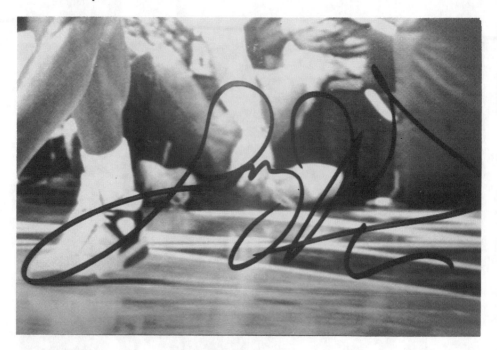

Johnson, Larry

Replicas of Johnson's jersey are the NBA's second best-selling item behind those of Michael Jordan. After being named the NBA's Rookie of the Year in 1991-92, Johnson led the team to its first-ever playoff appearance in 1992-93.

Johnson's autographing habits are still unpredictable, but he does do some private autographing sessions.

Johnson's three-stroke signature has one consistent break between the "L" and the "a" in Larry. His entire last name is nearly illegible. The "L" in Larry looks like the number 8 fallen on its side. His last name, if any formation can be determined at all, resembles a "2Y" or "JY" combination. His signature could prove to be another authenticator's nightmare in the future.

Basketball: $85 Photograph: $26

Address: c/o Charlotte Hornets, Hive Drive, Charlotte, N.C. 28217

---

* The subject's hand must be available for a signature - It is not unusual for your subject to be carrying an equipment bag, locker room bag, etc.. If you see that a subject has both hands occupied, you are going to have to find a way to free-up one of them so that he can autograph your items. The easiest way is to offer to hold the item for him while he signs your material.*
Learn a few basic phrases of common languages - Not everyone who plays professional sports in this country is fluent in English. Learning some basic phrases in Spanish, French and even Russian will prove to be particularly helpful in many instances.* Be courteous, yet firm, with your request - Always be courteous to your subject: "May I please have your autograph, Mr. Montana?" "Thank you very much. I really appreciate it." Respect your subject, but do not be timid with an autograph request. You must be aggressive, but not overbearing.

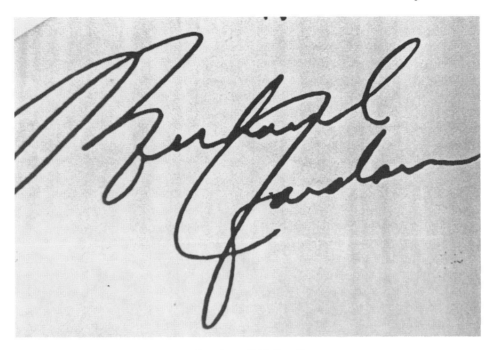

Jordan, Michael

"His Airness" went 2 for 5 with two RBI in his hometown Chicago White Sox debut on Thursday, April 7, 1994, against the crosstown rival Chicago Cubs. It was his first multi-hit, multi-RBI game after 13 spring exhibition games with the major league club. He was ticketed to spend the 1994 season playing Double A ball with the Birmingham Barons.

Jordan displayed his basketball prowess with the Chicago Bulls earlier in his professional athletic life, playing nine seasons with scoring 21,541 total points, an average of 32.3 points per game. He also led his team to three consecutive NBA titles.

Jordan's two-stroke signature was forced to evolve into a single-stroke variation due to his popularity. The single-stroke form exhibits no distinct character formations other than the "M" in Michael. His signature varies so frequently, due to the writing circumstance, that it is difficult to track alterations in style. Collectors hope that through the increased autograph access provided in minor league ballparks, more of his signatures will enter the market, thus reducing forgeries and giving collectors a better chance to observe any changes.

Baseball: $50 Photograph: $35

Address: c/o Birmingham Barons, Hoover Metropolitan Stadium, I-65 near U.S. 31, Birmingham, Ala. 35236

Hints for acquiring autographs through the mail

* Don't risk sending expensive items through the mail. Although I am astounded by the accuracy and promptness exhibited by the U.S. Postal Service, most collectors are not in position to replace lost merchandise.

Juneau, Joe

Juneau, in his first full NHL season with the Boston Bruins, finished the 1992-93 season with 102 total points. A member of the NHL All-Rookie team in 1992-93, the center/left winger shows tremendous potential as a playmaker. The Bruins dealt him to the Washington Capitals in 1994, in a monster trade for Al Iafrate.

Juneau has been an obliging signer in person. However, mail autograph requests can be unpredictable.

Juneau's five-stroke signature has two common breaks, between the "J" and the "o" in Joe, and between the "J" and the "u" in Juneau. The trademark of his signature has been the two large capitalized "J"s, which can resemble an enlarged "f" in their character formation. The "J" in Juneau is the only recognizable character in his last name. He often adds his uniform number, 49, underneath an upward stroke that represents all the lowercase letters of his last name.

Puck: $27 Photograph: $15

Address: c/o Washington Capitals, USAir Arena, Landover, Md. 20785

Justice, Dave

In 1993 Justice recorded 158 hits, including 40 home runs, and drove in 120 runs. He is a solid line-drive hitter with incredible power, and always finishes the season strong. With career high numbers in almost every offensive category, Justice is just beginning to show his potential with the Atlanta Braves.

Justice has been accessible to the public and is no stranger to baseball card shows, private autograph signings and the local golf course. His signature should be fairly easy to add to a collection.

The outfielder has undergone a transition in his signature over the past few years. His signature has evolved from a refined nine-stroke version in 1989, to the six-stroke highly-flamboyant example of today. The two-stroke "D" in Dave has evolved from what used to resemble an upside, backward "L," to a formation that now appears like an enlarged "Z." The "J" in Justice, originally a two-stroke version, is now a single stroke that resembles the letter "P." He has dropped the "ice" of Justice in most of the examples I have seen.

Baseball: $30 Photograph: $20

Address: c/o Atlanta Braves, P.O. Box 4064, Atlanta, Ga. 30302

Robert Mondavi Woodbridge
(Cabernet or Chardonnay)

Thanks
City Grill
memor
the year
coming
that's a
th

Kelly, Jim

A former Rookie of the Year in the USFL, Kelly has starred in the NFL, leading the Buffalo Bills to four straight Super Bowls. He passed for 3,382 yards and 18 TDs during the 1993 season. His 61.3 completion percentage was second only to John Elway among qualified quarterbacks in the AFC.

Send your self-addressed stamped envelope with your autograph request to Kelly and he'll stamp you a signature and mail it back. He was traditionally a very good signer of mail autograph requests, but apparently times have changed, at least by mail. But there is hope; stop by the Sports City Grill in Buffalo, N.Y., and you may catch a glimpse of #12 stocking the cooler with chicken wings. This multi-million dollar sports bar and restaurant is a treat to any sports fan, and a tribute to a great quarterback - Jim Kelly.

Kelly's four-stroke signature can vary in character formation, size and flamboyance. Trademarks of his signature are the large "J" in Jim, the two-stroke "K" in Kelly that resembles a "77" on occasion and the semi-circled 12 that he places underneath his last name.

Football: $80 Photograph: $21

Address: c/o Buffalo Bills, 1 Bills Drive, Orchard Park, N.Y. 14127

LaFontaine, Pat

The Buffalo center, named to his fifth NHL All-Star team in 1992-93, had 148 total points (second in the league) that season, 95 of which were assists. An injury during the 1993-94 season prevented LaFontaine from matching his career year from the season before, but LaFontaine is closing in on 1,000 career total points.

LaFontaine is a fairly good signer in person and will respond to autograph mail requests. The problem is that you may receive an authentic autograph or a stamped facsimile in response to mail requests.

LaFontaine's seven- or eight-stroke signature has five common breaks, between the "P" and the "a," and between the "a" and the "t" in Pat, also between the "L" and the "a," "a" and the "F," and between the "F" and the "o" in LaFontaine. The "P" resembles a "C" in its formation. The stroke that creates the "t" in Pat also creates the stem of the "L." His last name appears like "FaZ," primarily due to the "F" that resembles a "Z" and the slightly curved line that follows it that supposedly represents the "ontaine." He typically adds an "e" swirl underneath his last name and his uniform number - 16.

Puck: $27 Photograph: $15
Address: c/o Buffalo Sabres, Memorial Auditorium, Buffalo, N.Y. 14202

Hints for attending card shows

* Know what you are looking for - Know why you are attending the show. Always bring a compact, updated list that is readily accessible.

* Know what you are willing to pay - Before the show, know what you will pay for the items you want. Consult a price guide if necessary; bring it to the show.

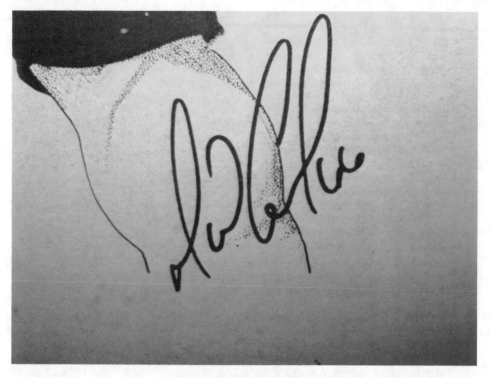

Lemieux, Mario

"Super Mario" is a six-time All-Star, four-time winner of the Art Ross Trophy, three-time winner of the Lester B. Pearson Award, and two-time Hart Trophy winner. He won the Calder Memorial Trophy in 1985, after being the Penguins' first choice in the 1984 draft. He had six consecutive 100-plus point seasons before being sidelined with an injury in 1991. Lemieux led the Pittsburgh Penguins to two consecutive Stanley Cup Championships and has become an inspiration to everyone as he fights a potential career-, if not life-, threatening illness.

Lemieux is an obliging signer, particularly in a favorable atmosphere. Mail requests for his signature have unpredictable results.

His autograph has shown a great degree of variation over the years, and thus is examined in the chapter about signature variations in this book.

Puck: $70 Photograph: $30

Address: c/o Pittsburgh Penguins, Civic Arena, Pittsburgh, Pa. 15219

Hints for acquiring autographs through auctions

* Any auction item not properly described - conditioning or grading, year, manufacturer - by the seller may be returned to the highest bidder. All items should be guaranteed authentic by the seller.

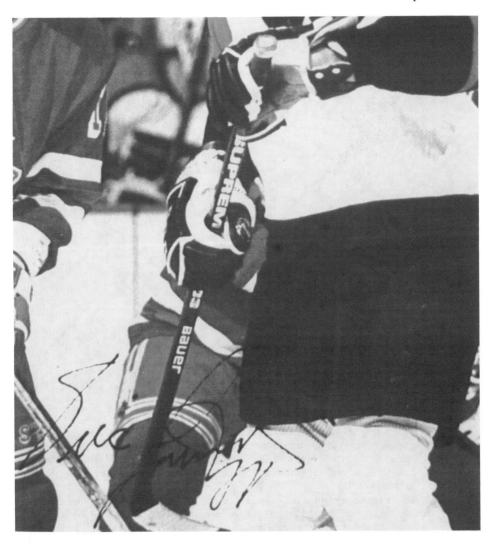

Lindros, Eric

The big center finished his first full NHL season with Philadelphia in credible fashion, notching 75 total points as part of a well balanced Flyer attack. Billed as a future NHL superstar, Lindros entered the 1993-94 season still underneath a magnifying glass, but finished the season in the top 10 in scoring in the league with 97 points.

Lindros is already an elusive signer, and autograph mail requests are answered by the team with color postcards bearing a facsimile autograph.

Lindros' three-stroke signature varies in size and character formation. The only common signature break falls between the "E" and the "r" in Eric. The "E" often resembles the number "8" in its formation. The "L" in Lindros is usually the largest letter of his signature. Following what appears to be the completion of his last name, the ending stroke swirls underneath his name, then upward to form a loop, which could be the "d" in Lindros, then back down below the signature's baseline and into two other formations that resemble a "W" or "yy." The stroke is unique, but I am still unsure of its significance.

Puck: $50 Photograph: $20

Address: c/o Philadelphia Flyers, The Spectrum, Pattison Place, Philadelphia, Pa. 19148

Lott, Ronnie

Lott is one of the league's most feared hitters. Lott once had a portion of a finger surgically removed so he wouldn't miss playing time during a season. A future Hall of Famer with more than 10 Pro Bowl appearances, Lott hopes to lead the New York Jets to a Super Bowl championship.

Lott can be an evasive and temperamental signer. Autograph requests by mail are often unpredictable or unanswered.

Lott's five- or six-stroke signature can vary in size and character formation. Common breaks occur between the two-stroke "R" and the "o" in Ronnie, also between the "L" and the "o" in Lott. The "nnie" in Ronnie and the "ott" in Lott are often undistinguishable. The "L" in Lott often resembles a "J" in his signature because of its large formation and the line he uses to cross the double "t"s. Like that of many professional athletes, the legibility of his signature will vary depending upon the signing conditions.

Football: $70 Photograph: $16

Address: c/o New York Jets, 1000 Fulton Ave., Hempstead, N.Y. 11550

---

* Block all accessible paths between you and the subject - Using other collectors, you can strategically place yourself so that there is no clear path between the subject and his destination. Similar to electricity, the subject is going to always choose the path of least resistance or, in this case, the trail that has the least amount of autograph seekers.

Maddux, Greg

Maddux, one of baseball's premier pitchers, posted his second straight 20-win season and added another Cy Young Award to his list of credentials in 1993. He exhibits excellent control with a variety of pitches and yields fewer than eight hits and two walks per nine innings. Maddux, who averages six-and-one-half strikeouts per game, entered the 1994 season with 1,134 strikeouts.

Maddux has not been as accessible to collectors as some of the other Atlanta starters have been. The demand for his signature still has not been met, driving up the price of what is available in the market.

His four-stroke signature has a common break between the "M" and the "a" in Maddux. The trademark of his signature is the "M" in Maddux, which begins with a stroke that resembles the number 2. The "a" and "u" in his last name are typically undistinguishable.

Baseball: $30 Photograph: $21

Address: c/o Atlanta Braves, P.O. Box 4064, Atlanta, Ga. 30302

* Always have flat items placed on a clipboard - Flat items are cumbersome to sign if a similar surface area is not available. Placing the items gently underneath the clip allows for the much needed support. Additionally, trading card collectors can place more than a single item, side by side, underneath the clip, possibly allowing for a quick, additional signature.

Malone, Karl

"The Mailman," another former U.S. Olympic "Dream Team" member, completed his ninth season with Utah in 1993-94 with 18,960 career points. Equally as impressive is that, after the 1993-94 season, he had only missed playing in four games in his career. His 25.8 career points per game average already ranks him among the top 10 players in this category in NBA history.

Malone is currently asking fans seeking autographs not to send any cards, pictures or objects. He will return a photo with his signature to those who request one, but you must include an SASE. "The Mailman" has been a very obliging signer throughout his career.

Malone's four- or five-stroke signature has three common signature breaks. The first break is between the "K" and the "a" in Karl and the second is between the "l" and the "o" in Malone. A sometimes difficult break to distinguish falls between the "M" and the "a" in Malone. The two stroke "K" and the large flamboyant loop of the "l" in Karl are both distinguishing elements in his first name. The unusually small "M" in Malone can be 10 times smaller than either of the "l"s in his name. The large and distinct "one" letter configuration resembles a large "m" with an extended "c" attached to the bottom of the letter. Malone often adds his uniform number, 32, to the bottom of his signature.

Basketball: $95 Photograph: $30
Address: c/o Utah Jazz, Delta Center, 301 W. South Temple, Salt Lake City, Utah 84101

Hints for acquiring autographs through the auctions

* Any unusual exception to common mail bid rules for an auction must be clearly stated by the seller in the auction catalog or advertisement.

Marino, Dan

Statistically speaking, Marino is the game's greatest quarterback. For Marino, who was injured during most of the season, 1993 was not a memorable year. He did, however, complete enough passes to overtake Johnny Unitas, putting him in third place on the NFL's all-time passing list.

Marino does numerous private signings, mainly for Upper Deck Authenticated. He's not shy about hawking his signature, so there is plenty of material available in the market.

Marino's two-stroke signature has varied little over the years. He has one consistent signature break that falls between the "M" and the "a" in Marino, and an inconsistent break that falls between the "D" and the "a" in Dan. The inconsistent break seems to be most evident on larger items such as footballs. The flamboyant ending stroke of the "o," which is characteristic of his signature, can vary significantly in size. The top of the second downward stroke in the "M" is usually the highest point in his signature. He often puts his uniform number, 13, below his last name.

Football: $90 Photograph: $27

Address: c/o Miami Dolphins, Joe Robbie Stadium, 2269 NW 199th St., Miami, Fla. 33056

---

* Local public golf course - Most professional athletes love to play golf, especially on off days, when no game is scheduled. Position yourself outside the pro shop and be aware that golfers start on either the first or ninth hole, depending upon how crowded the course is.

Mattingly, Don

A six-time All-Star and Gold Glove winner several times, Mattingly posted a .291 batting average in 1993, while driving in 86 runs. He is a solid contact hitter, who bats about .350 with players in scoring position. Mattingly entered the 1994 season with 1,908 hits and a career batting average of .309.

Mattingly's popularity slipped with his batting average in 1990. Injuries, especially his back and rib cage, began to effect his performance in the early 1990s. But during the last four years he has increased his batting average steadily to around the .300 mark. Last season he regained a lot of his strength and finally posted Mattingly-like numbers.

Regaining his popularity has met with increased autograph requests. He is a humble individual who does not attend baseball card shows and reluctantly obliges to occasional private autograph signings. The best time to catch him for his signature is during the off-season at his restaurant in Evansville, Ind. - Mattingly's 23. Mattingly does sell autographed memorabilia through his restaurant. He does attend some annual events, most of which are team sponsored or for certain charities. Don't be surprised if Mattingly refuses to sign certain types of equipment, especially jerseys.

Mattingly's five- or six-stroke signature has varied in size and character formation over the last 10 years. There are two common breaks in his signature, between the "D" and "o" in Don and between the "M" and "a" in Mattingly. His signature has always looked compressed, with very tight letter spacing. The capitalization in his signature often varies in size, usually depending upon what form of item he is signing. The "ly" in Mattingly also can vary significantly in character formation and flamboyance.

Baseball: $30 Photograph: $17

Address: c/o New York Yankees, Yankee Stadium, Bronx, N.Y. 10451

McDowell, Jack

The 1993 Cy Young Award winner in the American League, McDowell posted a 22-10 mark with the Chicago White Sox. He has a three-year average of 20-10, with a 3.32 ERA. He's struck out 791 batters in his career. "Black Jack" has an exceptional pick-off move that caught more than 10 runners off guard last year.

McDowell can be an evasive signer in person, and a bit avant-garde, perhaps due to his off-field love of progressive rock music. He will, however, respond to mail requests for his signature, and sometimes even include a flyer or information about his rock band. The best time to acquire his signature is during the off-season at a place where his band is playing, or at some of the local clubs in the cities where the White Sox are visiting.

McDowell has one of the most illegible signatures you'll ever see. Combined with significant character formation variances, his signature should prove to be extremely difficult to authenticate in the future. Should he continue to be an effective pitcher, there will no doubt be plenty of McDowell forgeries in the market because of his inconsistent signing habits.

Baseball: $28 Photograph: $14

Address: c/o Chicago White Sox, 333 West 35th St., Chicago, Ill. 60616

Hints for acquiring autographs through the auctions

* A seller has the right to reject an auction bid for any reason whatsoever.

* A bidder is obligated to honor any and all bids submitted.

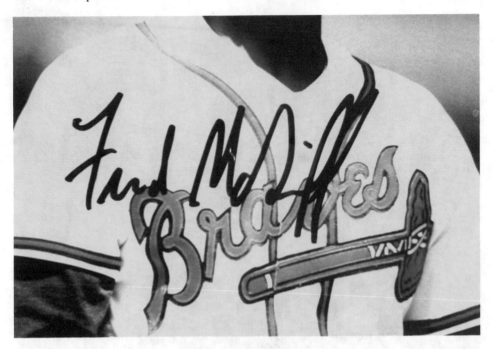

McGriff, Fred

McGriff's arrival was the key factor that led Atlanta to its 1993 National League championship. He terrorized pitchers during the month of July with a .413 average, nine homers and 22 RBI. "Crime Dog," considered by most to be baseball's most consistent power hitter, finished the 1993 season with 37 homers, 101 RBI and a .291 average.

McGriff is an obliging signer with a fairly consistent four-stroke signature. He is unique in that he believes signing autographs goes along with being a professional baseball player. He will impress you not only with his bat, but with his presence. The placement of the "c" in McGriff and the formation of the ending "ff" can be inconsistent. His signature exhibits large letter spacing, with little regard for closing a character.

Baseball: $27 Photograph: $14

Address: c/o Atlanta Braves, P.O. Box 4064, Atlanta, Ga. 30302

Hints for attending card shows

* Get there early - There's a lot to be said in the old adage "The early bird gets the worm." The best selection of autographed sports memorabilia is generally at the beginning of the show.

* Allocate plenty of time - You can not make clear, concise decisions if you are rushed. Concentrate on the task at hand; try not to get distracted.

Mirer, Rick

The former Notre Dame quarterback and first choice of the Seattle Seahawks in 1993, Mirer completed a successful first year at the helm, passing for 2,833 yards and 12 TDs. His Montana-like instincts were tested behind an offensive line that allowed 67 sacks in 1992.

Mirer is a gracious signer both in person and through mail autograph requests. He has done memorabilia shows and some private autograph signings. Collectors should have little trouble adding his signature to their collections.

Mirer's large four-stroke signature has only one consistent break, which falls between the "M" and the "i" in his last name. His signature has large character spacing, with each letter clearly legible. The trademarks of his signature are the large "R," which resembles an upside down "U," and the large "M," with its deep descending ending stroke. He also places a near-vertical line between the "R" and the "i" in Rick, perhaps as a way to identify the leg of the character.

Football: $65 Photograph: $16

Address: c/o Seattle Seahawks, 11220 NE 53rd St., Kirkland, Wash. 98033

Hints for acquiring autographs through the mail

* Be creative with your request. Before sending out a letter, collectors should ask these questions: What is unique about my request that will make a player respond? Will my request stand out among the hundreds of others he receives? What would be my reaction to such a request?

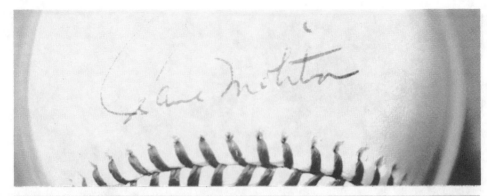

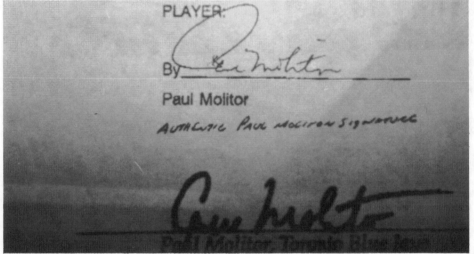

Molitor, Paul

For years Paul Molitor has been perhaps the most underrated player in the game. Not until he arrived in Toronto and became a World Series MVP in 1993 did fans outside of Milwaukee finally realize his tremendous offensive prowess. Molitor hit .332 during the 1993 season, with 22 homers and 111 RBI. He became the oldest player ever to post his first 100-RBI season. Molitor entered the 1994 season with 2,492 hits and a career batting average of .306.

"Molly" does make public appearances and occasionally will do a private signing. He is evasive at the ballpark, but may respond to mail autograph requests. In January of 1994, some forged Molitor autographed material was confiscated by the Metropolitan Toronto Police force. Two persons were arrested, charged and sentenced in the incident. The forged signatures bore little resemblance to an authentic Molitor autograph. Molitor has primarily signed World Series balls and bats that have the Blue Jays' team signatures on them. A lot of forged Molitor material still remains in circulation, so collectors beware!

Molitor's five-stroke signature has one common break between the "P" and the "a" in Paul. An occasional break also falls between the "M" and the "o" in Molitor. Over the years the most dramatic change in his signature has been the increased flamboyance and size of the "P." It is not unusual for the "P" in Paul to be two-and-a-half times the height of the "M" in Molitor, and greater in width than his complete last name. His lowercase characters have decreased in size over the years, the "au" in Paul is often unrecognizable.

Baseball: $29 Photograph: $17

Address: c/o Toronto Blue Jays, The SkyDome, 300 Bremner Blvd., Suite 3200, Toronto, Ontario, Canada M5V 3B3

Montana, Joe

After missing most of the 1991 and 1992 seasons with an elbow injury, Montana came back strong in 1993. The Kansas City Chiefs quarterback passed for 2,144 yards and 13 TDs. He and Terry Bradshaw are the only quarterbacks in NFL history to win four Super Bowls. The future Hall of Famer plans to finish his career in Kansas City.

Montana has been accessible through the years, but prefers now to market his signature through exclusive sources such as Upper Deck Authenticated. There is an incredible amount of his autographed memorabilia in the market. His popularity over the years and the lack of character definition in his signature make him a prime target for forgers. The anomalies of his signature also hamper the authentication process.

Montana's typical two-stroke signature, like those of most major sports personalities, was modified over the years to reduce his writing time and increase his autograph production. An occasional break can appear between the "M" and the "o" in Montana. The trademarks of his signature are the large flamboyant "J" in Joe and the ascending looped stroke that forms the "t" in Montana, then creates a new higher signature baseline before continuing with the "ana."

Football: $135 Photograph: $40

Address: c/o Kansas City Chiefs, 1 Arrowhead Drive, Kansas City, Mo. 64129

Moore, Rob

Moore has struggled through some tough injuries during the past few seasons, but still remains one of the league's most promising receivers. Despite these adversities, Moore compiled more than 1,500 receiving yards in the last two years. He has an amazing 45-inch vertical leap and runs the 40-yard dash in 4.4 seconds.

Moore is an obliging signer; collectors should have little difficulty in obtaining his signature. Moore also makes a considerable amount of public appearances, especially for charities.

His two-stroke signature typically has no breaks. The "o" in Rob gets intertwined with the "R" in Rob and can be difficult to distinguish. The beginning stroke of the "M" can resemble the number 2 and the second upward stroke of the letter is often four times larger than the first. Both "o"s in Moore will usually vary in size and formation. It is not unusual for the "r" in Moore to dip below the signature's baseline and for the "e" to be unrecognizable. Moore adds his uniform number, 85, which can resemble 05, to the end of his name.

Football: $45 Photograph: $10

Address: c/o New York Jets, 1000 Fulton Ave., Hempstead, N.Y. 11550.

---

* Be prepared - Often you will only have ONE autograph opportunity, so be prepared. Have both a new "Sharpie" and ballpoint pen immediately accessible. Know what you're going to have signed by each player and have it also at your fingertips.

Mourning, Alonzo

As a rookie, Mourning was second on the Charlotte Hornets in scoring and rebounding in 1992-93 and became the Hornets' all-time shot blocker in just his 49th game. At season's end, he was the only other rookie besides Shaquille O'Neal to place in the league's top 15 in scoring, rebounding and shot blocking. He completed the 1993-94 season at a 21.5 points-per-game scoring clip.

Mourning has been a gracious signer so far in his career. Autograph requests mailed to the club (one per person) have also proven successful. He also doesn't mind taking advantage of marketing his signature through private autograph signings or memorabilia shows.

Mourning's two-stroke signature exhibits no breaks and resembles "CloyoMorz" in its appearance. The large "A" that resembles a "C" is the largest letter in his signature. The "M" in Mourning begins from the top of the letter and can resemble a "W" at times because of its formation. A long wavy line extends from the "u" in Mourning, to the beginning of the "g," and apparently represents the "nin." This line can be 25-30 percent of the length of his signature. Mourning typically adds the "33" beneath the wavy line.

Basketball: $100 Photograph: $27

Address: c/o Charlotte Hornets, Hive Drive, Charlotte, N.C. 28217

---

* Don't be conspicuous - Blend into your surroundings as much as possible. Act like you belong in your environment. Wearing recognizable media clothing, such as NBC Sports, or ESPN, can help you in all professional-level facilities. Always look and act professional.

Mullin, Chris

Mullin was the second-leading scorer for the U.S. Olympic "Dream Team," trailing Michael Jordan. He finished his ninth season at Golden State in 1993-94 with 13,767 career total points, at a game average of 21.9 points.

Mullin is a temperamental signer. In-person autograph requests can be successful if the timing is appropriate. Autograph requests through the mail are often unpredictable.

Mullin's three-stroke signature has only one common break; it falls between the "M" and the "u." The hallmark of his signature is the large flamboyant "C," which extends from the bottom of the letter upward, to form an extremely large ascending loop, before then descending and creating the stem, and the bottom loop of the "h" in Chris. The "ris" in Chris is typically indistinguishable. The "M" in Mullin is normally half the height of the large "C" in Chris. The "in" at the end of his last name is usually dropped. The loop in the ascender of the "h" in Chris is large enough to house his uniform number 17, which he often conveniently places inside.

Basketball: $80 Photograph: $20

Address: c/o Golden State Warriors, Oakland Coliseum Arena, Nimitz Freeway and Hegenberger Road, Oakland, Calif. 94621

---

* You must stop the subject from moving - Do not allow the subject to walk while he is signing his autograph. As he walks he is decreasing his available signing space, causing other collectors to loose an autograph opportunity.

Murray, Eddie

Since he began his career with the Orioles in 1977, Murray, entering the 1994 season, has 2,820 career hits and 441 home runs. Just to prove that age can keep up with youth, he hit 27 homers, drove in 100 runs and batted .285 in 1993. Murray has had 17 straight seasons with at least 75 RBI, which is a record from the start of a player's career. He's considered by some baseball experts to be one of the most consistent run producers the game has ever seen.

Over the years, Murray has done his share of baseball card shows and charity appearances. His simple two-stroke signature has varied little over time. The hallmark of his signature is the strong left slant. Character formation will vary slightly with definition, and the double-backed strokes of the loops that make up the "d"s in Eddie may or may not be closed.

Watch Murray's stock soar as he approaches 3,000 hits and 500 home runs. Remember, only two players have ever had both 3,000 hits and 500 home runs - Hank Aaron and Willie Mays.

Baseball: $24 Photograph: $14

Address: c/o Cleveland Indians, Cleveland Stadium, Cleveland, Ohio 44114

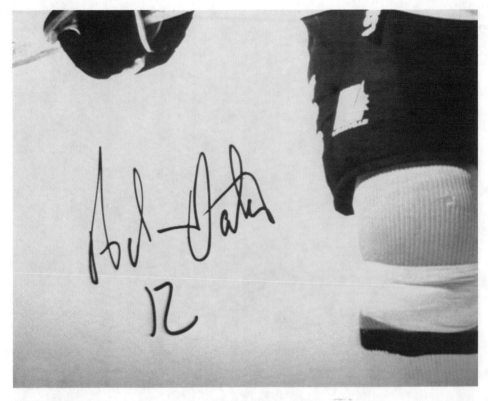

Oates, Adam

The Bruins center compiled 142 total points in 1992-93, leading the league in assists with 97. The former St. Louis Blues star has found a home in Boston; his scoring during the 1993-94 season (112 points) ranked in the top five at year's end.

Oates is a temperamental signer in person, and mail autograph requests can have unpredictable results.

His four-stroke signature has two common breaks, between the "A" and the "d" in Adam, and between the "O" and the "a" in Oates. The unique stroke of the "A" loops into the letter to finish its formation. The "am" in Adam is often dropped from his first name. He also double backs the finishing stroke of the "s," to cross the "t" in Oates. Oates will usually place his uniform number, 12, beneath his first name.

Puck: $34 Photograph: $18

Address: c/o Boston Bruins, Boston Garden, 150 Causeway St., Boston, Mass. 02114

---

* Exercise perseverance - Not everyone will comply with your request. In fact, some athletes will just choose to ignore your solicitations. These situations can be difficult, possibly requiring a different approach to a request, or repeated solicitations. Whatever the alternative, be patient and don't give up!

Olajuwon, Hakeem

Hakeem "The Dream" was the third player in NBA history to have 2,000 points, 1,000 rebounds and 300 blocked shots in the same season (1992-93). He put up MVP numbers in the 1993-94 season, too, averaging 27.3 points per game, while hauling down 955 rebounds and adding 287 assists. He was selected to his ninth All-Star team and captured the league's MVP award at the end of the season.

Olajuwon is unpredictable when it comes to autograph requests in person. Requests by mail will be sent back with a membership form for the Hakeem the Dream Fan Team. The Fan Team has four different membership levels. The first, with an autographed photograph, along with other items, is the "Lay-Up" at $25. Olajuwon could prove to be a difficult or expensive acquisition for your collection.

Olajuwon's four-stroke signature has been reduced simply to "Hakeem." Signature breaks occur between the "H" and the "a," and between the "e" and the "k" in Hakeem. The two stems of the "H" are crossed by the beginning stroke of the "e" to form the capitalized letter. The stylized "a" in Hakeem can vary in size, while the bottom loop of the letter may or may not be used. The "k" in Hakeem can be a single- or two-stroke variation and the "m" usually has little character definition.

In instances where Olajuwon signs his last name, signature breaks can occur between the "u" and the "w," and between the "w" and the "o." The one-and-a-half looped "O" in Olajuwon is usually the largest letter in his name. He typically places "#34" underneath his name.

Basketball: $100 Photograph: $30

Address: c/o Houston Rockets, 10 Greenway River Plaza E., P.O. Box 272349, Houston, Texas 77277

Olerud, John

Olerud won the American League batting title in 1993 with a .363 average. He had 200 hits, including 24 homers, while driving in 107 runs. Olerud, a patient hitter, walked about twice as often as he struck out last season. He began the 1994 season with 544 career hits, at the young age of 24.

Olerud is a very quiet and humble person, reminiscent in behavior to Lou Gehrig. He is obliging to in-person autograph requests, but prefers his privacy.

His four-stroke signature has changed only slightly in size and character formation over the last few years. The "n" in John, and both the "e" and "u" in Olerud, are nonexistent in most of his signatures. He will vary the slant of the "d" in Olerud, but for the most part his signature is very upright - at 90 degrees.

Baseball: $28 Photograph: $21

Address: c/o Toronto Blue Jays, The SkyDome, 300 Bremner Blvd., Suite 3200, Toronto, Ontario, Canada M5V 3B3

O'Neal, Shaquille

This runaway Rookie of the Year in 1992-93 led the Magic in scoring, rebounding, blocks and shooting. He was the only NBA player in the Top 10 in those four areas. "Shaq" has become the Madison Avenue endorsement king, and an awesome raw specimen at the young age of 22. In his second season, "Shaq" finished second in scoring, at 29.3 points per game, racking up 2,377 points during the year.

If you want to get his autograph in person, or on your basketball cards, well - Don't Even Think About It! "Shaq" should be a significant challenge to add to your autograph collection. He receives more than 1,000 pieces of mail per week!

If he simply signs "Shaq" as his signature it looks like "h6c" with the #32 added above the end of his name. With little character definition, and taking all the signing variables into consideration, this autograph could become the most forged signature in history. Collectors are better off waiting until this hot commodity cools off before purchasing his signature.

Basketball: $225 Photograph: $50

Address: c/o Orlando Magic, Orlando Arena, 1 Magic Place, Orlando, Fla. 32801

Hints for acquiring autographs through the mail

* Always include a self-addressed, stamped envelope (SASE) for convenient response through the mail. Please be sure the enclosed envelope is of proper size to house the returned material, and that the proper postage is affixed.

* Be brief, personal and sincere with your request. Exhibit in a few sentences your genuine interest in, and knowledge of, a player's career. Courtesy is paramount.

Palmeiro, Rafael

Palmeiro stroked 37 home runs and drove in 105 runs in 1993. The Texas Rangers' All-Star first baseman continues to develop his strength at the plate and has become a more selective hitter. At the age of 29, he has 1,144 hits and a .296 career average.

Over the years he has attended some baseball card shows and has done some private autograph signings. He remains a very underrated player in comparison to his peers.

Palmeiro's six-stroke signature can often be illegible. His last name occasionally resembles Frank Robinson's handwriting. The common breaks in his signature occur between the "R" and "a" in Rafael and between the "P" and "a" in Palmeiro. The "ae" in Rafael and the "eiro" in Palmeiro are often indiscernible.

Baseball: $20 Photograph: $12

Address: c/o Texas Rangers, P.O. Box 1111, Arlington, Texas 76010

Parish, Robert

Only Kareem Abdul-Jabbar (1,560) has played more games than the "Chief" (1,413) following the 1993-94 season. Parish is the ninth player ever to pass 13,000 career rebounds. "Chief" ranks in the top 15 on the all-time NBA scoring list.

Parish can be reluctantly obliging to in-person autograph requests. Collectors are urged to make out a $6 check payable to NEMPA and indicate you would like a Parish autographed photo. Mail the request, your phone number, and check to: NEMPA, c/o Boston Celtics, 151 Merrimac St., Boston, Mass. 02114. You will be surprised what happens, and your money will be put to a worthy donation - Sudden (Infant) Death Syndrome.

As Parish's court speed has diminished, so too has his signature, which has decreased in size and flamboyance. His four-stroke signature exhibits breaks between the "R" and the "o" in Robert and between the "P" and the "a" in Parish. The letter spacing in his signature has also decreased over the years, giving the autograph a more compressed look. The beginning stroke of the "R" will vary in position of origin. The "h" in Parish has decreased dramatically in both size and flamboyance. "Chief" does remember to dot his "i"s and cross his "t"s.

Basketball: $60 Photograph: $10

Address: c/o Boston Celtics, 151 Merrimac St., 5th Floor, Boston, Mass. 02114

* Know your subject - Doing a little biographical research on a subject can also be helpful. Knowing an athlete's hometown, his hobbies or even his alma mater can lead a subject into conversation with you, which can end with an autograph request.

Piazza, Mike

Piazza became the 13th Dodger to win the National League's Rookie of the Year award. He finished the season with 35 home runs, 112 RBI and a .318 batting average. He is Tommy Lasorda's godson, who ironically was drafted only as a favor to the Dodger manager. But Piazza has become a marquee player because of his play on the field and his endorsements off it.

Piazza was thoroughly hounded by autograph seekers in 1993. Look for a repeat performance in 1994, as the demand for his signature still has not been met. He can be an elusive signer, but is pleasant if he is approached correctly.

Halfway through the 1993 season he had modified his signature to a three-stroke autograph that appears as "MPiez." The beginning stroke of the "M" often resembles the number 2. The hallmark of his signature is the large flamboyant capital "P" in Piazza.

Baseball: $37 Photograph: $21

Address: c/o Los Angeles Dodgers, 1000 Elysian Park Ave., Los Angeles, Calif. 90012

Pippen, Scottie

Finally out of Michael Jordan's shadow, the All-Star Dream Teamer made his mark in 1993-94, scoring 1,587 points, or 22 points per game, and finishing third in the MVP voting. Entering the 1994-95 season, his eighth, Pippen is about 700 points short of 10,000 career points.

Now that Pippen is in the spotlight, his signature is even in greater demand. If you thought it was a difficult task to get a signature before, well just wait, and you will indeed do just that if you mail in a Pippen autograph request.

Pippen's flamboyant four-stroke signature exhibits only one common break; it falls between the "S" and the "c" in Scottie. The triangular formation of the "S" in Scottie is repeated in the loop of the "P" in Pippen. His last name resembles "Pw" rather than Pippen. The two "t"s in Scottie are typically crossed with a long curled stroke that intersects the loop of the "P" in his last name.

Basketball: $80 Photograph $21

Address: c/o Chicago Bulls, 1 Magnificent Mile, 980 N. Michigan Ave., Suite 1600, Chicago, Ill. 60611

---

* Conceal all the material you are going to have signed - Keep all of the material you are going to have signed concealed until the last possible minute.

Puckett, Kirby

Puckett is one of the most admired and popular players in baseball. A six-time Gold Glove Award winner, Puckett enters his 11th season with the Minnesota Twins a mere four hits shy of 2,000. A career .318 hitter, he has also smacked 164 home runs. He plays each game to the best of his ability and loves being a professional baseball player.

Puckett is not a frequent guest on the baseball card show circuit, but he does make public appearances on behalf of certain organizations. He can be an elusive signer, particularly if he's not in the mood. But when he has the time he doesn't mind giving out a few autographs.

His six-stroke signature has varied in size, character formation and flamboyance. The trademark of his signature is the large two-stroke "P" with its loop beginning far below the signature's baseline and extending to the "tt" in Puckett. Character variations in his signature are often due to writing expedience.

Baseball: $32 Photograph: $17

Address: c/o Minnesota Twins, 501 Chicago Ave. South, Minneapolis, Minn. 55415

Hints for acquiring autographs through the mail

* Avoid form letters. In addition to being impersonal and unflattering, the letters typically have a low response rate.

* To avoid confusion and disappointing responses, requests should be succinct and specific. If personalization is desired, please clearly indicate it in your request.

* Be conscious of a player's time by including no more than one or two items to be autographed.

Recchi, Mark

The Philadelphia right wing was acquired from Pittsburgh with hopes of complementing the play of Eric Lindros in 1992-93. The two-time All-Star did exactly that by logging 123 total points, including 70 assists. He followed up that season by finishing in the top 10 in scoring in 1993-94 with 107 points.

Recchi can be an evasive signer. Mail requests for his signature are answered by the team with a 4x6 color postcard that includes a facsimile autograph.

Recchi's three-stroke signature has only one common break, between the "M" and the "a" in Mark. His signature's trademarks are the large flamboyant second loop of the "M" in Mark and his large, backward looping, ending strokes.

Puck: $28 Photograph: $16

Address: c/o Philadelphia Flyers, The Spectrum, Pattison Place, Philadelphia, Pa. 19148

* Be timely with your request - The timing of an autograph request is the key element that will determine its success. Try to put yourself in the athlete's position. For example, a hockey team wins during overtime on a key goal. Who is more likely to be obliging to an autograph request following the game, the goalie who gave up the goal or the player who scored it?

Rheaume, Manon

The Sally Ride or Sandra Day O'Conner of her field, Manon Rheaume is a legitimate goaltender on a genuine team roster, the Tampa Bay Lightning. Rheaume signed as a free agent with Tampa Bay in August of 1992, and spent most of her time with Atlanta in the International Hockey League. It will be interesting to see if this 22 year old will be given an opportunity to fulfill a lifetime dream.

Taking advantage of her celebrity status, Rheaume has done some memorabilia shows and many charity events.

Rheaume's six- or seven-stroke signature can exhibit breaks between the "M" and the "a," and between the "n" and the "o" in Manon, also between the two-stroke "R" and the "h" in Rheaume. All the characters in her signature are clearly identifiable. The trademarks of her signature are the general legibility, the large second loop of the "M" in Manon and the two-stroke "R" of Rheaume.

If she plays a single game in the NHL, Rheaume will become an instant celebrity; every autograph collector in the United States and Canada will want her signature.

Puck: $16 Photograph: $8

Address: c/o Atlanta Knights, 100 Techwood Drive, Atlanta, Ga. 30303

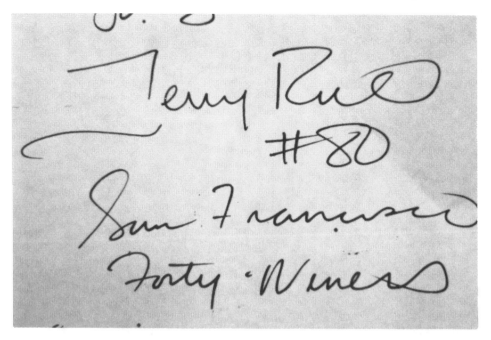

Rice, Jerry

Considered the greatest wide receiver in NFL history, Rice broke Steve Largent's career TD mark in 1992 with 103, and added 15 more to it in 1993. Rice was the NFL's MVP in 1987, after he caught 22 TD passes in a shortened 12-game season. He is an eight-time Pro Bowl selection and continues to rewrite the record books with each new season.

Rice, a good signer in person, does numerous private autograph signings and is no stranger to the show circuit.

Rice's signature can vary in character formation and has evolved with his popularity. Earlier signatures have no common breaks, while later variations have a break between the "J" and the "e" in Jerry. The most notable variation has been a complete change in the character formation of the "J" in Jerry. The "J" now can be either a two- or three-stroke process that resembles a "]." The top stroke of the letter often looks like a number 1 that has fallen over. His last name has remained very consistent, with only slight variation in the beginning stroke origin of the "R."

Football: $95 Photograph: $25

Address: c/o San Francisco 49ers, 4949 Centennial Blvd., Santa Clara, Calif. 95054

---

* Shopping malls - The primary shopping mall in any city is always an excellent place to meet professional athletes. Always position yourself at the central point of the mall, never at a specific exit. If the mall has multiple floors, stay on the main level. During the season players will shop between 11 a.m. to 2 p.m. - if there is a night game scheduled. If a day game is scheduled, they will shop or possibly attend a movie after the game. Many malls include movie theaters.

Ripken Jr., Cal

Still chasing Lou Gehrig's consecutive-game streak, Ripken knocked in 90 runs while hitting .257 in 1993. He began the 1994 season with 2,087 lifetime hits, 297 home runs and a career batting average of .275. Ripken makes solid contact with the ball, and still remains strong defensively.

His sub-par performance in 1992 hurt his popularity; many fans openly criticized Oriole management for starting Ripken. Although his average improved only slightly in 1993, his power jumped dramatically - he added 10 home runs and 18 RBI to his totals from the previous season.

Ripken did do several baseball card shows earlier in his career, but prefers private autograph signings. Ripken's not afraid to charge a baseball on the field or charge for one off the diamond. He has appeared on satellite shopping networks hawking autographed memorabilia. He also signed 5,000 Donruss cards for the company in the fall of 1991.

His signature has exhibited only slight changes in character size over the past few years. Common signature breaks fall between the "C" and the "a" in Cal and between the "R" and the "i" in Ripken. Both the "e" and the "n" in Ripken have always lacked character formations. The "J" for Jr. can vary in style and flamboyance.

Baseball: $30 Photograph: $15

Address: c/o Baltimore Orioles, 333 W. Camden St., Baltimore, Md. 21201

Hints for attending card shows

* Get there early - There's a lot to be said in the old adage "The early bird gets the worm." The best selection of autographed sports memorabilia is generally at the beginning of the show.

* Allocate plenty of time - You can not make clear, concise decisions if you are rushed. Concentrate on the task at hand; try not to get distracted.

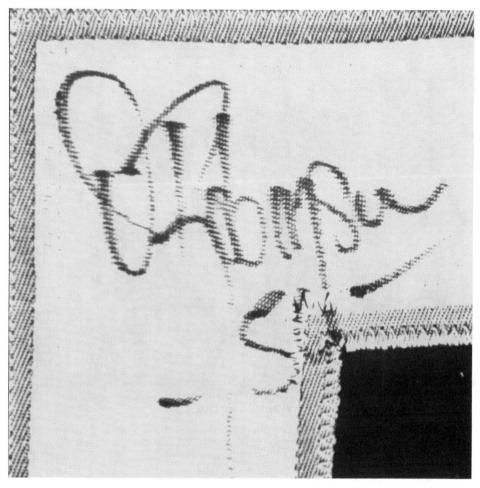

Robinson, David

"The Admiral," the league's top scorer at 29.8 points per game during the 1993-94 season, finished second in the MVP voting to Hakeem Olajuwon. He's pulled down 4,686 rebounds in his first five seasons, and has been an All-Star each season.

Robinson traditionally was a pretty good signer, but as his popularity has increased he has been unable to keep up with the demand. He occasionally does private autograph signings.

As the seasons change, so does Robinson's autograph. He typically signs "D. Robinson," which often resembles "PRobinF" or "OrobinA." The signature breaks are so inconsistent that they can occur between any letter. The beginning stroke of the "D" can originate at any point or direction. The often two-stroke "R" in Robinson has been consistent in formation, but earlier samples use a single stroke. The "in" in Robinson are the two lowercase letters that most often connect. The "s" in Robinson can be a stylized formation, or resemble an upside down "V." He often places "- 50 -" underneath his signature.

Most collectors would like to see "The Admiral" set a course for his signature.

Basketball: $110 Photograph: $26

Address: c/o San Antonio Spurs, 100 Montana St., San Antonio, Texas 78203

Robitaille, Luc

The quick left wing was drafted by Los Angeles in the 1984 draft. A six-time All-Star, he was awarded the Calder Memorial Trophy in 1987. Robitaille, who has put together eight very impressive seasons so far, finished the 1993-94 season as one of the league's best scorers off the power play, scoring 24 times, second best.

Robitaille is a temperamental signer. Mail autograph requests sent to him also yield unpredictable results.

Robitaille's two-stroke expedient signature has no breaks and only two clearly distinguished letters, the "L" and the "R." The lack of character definition in the signature, combined with many expedient collector requests and haphazard responses, makes his autograph another authentication nightmare to add to the growing list.

Puck: $27 Photograph: $15

Address: c/o Los Angeles Kings, Great Western Forum, 3900 West Manchester Blvd., Box 17013, Inglewood, Calif. 90306

Hints for acquiring autographs through auctions

* Any auction item not properly described - conditioning or grading, year, manufacturer - by the seller may be returned to the highest bidder. All items should be guaranteed authentic by the seller.

Roenick, Jeremy

A four-time All-Star, this Chicago center is known for his well-balanced attack. Roenick has had three straight 100-plus total point seasons.

Roenick is a good signer, but mail requests remain unpredictable. His five-stroke signature has two common breaks, between the "J" and the "e" in Jeremy and between the "R" and the "o" in Roenick. The large capitalization and his long descenders are trademarks of his signature. The two-stroke "R" in Roenick is often the largest letter in his name - measured from the furthest descending point to the highest ascending point. The "J," the "R" and the looped ending stroke of the "k" can be nearly equal in character height - measured from the baseline.

Puck: $26 Photograph: $14

Address: c/o Chicago Blackhawks, Chicago Stadium, 1800 W. Madison St., Chicago, Ill. 60612

Hints for acquiring autographs through the mail

* Be conscious of a player's time by including no more than one or two items to be autographed.

* Avoid form letters. In addition to being impersonal and unflattering, the letters typically have a low response rate.

* Be reasonable with your expectations. Some players receive hundreds of requests a day; they have little time to read a request, let alone respond to it.

Roy, Patrick

A five-time All-Star and three-time Vezina Trophy winner, Roy finished his ninth full season with Montreal in 1993-94 with a record of 260-146. He has also won the Conn Smythe Trophy twice and shared the William Jennings Trophy three times. When Roy finally retires, few doubt that he'll be the most decorated goaltender of all-time.

Roy is an obliging signer in person, but autograph requests can be unpredictable.

Roy's five- or six-stroke signature has three common breaks, between the "P" and the "a," "a" and the "t," and the "t" and the "k" in Patrick. The "ic" in Patrick is often dropped in his first name. The "a" in Patrick can resemble a "v" and usually intersects the "P." The stem of the "t" typically intersects the "P" and can extend beyond the capitalized letters' height. His single-stroke last name can resemble a number 3 tilted 45 degrees forward. Roy sometimes puts his uniform number, 33, underneath his last name.

Puck: $37 Photograph: $20

Address: c/o Montreal Canadians, Montreal Forum, 2313 St. Catherine St. W., Montreal, Quebec, Canada H3H 1N2

---

* Local public golf course - Most professional athletes love to play golf, especially on off days, when no game is scheduled. Position yourself outside the pro shop and be aware that golfers start on either the first or ninth hole, depending upon how crowded the course is.

Rypien, Mark

Although he's had two disappointing seasons, don't be surprised if Mark Rypien bounces right back. Only a few seasons ago he passed for 3,564 yards and 28 TDs and earned Super Bowl MVP honors. With his stock low, it might be a great time to buy!

Rypien can be obliging with his signature in person, but mail requests are often unpredictable. He loves to play golf, so tracking him down at the finest local area country club in Cleveland, home of his new team, may prove fruitful.

Rypien's autograph has evolved into a single-stroke format for increased signature production. Often this technique, which is common with many athletes, requires creating an alternate signature baseline below the first to accommodate the player's last name. Only the "ien" character combination is illegible in his signature. The "R" in Rypien is typically the largest character in his name, often four or five times larger than his lowercase letters. The beginning stroke in his first name starts with a curved line that originates from the top of the letter before descending downward to create the first stem in the letter "M." The descender of the "y" can vary in size, and may be six times the size of the looped formation of the letter. Rypien often adds his uniform number, 11, underneath his first name, which would be to the left of Rypien.

Football: $55 Photograph: $20

Address: c/o Cleveland Browns, Cleveland Stadium, Cleveland, Ohio 44114

---

* Be prepared - Often you will only have ONE autograph opportunity, so be prepared. Have both a new "Sharpie" and ballpoint pen immediately accessible. Know what you're going to have signed by each player and have it also at your fingertips.

Sakic, Joe

A four-time All-Star, Sakic has already logged 564 total career points during the last six seasons. The Nordiques' captain led the team in scoring in 1993-94 with 92 points and is considered one of the finest playmakers in the NHL.

Sakic is an obliging signer in-person, but autograph mail requests are often unpredictable.

Sakic's three- or four-stroke signature has a common break between the "S" and the "a" in Sakic. The large capitalized "S" in Sakic dominates his signature. The "J" in Joe, which can often resemble the number 8, is also a recognizable characteristic of his autograph. He typically places his uniform number, 19, underneath his last name.

Puck: $30 Photograph: $14

Address: c/o Quebec Nordiques, Colisee de Quebec, 2205 Ave. du Colisee, Quebec City, Quebec, Canada G1L 4W7

Sandberg, Ryne

Sandberg began the 1993 season with a cast on his left hand, which sidelined him until April 30. Although he managed to hit .309 in 117 games, his power was noticeably absent. The season ended for him Sept. 13, when he dislocated a finger. Since he's a tremendous athlete, all of Chicago awaits Sandberg's return in 1994. "Ryno" enters this season with 2,080 hits and 240 home runs.

Sandberg can also be an elusive signer; mail requests often are a waste of time. He has done some private autograph signings, but prefers to make his money doing endorsements. He signed 5,000 1992 Donruss cards at his home in Phoenix in 1991.

As his popularity increased, Sandberg altered his signature so that his entire name can be written with one stroke. Many collectors were caught by surprise when they first saw the alteration. It is far more flamboyant with the "S" in Sandberg resembling the number 8. Variations in the signature could prove difficult to authenticate. The advantage, however, is that any pen lifts will probably indicate a forgery.

Baseball: $35 Photograph: $27

Address: c/o Chicago Cubs, 1060 W. Addison St., Chicago, Ill. 60613

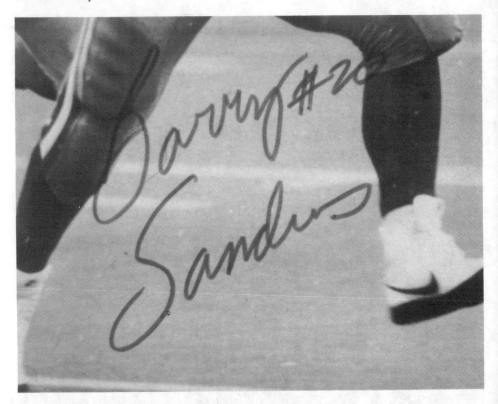

Sanders, Barry

Barry Sanders ran for 1,115 yards and three TDs in 1993, finishing as the league's fourth best rusher. His rushing production was down, but he had 40 fewer attempts than the league's leader. Many experts consider him one of football's best pure runners.

Sanders can be an evasive signer. He has attended a few shows. However, lately I have not seen a whole lot of his material in the market.

Sanders' signature can vary significantly, especially in character formation. This most often appears when he is being deluged with autograph requests. It is in these situations where he will, like most sports celebrities, begin dropping letters from his name. If Sanders is in a relaxed environment his signature is usually very legible, with nearly every letter distinguishable. There are two common breaks in his signature, between the "B" and the "a" in Barry, and between the "S" and the "a" in Sanders. The "S" in Sanders can be both traditional (usually a rushed signature) and stylized in its formation.

Football: $70 Photograph: $16

Address: c/o Detroit Lions, 1200 Featherstone Road, Pontiac, Mich. 48057

Hints for acquiring autographs through the mail

* Don't risk sending expensive items through the mail. Although I am astounded by the accuracy and promptness exhibited by the U.S. Postal Service, most collectors are not in position to replace lost merchandise.

Sanders, Deion

The versatile two-sport athlete made the Pro Bowl for the third straight year in 1993. "Prime Time," who led the league in interceptions in 1993 with seven, remains one of the league's strongest defensive backs. However, he appears headed toward focusing on just one sport, baseball, as an outfielder with the Atlanta Braves. An evasive signer both on and off the field, "Prime Time" does, however, manage to do a few private autograph signings each year.

Deion's signature can vary with the temperature; the only consistent elements over the years have been the two-stroke "D" in Deion and, the "$" or "S" and "d" in Sanders. Depending upon his time, he may draw a face inside the letter "D" of his signature.

Baseball/football: $29/$65 Photograph: $17
Address: c/o Atlanta Braves, P.O. Box 4064, Atlanta, Ga. 30302

Hints for attending card shows

* Know what you are looking for - Know why you are attending the show. Always bring a compact, updated list that is readily accessible.

* Know what you are willing to pay - Before the show, know what you will pay for the items you want. Consult a price guide if necessary; bring it to the show.

Selanne, Teemu

A unanimous selection for the 1992-93 Calder Memorial Trophy, Selanne led all rookies in scoring with 132 points. He appeared in all 84 games with the Winnipeg Jets and shattered Mike Bossy's single-season rookie scoring record. Selanne also led all NHL rookies in six offensive categories.

Selanne is an obliging signer in person, but mail autograph requests are slow, but often fruitful.

Selanne's four-stroke signature has two common breaks, between the "T" and the "e" in Teemu, and between the "S" and the "e" in Selanne. The "u" in his first name connects to the "S" in Selanne. His capitalized letters, the two-stroke "T" and the single-stroke "S," are typically the largest characters in his signature. The flamboyant finishing upward stroke of the "e" in Selanne can extend backward, as far as the letter "l." He often places his uniform number, 13, underneath his last name.

Puck: $32 Photograph: $20

Address: c/o Winnipeg Jets, Winnipeg Arena, 15-1430 Maroons Road, Winnipeg, Manitoba, Canada R3G 0L5

---

* Don't be conspicuous - Blend into your surroundings as much as possible. Act like you belong in your environment. Wearing recognizable media clothing, such as NBC Sports, or ESPN, can help you in all professional-level facilities. Always look and act professional.

Smith, Emmitt

Smith led the NFC in rushing in 1993 with 1,486 yards and nine TDs, despite having missed the first few games of the season in a contract dispute. In collecting his third straight NFL rushing title, Smith has sets the standard as a "franchise" player. The NFL's Rookie of the Year in 1990, Smith also collects Super Bowl championship rings.

Taking full advantage of his popularity, Smith remains active on the show circuit. His signature may cost you between $35 and $45 to put on an 8x10 color photograph. If you can't make it to a show, you can purchase an Emmitt Smith autographed authentic NFL jersey through "The Official Dallas Cowboys Catalog" for only $199.99, or an autographed authentic helmet for $319.99.

Smith's flamboyant six- or eight-stroke signature can vary in size, especially when he's signing uniforms or trading cards, and character formation. Typical breaks are between the "E" and "mmitt" in Emmitt, and between the "S" and the "m" in Smith. The "mith" in his last name varies in size, character formation and positioning. Smith also typically puts "22" beneath his last name. His large signature usually dominates a color photograph - often half the height of the item.

Football: $125 Photograph: $45

Address: c/o Dallas Cowboys, Cowboys Center, 1 Cowboys Parkway, Irving, Texas 75063

* Block all accessible paths between you and the subject - Using other collectors, you can strategically place yourself so that there is no clear path between the subject and his destination. Similar to electricity, the subject is going to always choose the path of least resistance or, in this case, the trail that has the least amount of autograph seekers.

Stevens, Kevin

The three-time All-Star left wing has already compiled 500 career total points, after only five full seasons. A stronger than anticipated offensive threat, his 111 total points in 1992-93 was a big factor in the Pittsburgh Penguin offensive attack. He tailed off a bit in 1993-94, with but 88 points, but remains an integral scoring option in the team's offense.

Stevens is a good signer in person, but mail autograph requests are unpredictable.

His four-stroke signature exhibits two common breaks, between the "K" and the "e" in Kevin, and between the "S" and the "t" in Stevens. The "v" and the "n" in Kevin are often dropped from his first name, and the "en" in Stevens is difficult to distinguish. The two-stroke "K" in Kevin is usually the largest letter in his name. The stem of the "t" in Stevens often extends beyond the character height of the capitalized "S." He usually dots his "i" and crosses his "t," before adding his uniform number, 25, underneath the "s" in Stevens.

Puck: $24 Photograph: $12

Address: c/o Pittsburgh Penguins, Civic Arena, Pittsburgh, Pa. 15219

Thomas, Frank

Frank Thomas was the American League's Most Valuable Player in 1993. He hit .317 with 41 homers and 128 RBI. "The Big Hurt" struck out a mere 54 times; his .426 on-base percentage ranked fourth in the American League. He is one of the few players in baseball who could make a legitimate attempt at the Triple Crown.

Other than a fellow minor league teammate of his, Michael Jordan, Thomas is the endorsement king of Chicago. Thomas occasionally hits the show circuit, which is helpful to collectors who find him a difficult signature to obtain at the ballpark. He is a reasonably good signer in spring training, but is finicky about autographing certain types of equipment. Thomas penned his name to 3,500 Leaf/Donruss signature cards during a 10-day period last fall. He also remains a company spokesman for the card manufacturer.

"The Big Hurt" has reduced signature time by eliminating the "an" in Frank and the "omas" in Thomas. "Fk Th" is now his hallmark and he doesn't hesitate to add "35" to his signature. Like most signatures with reduced characters for comparison purposes, his autograph should prove to be an authentication nightmare in the future.

Baseball: $40 Photograph: $23

Address: c/o Chicago White Sox, 333 W. 35th St., Chicago, Ill. 60616

Thomas, Isiah

Thomas ranks third all-time in assists, fourth all-time in steals, and made 11 All-Star Game starts in 13 seasons. He led the Pistons to 1989 and 1990 World Championships and is the team's all-time leader in points, assists and steals.

Thomas has always been a good signer, whether in person or through the mail. It's not unusual for him to sign just "Isiah," dropping his last name.

His four-stroke signature has breaks between the "I" and the "s" in Isiah, and between the "T" and the "h," and the "m" and the "a" in Thomas. He typically adds "#11" underneath his signature. The formation of his capitalized letters resembles the letter "C," with looped ending strokes. The slant of the "I" and the "h" in Isiah, and the "T" and the "h" in Thomas, should be almost identical.

Basketball: $65 Photograph: $14

Address: c/o Detroit Pistons, Palace of Auburn Hills, 2 Championship Drive, Auburn Hills, Mich. 48057

Thomas, Thurman

Thomas ran the ball 355 times for 1,315 yards and six TDs in 1993 - tops in the AFC. Selected to his fifth straight Pro Bowl, he continues to be the dominant total yard gainer in the NFL.

He does make appearances, but can be an evasive signer. Your best bet is to catch him at Jim Kelly's "Sport City Grill" after the game. In fact, while you're there you will probably run into the rest of the team and half the city of Buffalo, N.Y.

Thomas's four- or five-stroke signature has been as consistent as his ground game, varying only slightly in size and character formation. Common signature breaks occur between the "h" and the "u" and the "m" and the "a" in Thurman, and between the "h" and the "o" in Thomas. There is often little definition in the "n" of Thurman and in the "a" in Thomas.

Football: $75 Photograph: $23

Address: c/o Buffalo Bills, 1 Bills Drive, Orchard Park, N.Y. 14127

---

* Exercise perseverance - Not everyone will comply with your request. In fact, some athletes will just choose to ignore your solicitations. These situations can be difficult, possibly requiring a different approach to a request, or repeated solicitations. Whatever the alternative, be patient and don't give up!

Tocchet, Rick

The four-time All-Star right wing compiled career high numbers in 1992-93 - his first full season as a Pittsburgh Penguin. He logged 61 assists on his way to 109 total points.

Tocchet is a good signer in person, but mail autograph requests can be a bit unpredictable.

Tocchet's three-stroke signature typically has two breaks, between the "o" and the "c" and between the "e" and the "t." The "ick" of Rick is completely indiscernible. An interesting element to his signature is that the leg of the "R" also serves as the arm, or top, of the letter "T." The formation of the downward strokes that form the stems of the "R" and the "T" loop and make good comparison points, since the slant and formation is similar in both. He also adds his uniform number, 22, which resembles a "w" underneath his last name.

Puck: $22 Photograph: $11

Address: c/o Pittsburgh Penguins, Civic Arena, Pittsburgh, Pa. 15219

Hints for acquiring autographs through the mail

* Be creative with your request. Before sending out a letter, collectors should ask these questions: What is unique about my request that will make a player respond? Will my request stand out among the hundreds of others he receives? What would be my reaction to such a request?

Turgeon, Pierre

Turgeon enjoyed career high scoring totals in 1992-93, posting 132 points to finish sixth in the NHL. He was awarded the 1992-93 Lady Byng Memorial Trophy for his sportsmanship and helped guide the Islanders into the playoffs for the first time since 1990. He added 94 points in 1993-94.

Turgeon is a gracious signer in person and responds promptly to autograph mail requests sent to him.

Turgeon's four-stroke signature exhibits two common breaks that occur between the "P" and the "i" in Pierre and also between the "T" and the "u" in Turgeon. The "erre" in Pierre is often dropped from his first name, and the "eon" is typically replaced with a slightly curved line extending from the "g" in Turgeon. The hallmarks of his signature are the large "P" in Pierre and the flamboyant "T" in Turgeon with its long extended arm, which can reach the "g" in his last name. He often adds his uniform number, "#77," underneath his signature.

Puck: $25 Photograph: $13

Address: c/o New York Islanders, Nassau Coliseum, Uniondale, N.Y. 11553

* Be timely with your request - The timing of an autograph request is the key element that will determine its success. Try to put yourself in the athlete's position. For example, a hockey team wins during overtime on a key goal. Who is more likely to be obliging to an autograph request following the game, the goalie who gave up the goal or the player who scored it?

Walker, Herschel

Walker seems to have found a home in Philadelphia. In 1992 he became the first Eagle since 1985 to gain 1,000 yards in a season. In 1993, he gained 746 yards on the ground, which was ninth in the NFC. If he can stay healthy, there could be a few more 1,000-yard seasons in his legs.

Walker's four- or five-stroke signature has two common breaks. The first is between the "H" and the "e" in Herschel, and the second is between the "W" and the "a" in Walker. Walker's flamboyant signature's hallmark is the large, unique two-stroke formation of the first letter in Herschel. The capitalized "H" can resemble a "zC" in its appearance. The first stroke creates an elongated loop that can be the same size as his signature. Nearly every letter in his autograph is legible. The "l" in Herschel has a flamboyant curled ending stroke, which allows it to resemble a "d" when it finishes near the "e" in Herschel. The second loop of the "W" in Walker is often twice the height of the first. The slant of the stem's "h" and "k" should be very similar. Fortunately for collectors, Walker's signature has been fairly consistent over the years, making it easier to authenticate. He typically adds his uniform number, 34, underneath his name.

Football: $60 Photograph: $12

Address: c/o Minnesota Vikings, 9520 Viking Drive, Eden Prairie, Minn. 55344

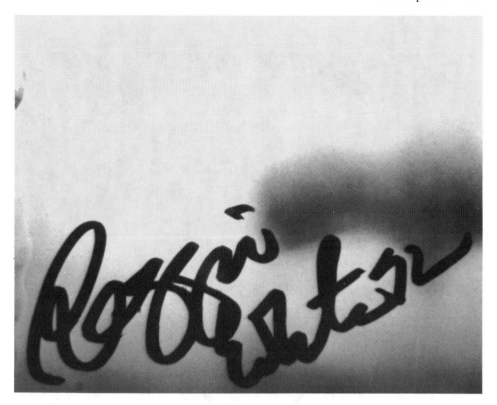

White, Reggie

White, the most coveted free agent in 1993, eventually signed with the Green Bay Packers. Considered to be the best defensive lineman in the league today, White came on strong in 1993 to help lead his team into the playoffs. "The Minister of Defense" was the only player in NFL history with more sacks than games played going into the 1993 season.

White, who is a licensed Baptist minister, is an extremely popular individual both on and off the field. He is a good signer in person, especially away from the stadium. He makes numerous appearances on behalf of certain charities and his church.

White's two-stroke signature typically has no breaks. The trademark of his signature is the well rounded "R" in Reggie, which has about a 60-degree right slant, and the "W" in White that is connected to the top of the letter "h."

Football: $80 Photograph: $25

Address: c/o Green Bay Packers, 1265 Lombardi Ave., Green Bay, Wis. 54304

---

* Always have flat items placed on a clipboard - Flat items are cumbersome to sign if a similar surface area is not available. Placing the items gently underneath the clip allows for the much needed support. Additionally, trading card collectors can place more than a single item, side by side, underneath the clip, possibly allowing for a quick, additional signature.

Winfield, Dave

On Sept. 16, 1993, Winfield became the 19th player to collect 3,000 hits. The future Hall of Famer hit .271 with the Twins and reached 20 homers for the 15th time, leaving him just 47 shy of 500. A remarkable athlete, he entered the 1994 season at the age of 41.

Winfield has done shows during his career, but still remains elusive to autograph seekers. He would rather sit in the dugout than to have to deal with all the requests for his signature.

Winfield's four-stroke signature has varied in size and character formation. The "ave" in Dave has been virtually eliminated. He may or may not break his signature between the "f" and "i" in Winfield.

Baseballs: $32 Photographs: $17

Address: c/o Minnesota Twins, 501 Chicago Ave. South, Minneapolis, Minn. 55415

Worthy, James

A seasoned 12-year veteran, Worthy added leadership to a young Lakers' team in 1993-94. He finished the season with 16,320 total career points. He posses a strong half-court, one-on-one ability and has consistently averaged 17.6 points per game.

As the Lakers faded from the limelight, which the Bulls now possess, the popularity of many of the team's players has decreased. Although the demand for his signature may be at an all-time low, it might be an excellent time to add Worthy's signature to your collection. Why? Because it's a bargain considering his achievements.

Worthy's four-stroke signature has varied slightly in character formation over the years, but still remains highly legible. Common signature breaks occur between the "J" and the "a" in James and between the "W" and the "o" in Worthy. The "J" in James is very stylized, and the "W" in Worthy resembles a "UE" in its formation.

Basketball: $60 Photograph: $15

Address: c/o L.A. Lakers, Great Western Forum, 3900 Manchester Blvd., P.O. Box 10, Inglewood, Calif. 90306

Young, Steve

Young, named NFL Player of the Year in 1992, led the San Francisco 49ers to a 14-2 record, and, in doing so, escaped the formidable shadow of Joe Montana. He passed for 3,465 yards and 25 TDs in 1992, and only had seven interceptions. Just in case this wasn't enough to prove his legitimacy as an NFL superstar, he topped those marks in 1993, throwing for 4,023 yards and 29 TDs. He was the NFC's highest rated quarterback in 1993.

Young is a good signer in person, but requests via mail are often unpredictable. He is no stranger to private autograph signings; his signature should be fairly easy to add to your collection. If you would like a Steve Young autographed authentic NFL jersey, don't bother calling the 49ers. Instead, refer to "The Official Dallas Cowboys Catalog" and you'll find one for $199.99.

Young's four- or five-stroke signature can vary in size, slant and character formation. The "S" in Steve is usually very large and can extend the entire length of his first name. He often varies the way he loops the bottom of the "S" in Steve. The beginning stroke of the "Y" in Young can vary its point of origin, and the stroke often forms a loop to complete the top of the letter that is often at the pinnacle of the signature. The common break in his signature is between the "S" and the "t" in Steve. There is also an occasional break between the "Y" and the "o" in Young. The slant and character formation of his signature can vary depending upon the expedience of the autograph. He has a very upright signature, with greater character definition, when he is not being pressured.

Football: $85 Photograph: $21

Address: c/o San Francisco 49ers, 4949 Centennial Blvd., Santa Clara, Calif. 95054

Yzerman, Steve

An eight-time All-Star, the Red Wings center finished the 1993-94 season with more than 1,000 career total points. He was the Lester B. Pearson Award winner in 1989 with 155 total points, 90 of them assists.

Yzerman can be a temperamental signer. Mail autograph requests sent to him are often unpredictable.

Often signing simply "S. Yzerman," he makes a very large three-stroke signature which has a common break between the "r" and the "m" in his last name. Sample signatures on 8x10 photographs often measure 2.5x6.5.

Puck: $35 Photograph: $19

Address: c/o Detroit Red Wings, Joe Louis Sports Arena, 600 Civic Center Drive, Detroit, Mich. 48226

* The subject's hand must be available for a signature - It is not unusual for your subject to be carrying an equipment bag, locker room bag, etc.. If you see that a subject has both hands occupied, you are going to have to find a way to free-up one of them so that he can autograph your items. The easiest way is to offer to hold the item for him while he signs your material.* Learn a few basic phrases of common languages - Not everyone who plays professional sports in this country is fluent in English. Learning some basic phrases in Spanish, French and even Russian will prove to be particularly helpful in many instances.* Be courteous, yet firm, with your request - Always be courteous to your subject: "May I please have your autograph, Mr. Montana?" "Thank you very much. I really appreciate it." Respect your subject, but do not be timid with an autograph request. You must be aggressive, but not overbearing.

Chapter 11

Professional Team Profiles

**Major League Baseball, National Basketball Association,
National Football League, National Hockey League**

Notes:

★ Team addresses and telephone numbers are subject to change.

★ Club response is based solely on one written request and one to three phone requests for information. No additional requests were made because normally fans and collectors seeking information do not go beyond this point. Responses may vary due to the seasonal aspect of the particular sport and post-season activity. Irregularities in mail delivery, or phone system variations, can also effect outcome and response rating.

★ The marketing rating given is subjective and is based solely on this specific project and no others. All sample prices are subject to change. Please bear in mind that teams periodically issue new merchandise catalogs, brochures or price lists. Many of the teams I contacted were in this process and therefore could not provide the requested information. Also, team programs are subject to change or discontinuance. Hours and location of team gift shops are also subject to change.

★ A team's autograph policy is subject to change and often varies from stadium to stadium. No teams accept responsibility for items mailed or delivered to them. A club may or may not forward mail once a player is no longer part of the team. There are no guarantees that a player will ever receive or respond to your autograph request. Also, if you receive a signature from a player there is no guarantee that it is authentic.

★ The comments listed are subjective and based upon fan and collector needs that I am familiar with.

★ Business establishments listed in the "After the Game" section were recommendations from professional athletes, hotel employees, fans, collectors and employees of a city's Chamber of Commerce or Bureau of Tourism. They by no means constitute any associated guarantees.

★ All visiting team hotels are subject to change. The hotel(s) listed are those where professional teams have been known to stay. Please understand that once you set foot on a hotel's property, you are only a visitor; you are not subject to guest privileges. Also, you must dress and act in accordance with hotel regulations. Always be courteous and respect an individual's right to privacy.

Major League Baseball

Team address

Atlanta Braves
Atlanta-Fulton County Stadium
521 Capitol Ave. S.W.
Atlanta, Ga. 30302

Phone: (404) 522-7630

Club mail response

Good - A typical reply to an information request will include a Braves bumper sticker, current schedule, Braves Clubhouse Store catalog, Braves "Fan Facts" (an information sheet) and Braves Historical Highlights (one sheet chronological team review).

Marketing

Very Good - The club is expanding its souvenir outlets, which are located at the CNN Center and the North Point Mall. No autographed material is available at these outlets, which is a real weakness considering the team's popularity. The Braves issue a 16-page comprehensive color catalog. To obtain a copy of the catalog, or to order merchandise, call 1-800-433-BRAVES • • - Final two digits unnecessary.

Autograph policy

The club does not guarantee autograph requests will be answered and asks that fans refrain from mailing any personal items to have signed; the team accepts no responsibility for them. Fans are permitted to assemble in the area directly behind the dugouts from the time the gates open until one hour before the game.

Comments

Braves game-used equipment is plentiful in the market, due to large dealer acquisitions. Also, several players attend sports memorabilia shows during the off-season. It would be nice to have a selection of autographed memorabilia, limited-edition collectibles and game-used equipment in future catalogs.

After the game

Jocks 'n' Jills is a hot sports spot after the game. Many visiting players make it a point to visit Underground Atlanta before they leave town. Like all major cities, Atlanta has its fair share of fine dining and popular night spots, making it difficult to determine a player's exact whereabouts. Start first with the dining areas one hour after the game, then with the night clubs. Some of Atlanta's hottest night spots may not be appropriate for families or small children.

Probable visiting team hotel

Marriott Marquis

Team address

Baltimore Orioles
333 West Camden St.
Baltimore, Md. 21201

Phone: (410) 685-9000 •

• Digital voice mail system - a listing of player appearances available on-line.

Club mail response

Slow in responding to written requests for information.

Marketing

Good - The Orioles were producing a 1994 merchandise catalog when I contacted them. The team operates a baseball store at the ballpark that carries a variety of team-related collectibles. For specific information, call 1-410-332-4633, ext. 158; this ARA Services number will put you in contact with the baseball store. The store does not sell any autographed memorabilia.

Autograph policy

Requests for player autographs should be sent directly to the player's attention at the address listed above. Many requests are answered with a player postcard. For example: "Dear Orioles Fan: The Baltimore Orioles and I are so happy that you take an active interest in our team. We truly appreciate the support our fans give us. We hope you will enjoy adding this photo card to your Orioles memorabilia collection. Thanks again, and we look forward to seeing you at Orioles Park at Camden Yards in the near future! Sincerely, Brady Anderson" - with a facsimile signature

Comments

Collectors and fans would like the Orioles to expand team-related merchandise to include a variety of limited-edition collectibles and autographed memorabilia.

After the game

Many of the players like to dine at Obrycki's Crab House and Seafood Restaurant, or restaurants along the inner harbor.

Probable visiting team hotels

Baltimore Marriott Inner Harbor, Omni

Team address

Boston Red Sox
Fenway Park
Boston, Mass. 02215

Phone: (617) 267-9440

Club mail response

Slow in responding to written requests for information.

Marketing

Good - There are three conveniently located Red Sox Clubhouse shops that sell a variety of team-related merchandise. They are located at the Burlington (1-617-273-0883), Emerald Square (1-508-695-6462) and North Shore malls (1-508-538-0345). These shops carry a large inventory of Upper Deck Authenticated merchandise and a good supply of Boston Red Sox player autographs. They also schedule two or three player autograph sessions in the store each season. An autographed Roger Clemens baseball will cost you $80. The Lansdowne Shop, located in Fenway Park, issued a two-fold, single-sheet color brochure with a variety of team-related souvenirs. The catalog does not contain any autographed memorabilia.

Autograph policy

Requests for player autographs should be sent directly to the player's attention at the address listed above.

Comments

Collectors and fans would like the Red Sox to upgrade team-related merchandise to include limited-edition collectibles and a larger variety of autographed memorabilia.

After the game

Popular sports spots after the game include Who's on First (across from Fenway), Champions Bar, Sports Salon, and T's Pub. Some finer dining spots include Anthony's Pier 4, Jimmy's Harborside, and Ye Olde Union Oyster House. Many players head downtown to eat and shop at the Faneuil Hall Marketplace.

Probable visiting team hotels

Westin Hotel, Marriott Copley Place

Team address

California Angels
P.O. Box 2000
Anaheim, Calif. 92803
Phone: (714) 937-7200

Club mail response

Slow in responding to written requests for information.

Marketing

Good - You can begin your souvenir hunting at the California Angels Clubhouse Shop located in the Main Place Mall. It offers a wide variety of team-related souvenirs and collectibles and carries the Upper Deck Authenticated line of autographed merchandise. The shop schedules one player autograph session each month during the season. At these sessions, it is common to have players sign a few dozen baseballs or other related merchandise for the shop, which later sells them at retail prices. A sample price is a Tim Salmon autographed baseball for $39.95.

Autograph policy

Requests for player autographs should be sent directly to the player's attention at the address listed above.

Comments

The autograph sessions in the Clubhouse Shop provide fans and collectors with an excellent opportunity to meet their favorite players. The Angels may want to add a larger assortment of team-related, limited-edition collectibles and expand the selection of autographed memorabilia.

After the game

Popular restaurants with the players include Benihana's of Tokyo, Casa Maria, and Cattleman's Wharf.

Probable visiting team hotels

Marina del Rey Marriott

Team address

Chicago Cubs
Wrigley Field
1060 W. Addison St.
Chicago, Ill. 60613

Phone: (312) 281-5050 •

• Digital voice mail system - press 5 for events.

Club mail response

Mail response can be slow and unpredictable, but phone information requests are answered promptly.

Marketing

Good - The team offers a two-fold, single-sheet color Cubs Gift Catalog that highlights the new uniforms for 1994. Information on catalog merchandise can be obtained by calling 1-800-248-9467 (Monday through Friday, 9 a.m. to 5 p.m., CST). The team generally issues two catalogs per year; the larger spring catalog offers autographed merchandise. Sample prices from the catalog include an official Cubs jersey ($115) and an official Cubs team jacket ($120).

Autograph policy

Requests for player autographs can be sent directly to the player's attention at the address listed above.

Comments

The team seems to respond very well to the needs of fans and collectors.

After the game

Harry Caray's is a nice place to begin your autograph hunt. The restaurant, with its Italian cuisine and baseball display, usually attracts the media. Fine dining spots include Gene & Georgetti, Leona's and the Red Tomato.

Probable visiting team hotel

The Westin

Team address

Chicago White Sox
333 W. 35th St.
Chicago, Ill. 60616

Phone: (312) 924-1000

Club mail response
Slow in responding to written requests for information.

Marketing

Weak - A limited amount of clothing is available through Sportservice Corp. at White Sox Park. For product information or a two-fold, single-sheet color brochure, call 1-800-944-SOX7. The service does sell minor league affiliates' caps for $20 each. There is no autographed memorabilia for sale in the brochure. A gift shop also sells souvenirs and merchandise at the ballpark. Sample prices from the brochure include a Russell batting practice jersey ($70) and a Frank Thomas T-shirt ($20). There is also a Chicago White Sox Clubhouse Shop, located in Oakbrook, that carries a wide variety of team-related merchandise.

Autograph policy

Requests for player autographs can be sent directly to the player's attention at the address listed above.

Comments

As popular as the Chicago White Sox are, it's disappointing to see such a poor attempt at merchandising. Collectors and fans would like a greater selection of souvenirs, limited-edition collectibles and autographed sports memorabilia. A replica Birmingham Barons jersey, #45, might also prove to be a strong offering.

After the game

After the game, try America's Bar, owned by Walter Payton. (Also see the Cubs' list above).

Probable visiting team hotels

Westin, The Drake, Hyatt Regency

Team address

Cincinnati Reds
Riverfront Stadium
100 Riverfront Stadium
Cincinnati, Ohio 45202

Phone: (513) 421-4510

Club mail response

Slow in responding to written requests for information.

Marketing

Poor - The Reds issue a flier that contains team-related merchandise. There is no autographed memorabilia in the flier, and no autographed items are sold at the stadium.

Autograph policy

Requests for player autographs can be sent directly to the player's attention at the address listed above.

Comments

Fans and collectors would like the Reds to expand the flier into a catalog that would include limited-edition collectibles, game-used equipment and autographed memorabilia.

After the game

Some of the popular sports spots after the game are Barleycorn's, Flanagan's Landing, the Waterfront Sports Cafe and Willie's Bar and Grill. For finer dining, try Crockett's River Cafe, Mike Fink's or the Montgomery Inn at the Boathouse.

Probable visiting team hotel

The Westin

Team address

Cleveland Indians
Indians Park
2401 Ontario Ave.
Cleveland, Ohio 44115

Phone: (216) 420-4200

Club mail response

Slow in responding to written requests for information - could be due to the confusion surrounding the relocation of the club.

Marketing

Good - The Indians issue a 16-page color catalog filled with a nice selection of team-related merchandise. Many of the items, including some limited-edition collectibles, focus on the Indians' inaugural season at Jacobs Field. The team is doing a nice job marketing a selection of the new 1994 uniforms. For local shopping convenience, the team operates three Indians team shops (at the ballpark, Belden Village Mall, and the Galleria at Erieview) that offer a selection of merchandise. Sample prices from the price list include an authentic leather-sleeved jacket ($240) and an authentic jersey ($135).

Autograph policy

Requests for player autographs can be sent directly to the player's attention at the address listed above.

Comments

Fans and collectors would like to see a comprehensive mail-order catalog that includes limited-edition collectibles and autographed memorabilia.

After the game

Popular sports spots after the game include Rascal House Saloon and the Grand Slam Grille & Power Play. For finer dining establishments, try Morton's of Chicago/Cleveland or Sammy's. Shooters Waterfront Cafe is also popular with some players.

Probable visiting team hotel

Cleveland Hilton South

Team address

Colorado Rockies
Mile High Stadium
1900 Eliot St.
Denver, Colo. 80204

Phone: (303) 292-0200

Club mail response

Good - Written requests for information are responded to promptly.

Marketing

Good - The Rockies issue a 16-page color catalog that includes a wide variety of team-related merchandise. The team also operates five Dugout stores, located in Denver, Greeley, Fort Collins, Tucson and Colorado Springs. The catalog does not contain any autographed memorabilia. Team players do, however, occasionally appear at the stores to sign autographs.

Autograph policy

Requests for player autographs can be sent directly to the player's attention at the address listed above.

Comments

Fans and collectors enjoy the accessibility of the team stores and are delighted that team members occasionally visit these locations, especially during the Rockies "Winter Caravan." Including more limited-edition collectibles and possibly some game-used equipment or autographed memorabilia in future catalogs would be appreciated.

After the game

Some of the players' favorite restaurants are Marlowe's, Rock Bottom Brewery, and Strings. The Broker Restaurant is an excellent choice for fine dining.

Probable visiting team hotel

The Westin

Team address

Detroit Tigers
Tiger Stadium
2121 Trumbull
Detroit, Mich. 48216

Phone: (313) 962-4000

Club mail response

Good - Mail response can be slow, but usually contains the material or information requested.

Marketing

Fair - The club offers fans a two-fold, single-sheet color brochure with 15 different clothing items highlighting the new team logo. To receive a catalog or place an order, you can dial 1-800-221-2324 (outside Michigan) or in state 1-313-963-5216. Sample prices from the brochure include a Tigers adult jacket ($75) and an official Tigers uniform cap ($22).

Autograph policy

Requests for player autographs can be sent directly to the player's attention at the address listed above.

Comments

Collectors and fans would like to ask the "new tiger on the prowl" to consider expanding the team's merchandising efforts to include other non-clothing based souvenirs. Limited-edition collectibles and autographed memorabilia would be a nice addition to the current catalog.

After the game

Popular sports spots after the game include Hoot Robinson's, Lindell Athletic Club and Reedy's Saloon.

Probable visiting team hotel

Omni International, Hilton Suites

Team address

Florida Marlins
Joe Robbie Stadium
2267 N.W. 199th St.
Miami, Fla. 33056

Phone: (305) 626-7428

Club mail response

Very Good - The team responds promptly and accurately to mail information requests.

Marketing

Good - Like most newer teams, the Marlins marketing approach is much stronger than most older established teams. Through Benchwarmers Catalog, the team's official merchandiser, the Marlins offer 12 color pages of souvenirs and collectibles. There is a wide variety of merchandise available, some of which is autographed. Sample prices from the catalog include a Marlins authentic jersey ($119.95) and a Marlins travel bag ($49.95).

Autograph policy

Requests for player autographs can be sent directly to the player's attention at the address listed above. Additionally, fans who wish to seek autographs are encouraged to do so before the game - up to 40 minutes before game time or at the end of batting practice. Two Marlin players will also sign autographs before each Sunday home contest. Fans must have their own items for the players to sign.

Comments

The Marlins approach to having two players sign before each Sunday home contest is an excellent idea, and one which every collector and fan appreciates. It is a shame that more ball clubs do not approach their fans with a similar process.

After the game

There is a significant amount of night spots available to Miami visitors. The most popular dining spot is Joe's Stone Crab Restaurant. Some players head to Benihana's after the game.

Probable visiting team hotels

Sheraton Bal Harbour Resort, Don Shula's Hotel, Biscayne Bay Marriott

Team address

Houston Astros
P.O. Box 288
Houston, Texas 77001-0288

Phone: (713) 799-9794

Club mail response

Slow in responding to written requests for information. Phone requests, however, are prompt and accurate, and very politely handled.

Marketing

Fair - The team offers only a small souvenir list. For a copy of this list, send a self-addressed stamped envelope to the address above.

Autograph policy

Requests for player autographs can be sent directly to the player's attention at the address listed above.

Comments

Because a brand new logo appears on everything from cups to uniforms, one would think that the team would have had an aggressive marketing campaign, like the Chicago Cubs, to capitalize on its new look.

After the game

First stop is Shucker's Sports Bar at the Westin Hotel, because most of the teams stay at the hotel. Most of the visiting team's players will wander through the 300-plus shops at the Galleria.

Probable visiting team hotel

Westin Galleria

Team address

Kansas City Royals
P.O. Box 419969
Kansas City, Mo. 64141-6969

Phone: (816) 921-2200

Club mail response

Good - A typical request for information can include a single-sheet, three-fold color brochure with a selection of Royals' souvenirs and products. There is no authentic autographed memorabilia for sale through the organization.

Marketing

Good - Another team whose marketing potential hasn't been realized. The selection of souvenirs being marketed now is good, but needs to be updated to meet current collector needs. Sample prices from the catalog include an authentic team jacket ($95) and a Royals polo shirt ($36).

Autograph policy
Requests for player autographs can be sent directly to the player's attention at the address listed above.

Comments
Fans and collectors would like a selection of limited-edition merchandise and autographed memorabilia added to the next Royals catalog.

After the game
Chappell's Bar & Grill is a good sports bar and restaurant to begin with in your autograph hunt. The Bristol Bar and Grill, Plaza III Steakhouse and Savoy Grill and Restaurant all offer excellent dining and are popular among many athletes.

Probable visiting team hotels
The Westin Crown Center, Hyatt Regency Crown Center

Team address
Los Angeles Dodgers
Dodger Stadium
1000 Elysian Park Ave.
Los Angeles, Calif. 90012

Phone: (213) 224-1500

Club mail response
Good - Written requests for information are answered promptly and accurately.

Marketing
Good - The Dodgers issue a five-fold, single-sheet color brochure that contains 74 team-related items, from bomber jackets ($295) to a Dodgers old-timer jacket ($995). In a 1993 catalog the Dodgers offered autographed baseballs of Sandy Koufax ($100), Don Drysdale ($55), Duke Snider ($55) and Mickey Mantle ($85). An autographed Darryl Strawberry plaque sold for $60. The Dodgers also had some autographed bats available. To obtain an official gift catalog, or to order merchandise, call 1-800-762-1770.

Autograph policy
Requests for player autographs should be sent directly to the player's attention at the address listed above. The stadium opens 1 1/2 hours before game time for fans to watch batting practice. Most of the players are on the field then; if a fan is on the field level he might be able to get an autograph. After the game, many fans wait outside of the players parking lot to obtain autographs.

Comments
Fans and collectors are delighted that the Dodgers offer autographed memorabilia for sale, but would like the concept expanded. Also, a selection of limited-edition collectibles, 8x10 color photographs, game-used equipment and Dodger baseball card team sets would be good additions to the catalog.

After the game
Little Joe's Restaurant is a popular sports spot after the game.

Probable visiting team hotel
Hyatt Regency Broadway Plaza

Team address
Milwaukee Brewers
Milwaukee County Stadium
201 S. 46th St.
Milwaukee, Wis. 53214

Phone: (414) 933-4114

Club mail response
Slow in responding to written requests for information.

Marketing
Good - You may want to begin your souvenir shopping at the Milwaukee Brewers Clubhouse Shop located in the Brookfield Square Mall. It carries a wide selection of team-related merchandise. The shop does schedule player autographing sessions - one per month during the season - but does not sell any autographed memorabilia.

Autograph policy
Requests for player autographs can be sent directly to the player's attention at the address listed above.

Comments
Fans and collectors would like the Brewers to expand team-related merchandise to include limited-edition collectibles and autographed memorabilia.

After the game
Some popular sports spots after the game include Saz's (near the stadium) and Luke's Sports Spectacular. If fine dining is in order, try Alioto's, Benson's Steakhouse, which is popular with some players, Jake's or some of the finer German restaurants, such as Karl Ratzsch's or Mader's. After day games, many of the players head for to the Geneva Lakes Kennel Club to watch the dog races.

Probable visiting team hotel

Hyatt Regency Milwaukee

Team address

Minnesota Twins
The Metrodome
501 Chicago Avenue South
Minneapolis, Minn. 55415

Phone: (612) 375-1366

Club mail response

Good - The team responds timely and accurately to information requests.

Marketing

Good - The Twins have two Pro Shops in the area to cater to fan and collector needs. The Twins have a color sheet that offers a range of souvenirs and collectibles for sale. The team does offer game-used equipment for sale. For a list of the jerseys, bats and hats available, call (612) 635-0777. Sample prices from the sheet include an Twins authentic jersey ($114.95) and a Twins satin jacket ($91).

Autograph policy

Requests for player autographs can be sent directly to the player's attention at the address listed above.

Comments

Collectors and fans appreciate the fact that the Twins offer game-used memorabilia for sale and hope that this marketing technique becomes a trend with professional clubs.

After the game

Hoops on Hennepin is a good sports spot to visit. Minneapolis has a variety of fine dining, including Pronto Ristorante, Rudolph's and J.D. Hoyt's - just to name a few.

Probable visiting team hotel

Marriott Downtown

Team address

Montreal Expos
Olympic Stadium
4549 Avenue Pierrre de Coubertin
Montreal, Quebec, Canada H1V 3N7

Phone: (514) 253-3434

Club mail response

Slow in responding to written requests for information, but phone requests are handled promptly and courteously.

Marketing

Good - The Expos issue a 16-page color catalog that contains 56 team-related items and a centerfold insert that offers 40 different caps. There is no autographed memorabilia contained in the catalog. The team operates a gift shop in the stadium for the convenience of Expos fans.

Autograph policy

Requests for player autographs can be sent directly to the player's attention at the address listed above. There is also a "Fan Fest" area located inside Olympic Stadium where fans can gather and test their athletic prowess. Before every Sunday home game, two members of the team conduct autograph sessions in this area.

Comments

Expos fans and collectors appreciate meeting, and getting an autograph from, their favorite players at the stadium during Sunday's home games. Fans and collectors would also like the team to add some limited-edition collectibles and autographed memorabilia to future catalogs. The Montreal Expos genuinely care about their fans and strive to meet their needs, whenever and wherever they can.

After the game

After the game you can always stop at one of the 10 La Cage aux Sports bar and restaurants located around Montreal. Many of the visiting players will head to Old Montreal during their visit to the city. The area is filled with many unique shops and restaurants. Some of the finer dining areas are Le St. Amable, Les Chenets and Les Halles.

Probable visiting team hotel

Le Centre Sheraton

Team address

New York Mets
Shea Stadium
Flushing, N.Y. 11368

Phone: (718) 565-4305

Club mail response

Fair - Provides a prompt, but often incomplete, answer to specific written requests for information.

Marketing

Poor - Does not produce specific team product/souvenir catalogs. Does not direct fans as to where to find specific team products. If there are souvenir stands in the stadium, the club does a poor job of providing this information to the fans. There are no attempts to entice fans who contact the club via mail with any direct marketing pieces - schedules, ticket information, etc.. There are five Mets Clubhouse stores located in various parts of the tri-state area. Many of the shops, especially the one at 575 Fifth Ave., schedule periodic visits by Mets players.

Autograph policy

"Autographs of our players are owned by the men themselves and I have no control or rights to them." - Mets' vice president of marketing

Requests for player autographs can be sent directly to the player's attention at the address listed above.

Comments

The club needs to improve its communication and image with fans. It often takes several phone calls and letters to receive the proper information requested.

After the game

You might want to begin your autograph hunt at the better sports spots in the city, including Jimmy Weston's, Mickey Mantle's, Runyon's and the Sporting Club.

Probable visiting team hotel

Grand Hyatt

Team address

New York Yankees
Yankee Stadium
Bronx, N.Y. 10451

Phone: (718) 293-4300

Club mail response

Slow in responding to written requests for information. The Yankees win no awards for phone congeniality, with short responses and rude undertones.

Marketing

Good - The Yankees market souvenirs through an outside firm (Volume Services) which publishes the New York Yankee Catalog. Ordering information is available at 1-800-223-8479 or 1-212-244-3262. The person I spoke to by phone at this number was very pleasant and accommodating with my request. The catalog is 16 color pages of souvenirs and merchandise, but has no autographed memorabilia. The Yankees also have two Clubhouse stores in Manhattan that sell team souvenirs and merchandise. Sample prices from the catalog include a classic canvas jacket ($120) and a navy blue embroidered sweater ($35).

Autograph policy

Requests for player autographs can be sent directly to the player's attention at the address listed above. Serious collectors are encouraged to attend the Yankee Fan Festival held annually. This year the three-day festival was held during the first week of February at the Jacob Javits Convention Center. More than 35 current and former Yankees signed autographs free of charge. There are several card dealers, memorabilia exhibits and special booths. Also, many authentic and unique Yankee items are offered in daily auctions. If you attend the festival there is no guarantee of any specific autograph. Each player will sign only one item per person, but no bats or uniforms will be autographed.

Comments

The Yankee Fan Festival, now entering its fifth year, is an excellent marketing concept. The shows net proceeds benefit local charities, and the support given to this annual event by the players and the fans is commendable. The team is rich in tradition; it would be nice if historical souvenirs, limited-edition items and autographed memorabilia were offered.

After the game

There are plenty of sports spots to hit after the game, including Jimmy Weston's, Legends, Mickey Mantle's, Runyon's and the Sporting Club.

Probable visiting team hotels

Grand Hyatt, Embassy Suites

Team address

Oakland Athletics
Oakland-Alameda County Coliseum
Oakland, Calif. 94621

Phone: (510) 638-4900

Club mail response

Slow in responding to written requests for information.

Marketing

Good - Begin your souvenir shopping at either of the two Oakland A's Clubhouse shops, conveniently located in Hayward and Richmond. They carry a wide variety of team-related merchandise. Players appear periodically at the shops to greet fans and sign autographs.

Autograph policy

Requests for player autographs can be sent directly to the player's attention at the address listed above.

Comments

Fans and collectors would like the A's to expand team-related merchandise to include limited-edition collectibles, game-used equipment and more autographed memorabilia.

After the game

Some sports spots you might want to briefly stop by are Rickey's Sports Lounge and Restaurant or Mac's Sports Bar and Grill. Scott's Seafood Grill and Bar is an excellent dining establishment to visit after the game. It's popular with players because it's along the waterfront.

Probable visiting team hotel

Oakland Airport Hilton

Team address

Philadelphia Phillies
Veterans Stadium
P.O. Box 7575
Philadelphia, Pa. 19101

Phone: (215) 463-6000

Club mail response

Slow in responding to written requests for information.

Marketing

Undetermined - The team has been unresponsive to both phone and mail requests for information.

Autograph policy

Requests for player autographs can be sent directly to the player's attention at the address listed above.

Comments

The ball club needs to implement a better communication system with its fans.

After the game

Some of the finer restaurants in Philadelphia include Bookbinders Seafood House, Cafe Nola, DiLullo Centro, Downey's Pub, and La Famiglia.

Probable visiting team hotels

Sheraton Society Hill, Embassy Suites

Team address

Pittsburgh Pirates
Three Rivers Stadium
600 Stadium Circle
Pittsburgh, Pa. 15212

Phone: (412) 323-5000

Club mail response

Slow in responding to written requests for information.

Marketing

Good - Begin your Bucs souvenir shopping at either of the team's Clubhouse shops located in the Monroeville and Ross Park malls. The shops carry a wide variety of team-related merchandise, including game-used baseball bats. The team also has three franchised shops conveniently located in the area. Two color catalogs are also issued annually - a Spring/Summer, 12 pages, and a Fall/Winter, 16 pages. The additional pages in the later catalog also contain Steeler and Penguin merchandise.

Autograph policy

Requests for player autographs should be sent directly to the player's attention at the address listed above. The team sponsors "Autograph Sunday," an autograph session held from 12:15 p.m. to 12:45 p.m. at the "Pirates Boardwalk" concourse of the stadium. Two players generally attend this event.

Comments

"Pirate Fest," an annual three-day collectors convention sponsored by the team in January, attracts collectors nationwide. The 1994 convention had 15 current Pirates signing autographs and several former Bucs. It is highly recommended that all Pirates fans plan attending next year's convention.

After the game

The first stop after the game, and possibly your last, is the Pittsburgh Sports Garden. It's a great place to run into athletes, so bring plenty of items to have signed.

Probable visiting team hotel

Vista International

Team address

St. Louis Cardinals
Busch Stadium
250 Stadium Plaza
St. Louis, Mo. 63102

Phone: (314) 421-3060

Club mail response

Slow in responding to written requests for information.

Marketing

The Cardinals issue a three-page color brochure that includes a variety of team-related collectibles, but no autographed memorabilia.

Autograph policy

Requests for player autographs should be sent directly to the player's attention at the address listed above.

Comments

Fans and collectors would like the Cardinals to expand the brochure to include limited-edition collectibles, game-used equipment and autographed memorabilia.

After the game

The first stop after the game has to be Charlie Gitto's Pasta House. This casual downtown restaurant attracts players, sportswriters and other celebrities. From there, head toward Mike Shannon's, Ozzie's Restaurant or St. Louis Live & Lou Brock's Sports City Grille.

Probable visiting team hotel

Adam's Mark

Team address

San Diego Padres
Jack Murphy Stadium
9449 Friars Road
San Diego, Calif. 92108

Phone: (619) 283-4494

Club mail response

Slow in responding to written requests for information.

Marketing

Good - Begin your souvenir shopping at the San Diego Padres Clubhouse Shop (1-619-745-9656) located in the North County Fair Mall. The shop has a nice selection of team-related merchandise. Periodic autograph sessions with Padre players are also scheduled during Saturday home games. The shop carries the Upper Deck Authenticated line of autographed merchandise and a variety of other Padre autographed memorabilia.

Autograph policy

Requests for player autographs can be sent directly to the player's attention at the address listed above.

Comments

The Padre Clubhouse Shop does a nice job in marketing team-related collectibles. Fans and collectors would like the shop to carry game-used memorabilia and a larger selection of limited-edition collectibles.

After the game

Most of the visiting teams head to the waterfront restaurants after the game. Mister A's Restaurant and the Boatview are the finer stops along the waterfront.

Probable visiting team hotel

Marriott Hotel and Marina

Team address

San Francisco Giants
Candlestick Park
San Francisco, Calif. 94124

Phone: (415) 468-3700

Club mail response

Excellent - The Giants reply promptly and accurately to information that is requested. Also, the team provides many direct marketing pieces, such as schedules, team photographs and ticket information, to entice fans.

Marketing

Very Good - The San Francisco Giants produce a small, but diverse, brochure of team souvenirs and merchandise. No autographed memorabilia is included in the catalog.

Autograph policy

Requests for player autographs can be sent directly to the player's attention at the address listed above. Also, the Giants asked me to provide information about Willie Mays. Mays will autograph your item(s) for a contribution to his Say Hey

Foundation, which benefits underprivileged children. Minimum donations are $100 for each baseball and $50 for each flat item, such as baseball cards, photos, books, etc.. Please do not send bats or any other items. Please mail your item(s) to: Willie Mays' Say Hey Foundation, c/o New York Giants, Candlestick Park, San Francisco, Calif. 94124

Comments

The Giants do not hesitate to ask their players to cooperate with as many autograph requests as possible, whether in person or through mail requests.

After the game

Fisherman's Wharf is popular with the players, especially visiting teams, with the outdoor seafood stands, dozens of seafood restaurants, shopping and bay cruises.

Probable visiting team hotels

Parc 55, Hilton, Westin St. Francis, Grand Hyatt

Team address

Seattle Mariners
The Kingdome
P.O. Box 4100
411 1st Ave. S.
Seattle, Wash. 98104

Phone: (206) 628-3555

Club mail response

Slow in responding to written requests for information.

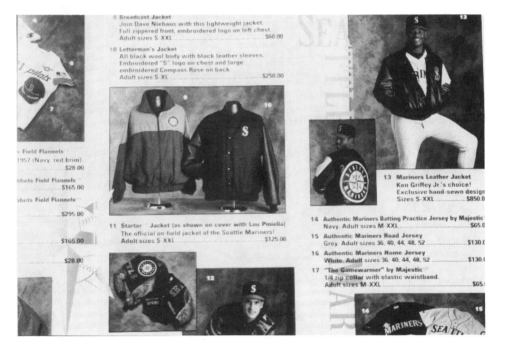

Marketing

Good - Official Mariners merchandise is marketed by Ogden Entertainment Services, which prints an attractive five-fold, single sheet, color brochure packed with souvenirs. The brochure offers 82 pieces of merchandise, from nostalgic offerings such as old Pilots replica jerseys ($165) to an exclusive hand-sewn Mariners leather jacket ($850). The company also operates a new gift store, The Batters Box, located on the 100 level concourse of the Seattle Kingdome.

Autograph policy

Requests for player autographs can be sent directly to the player's attention at the address listed above.

Comments

The team, through Ogden Entertainment Services, has brought collectors and fans a nice selection of Mariners merchandise. The catalog is current with market needs and avoids the "key chain and ashtray" approach to collectibles. The only improvements would be to offer color player photographs, posters, limited-edition souvenirs or artwork and autographed memorabilia.

After the game
A great stop after the game is F.X. McRory's Steak, Chop and Oyster House. The restaurant recreates a classic New York City chop house. Another fine dining spot is the Metropolitan Grill, specializing in steak and seafood. If sports bars are your fancy, try Swannie's at 222 South Main St..

Probable visiting team hotel
Stouffer Madison

Team address
Texas Rangers
The Ballpark in Arlington
1000 Ballpark Way
Arlington, Texas 76011

Phone: (817) 273-5222 •
• - very accommodating over the phone.

Club mail response
Slow in responding to written requests for information.

Marketing
Good - The Rangers issue a color catalog of team-related merchandise which was not available when I spoke to them. They have just opened a Grand Slam Shop which will offer a variety of team collectibles. For a listing of those items, contact the store at P.O. Box 90111, Arlington, Texas 76004, or call 1-817-273-5001. The Rangers souvenir publication also offers a Nolan Ryan commemorative "no-hitter" poster (autographed for $30), at the address listed above. Please allow four to eight weeks for delivery.

Autograph policy
Requests for player autographs should be sent directly to the player's attention at the address listed above. From 6:15 p.m. to 6:45 p.m. before Wednesday home games at the stadium the Rangers hold an autograph session that usually includes four or five players.

Comments
Fans and collectors enjoy the opportunity to meet their favorite Ranger players during the Wednesday autograph session. Also, the club is providing a wonderful service to collectors by offering the Nolan Ryan autographed poster. It is hoped the team's merchandise catalog and Grand Slam Shop will offer autographed memorabilia for sale.

After the game
A popular spot after the game is Bobby Valentine's Sports Gallery Cafe. A couple of other fine dining areas, Bay Street and Key West Grill, could also prove to be a worthwhile visit.

Probable visiting team hotels
Marriott Courtyard, Arlington Marriott

Team address
Toronto Blue Jays
SkyDome
One Blue Jays Way
Suite 3200
Toronto, Ontario M5V 1J1, Canada

Phone: (416) 341-1000

Club mail response
Slow in responding to written requests for information.

Marketing
Fair - The Blue Jays issue a sheet listing team-related merchandise. Upon request, the team also offers a sheet listing World Series souvenirs. The team operates two gift shops. One, open only during Blue Jay home games, is in the SkyDome; one services downtown Toronto. These shops rarely offer autographed memorabilia. Not unlike some other professional teams, the Blue Jays believe offering autographed memorabilia could be considered a conflict of interest. Blue Jay players do, however, occasionally appear at the gift shops to sign autographs.

Autograph policy
Requests for player autographs can be sent directly to the player's attention at the address listed above. According to a 1994 fan information flier, "players are not permitted to sign autographs during a game or 45 minutes prior to a game."

Comments
Labatt's, who is the primary stockholder of the club, used to sponsor monthly luncheons honoring its "Player and Pitcher of the Month." These luncheons, held at a Toronto hotel, were open to the public. Fans and collectors would like these luncheons to be resumed so they can meet and obtain autographs from the players. Also, the team needs to upgrade its marketing approach to be more in line with fan and collector needs.

After the game
A sure bet after the game is Alice Fazooli's Italian Crabshack Saloon, so bring plenty of things to have autographed. A few other stops, such as Fisherman's Wharf, the Old Spaghetti Factory and Whistling Oyster, might prove worthwhile.

Probable visiting team hotels
The Westin Hotel, Radisson Hotel Plaza

National Basketball Association

Team address

Atlanta Hawks
One CNN Center
South Tower Suite 405
Atlanta, Ga. 30303

Phone: (404) 827-3800

Club mail response

Slow in responding to written requests for information.

Marketing

Weak - The Atlanta Hawks do not sell team-related merchandise. Some souvenirs, however, are sold in the arena by a merchant who is unaffiliated with the team.

Autograph policy

Requests for player autographs can be sent directly to the player's attention at the address listed above.

Comments

Providing team-related merchandise to fans and collectors is not a requirement of an NBA basketball franchise. Most teams offer products to the public to increase team awareness and hopefully entice fans into attending a game. The Hawks choice in not offering team-related merchandise is in sharp contrast to other clubs, such as the Orlando Magic, who have found it a worthwhile and lucrative venture.

After the game

A popular sports spots after the game is Jocks 'n' Jills, especially for a basketball fan. Autograph seekers should head to Champions, a sports bar and restaurant that is conveniently located inside the hotel where most of the visiting clubs stay while in Atlanta.

Probable visiting team hotel

Marriott Marquis

Team address

Boston Celtics
151 Merrimac St.
Boston, Mass. 02114

Phone: (617) 523-6050

Club mail response

Excellent - The Celtics react promptly to mail information requests.

Marketing

Good - The Celtics will be moving into the new Shawmut Center next season, and intend to increase product and souvenir offerings. Celtics souvenirs and gift items can be purchased from the Boston Garden Pro Shop by calling (617) 557-1315.

Autograph policy

Each player is responsible for the mail addressed to him and sent to the club. The Celtics, in association with the New England Monitoring Parents Association (NEMPA), an affiliate of the National Sudden Death Syndrome Foundation, have a program by which fans can, for a $6 donation, acquire an autographed player photograph. If this interests you, please make your check payable to NEMPA and indicate your choice of players, with alternates in case of a shortage. Mail your request to: NEMPA, c/o Boston Celtics, 151 Merrimac St., Boston, Mass. 02114. Please include your phone number and allow six to eight weeks for delivery. This program is for current players only. Therefore, Larry Bird and Kevin McHale are NOT available.

Comments

The Celtics charity efforts are certainly applauded and hopefully will continue each season. It remains to be seen, however, what future marketing efforts will be made to entice collectors who not only visit the new facility, but may want to acquire mail order items.

After the game

Faneuil Hall Marketplace, with its shops and restaurants housed in 19th-century warehouses, is popular and near the Boston Garden. Anthony's Pier 4 and Jimmy's Harborside are very popular with visiting teams, but may be a bit out of line for your pocketbook.

Probable visiting team hotel

Marriott Copley Place

Team address

Charlotte Hornets
Hive Drive
Charlotte, N.C. 28217

Phone: (704) 357-0252

Club mail response

Slow in responding to written requests for information.

Marketing

Good - The Hornets do not directly market team-related merchandise. The team authorizes an outside service - Sportservice Corp. - to sell souvenirs in the arena. This service issues a 16-page souvenir catalog which contains a wide variety of team-related merchandise, but no autographed memorabilia. It's available by calling 1-704-357-3346.

Autograph policy

Requests for player autographs can be sent directly to the player's attention at the address listed above.

Comments

Charlotte is a team with tremendous marketing potential, as evidenced by the fact that Larry Johnson replica jerseys sell more than any other active player in the league. The fact that the team has not taken a more active role in offering team-related merchandise to collectors and fans is disappointing.

After the game

After the game, start at Champions Sports Bar inside the Marriott. Some of the visiting players also dine at Slugs Thirtieth Edition, which is close to the hotel. The Lamplighter, often considered the finest restaurant in town, is also popular with many players.

Probable visiting team hotel

Marriott City Center

Team address

Chicago Bulls
1 Magnificent Mile
980 N. Michigan Ave.
Suite 1600
Chicago, Ill. 60611

Phone: (312) 943-5800

Club mail response

Slow in responding to written requests for information.

Marketing

Poor - The Bulls do not directly market team-related merchandise. The team uses a merchandising service that offers just basic souvenirs - mostly clothing items. When I contacted the service it informed me that there were no product listings or team catalogs available for fans.

Autograph policy

Requests for player autographs can be sent directly to the player's attention at the address listed above.

Comments

The many vendors who sell unlicensed or counterfeit Chicago Bulls products must be laughing all the way to the bank. The team desperately needs a sophisticated marketing approach to its merchandising, which is extremely disappointing to fans and collectors. Add to this the disorganization of the team's current merchandiser and you have a real enigma.

After the game

After the game you can head to America's Bar, owned by Walter Payton, or try some of Chicago's fine dining at places such as Gene & Georgetti or, of course, Michael Jordan's.

Probable visiting team hotel

Hyatt Regency Chicago

Team address

Cleveland Cavaliers
2923 Streetsboro Drive
Richfield, Ohio 44286

Phone: (216) 659-9100

Club mail response

Slow in responding to written requests for information.

Marketing

Good - The Cavs issue a 12-page color catalog loaded with a variety of souvenirs, from vanity night lamps ($37.99) to a Cavs clock ($27.99). Most of the merchandise is marketed toward fans, but not collectors.

Autograph policy

Requests for player autographs can be mailed directly to the player's attention at the address listed above.

Comments

Fans and collectors would like the Cavs to offer these items in the next team merchandise catalog: 8x10 color photographs, Cavs trading card team sets, limited-edition collectibles, autographed memorabilia and game-used equipment.

After the game

Some good sports spots to visit after the game are the Rascal House Saloon and the Grand Slam Grille & Power Play. Some of the player's favorite restaurants include Shooter's Waterfront Cafe, Morton's of Chicago/Cleveland and Sammy's.

Probable visiting team hotel

Cleveland Hilton South

Team address

Dallas Mavericks
Reunion Arena
777 Sports St.
Dallas, Texas 75207

Phone: (214) 748-1808

Club mail response

Slow in responding to written requests for information.

Marketing

Poor - The Mavericks have a black-and-white order form that includes 13 items. Sample prices from the form include a Mavericks T-shirt ($15) and a replica Jackson or Mashburn jersey ($40 each). The order form does not include any autographed memorabilia.

Autograph policy

Requests for player autographs can be sent directly to the player's attention at the address listed above.

Comments

Fans and collectors would like the team to make a serious attempt at merchandising team-related items.

After the game

After the game, go to the West End, which is a warehouse section that has been renovated. There are many nice shops, restaurants and night clubs. This area is a favorite among the players.

Probable visiting team hotel

Hyatt Regency Reunion

Team address

Denver Nuggets
1635 Clay St.
Denver, Colo. 80204

Phone: (303) 893-6700

Club mail response

Slow in responding to written requests for information.

Marketing

Good - The Nuggets issue a single-page color merchandise catalog that includes 32 different souvenirs, but no autographed memorabilia. The Nuggets Sports Gallery, located in the Cherry Creek Shopping Center (Denver), and the Nuggets Locker Room, located in the 16th Street Mall (Denver), are owned and operated by the team and carry a wide selection of sports merchandise.

Autograph policy

Requests for player autographs can be sent directly to the player's attention at the address listed above.

Comments

The team needs to expand its merchandising to include limited-edition collectibles, 8x10 color photographs, authentic Nuggets jerseys, sports trading card team sets and autographed memorabilia.

After the game

After the game, start at Marlowe's, then head to the Broker Restaurant, Rocky Mountain Diner and Strings.

Probable visiting team hotel

Westin Hotel

Team address

Detroit Pistons
Palace of Auburn Hills
Two Championship Drive
Auburn Hills, Mich. 48057

Phone: (313) 377-0100

Club mail response

Slow in responding to written requests for information.

Marketing

Good - The Pistons issue a 10-page color merchandise catalog which offers a wide variety of team-related merchandise, including a Starter Pistons jacket ($95) and an official Spalding leather NBA ball ($79). For a copy of the catalog, or to order merchandise, call 1-313-377-0100. The catalog contains no autographed memorabilia.

Autograph policy

Requests for player autographs can be sent directly to the player's attention at the address listed above.

Comments

Collectors and fans would like the Pistons to include in the next catalog the following items: authentic Pistons jerseys, limited-edition collectibles, 8x10 color photographs, game-used equipment and autographed memorabilia.

After the game

Some good sports spot after the game are Reedy's Saloon and the Lindell Athletic Club. For fine dining, try Joe Muer's Restaurant or the Whitney.

Probable visiting team hotel

Hilton Suites

Team address

Golden State Warriors
Oakland Coliseum Arena
Nimitz Freeway and Hegenberger Road
Oakland, Calif. 94621

Phone: (510) 638-6300

Club mail response

Slow in responding to written requests for information.

Marketing

Good - The team issues an eight-page color catalog of official team merchandise; it contains a wide variety of souvenirs and clothing items but does not contain any autographed memorabilia. Sample prices from the catalog include an NBA authentic game jersey by Champion ($115), and an NBA replica jersey by Champion ($40). For a copy of the catalog, or to order merchandise, call 1-800-833-9800.

Autograph policy

Requests for player autographs can be sent directly to the player's attention at the address listed above.

Comments

The team needs to implement a better communications system with its fans.

After the game

After the game, try Mac's Sports Bar and Grill, Rickey's Sports Lounge and Restaurant, and the Sports Edition Bar. For fine dining, try Scott's Seafood Grill and Bar.

Probable visiting team hotel

Oakland Airport Hilton

Team address

Houston Rockets
10 Greenway River Plaza E.
P.O. Box 272349
Houston, Texas 77277

Phone: (713) 627-0600

Club mail response

Slow in responding to written requests for information.

Marketing

Good - The Rockets issue a single color sheet of team-related merchandise. The "Arena Collection" includes 33 different items, but does not include any autographed memorabilia. Sample prices include an authentic replica jersey ($60) and an Elite jacket ($125). For a copy of the sheet, or to order merchandise, call 1-800-228-4364.

Autograph policy

Requests for player autographs can be sent directly to the player's attention at the address listed above.

Comments

The team needs to implement a better communications system with its fans.

After the game

Shucker's Sports Bar, located in the Westin Hotel, is a good spot to try after the game. Brennan's of Houston, known for its outstanding creole cuisine, is popular with the players.

Probable visiting team hotel

Stouffer's Presidente

Team address

Indiana Pacers
300 E. Market St.
Indianapolis, Ind. 46204

Phone: (317) 263-2100

Club mail response

Slow in responding to written requests for information.

Marketing

Good - The team issues a six-page color catalog that includes a variety of team-related merchandise. The club also owns and operates the Homecourt Gift shop in the Market Square Arena. The Pacers do not sell any autographed memorabilia.

Autograph policy

Requests for player autographs can be sent directly to the player's attention at the address listed above. Some autographed items are available for certain events or charities through the club's Community Relations Department.

Comments

Fans and collectors would like the Pacers to expand team-related merchandise to include limited-edition collectibles and autographed memorabilia.

After the game

After the game, some of the visiting team players will dine at the Eagles Nest, which is the revolving restaurant at the top of the Hyatt Regency. Del Frisco's is also a popular restaurant within a few blocks of the hotel. Some players also head to Union Station, which has a variety of restaurants and clubs. Players, Hooters and Rick's Cafe are all popular spots within Union Station.

Probable visiting team hotel

Hyatt Regency Indianapolis

Team address

Los Angeles Clippers
Los Angeles Sports Arena
3939 S. Figueroa
Los Angeles, Calif. 90037

Phone: (213) 748-8000

Club mail response

Slow in responding to written requests for information.

Marketing

Undetermined - The team has been unresponsive to both phone and mail requests for information.

Autograph policy

Requests for player autographs can be sent directly to the player's attention at the address listed above.

Comments

The team needs to implement a better communications system with its fans.

After the game

Similar to New York City, Los Angeles has so many great places to go after the game. As far as sports bars, Legends or Little Joe's Restaurant are good spots to hit after the game. For dining, Bernard's, inside the Biltmore Hotel, attracts its fair share of celebrities. Also head to the dozens of restaurants in the marina district.

Probable visiting team hotel

Marina del Rey Marriott

Team address

Los Angeles Lakers
Great Western Forum
3900 Manchester Blvd.
P.O. Box 10
Inglewood, Calif. 90306

Phone: (310) 419-3100

Club mail response

Slow in responding to written requests for information.

Marketing

Undetermined - The team has been unresponsive to both mail and phone requests for information.

Autograph policy

Requests for player autographs can be sent directly to the player's attention at the address listed above.

Comments

The team needs to implement a better communications system with its fans.

After the game

The vastness of the city makes it difficult to pinpoint the places to catch players after the game. The hotel lounge and restaurant can be a safe haven for the bigger name athletes, who can sometimes be less adventuresome because they are easier to recognize.

Probable visiting team hotel

Marina del Rey Marriott

Team address

Miami Heat
Miami Arena
Miami, Fla. 33136-4102

Phone: (305) 577-4328

Club mail response

Slow in responding to written requests for information.

Marketing

Poor - The Heat does not directly market team-related merchandise.

Autograph policy

Requests for player autographs can be sent directly to the player's attention at the address listed above.

Comments

Fans and collectors would like the Heat to market a nice selection of team-related merchandise.

After the game

Joe's Stone Crab Restaurant is popular among the visiting players, as well as many tourists. Benihana's and the Outpost Steakhouse are also good dining spots after the game.

Probable visiting team hotel

Biscayne Bay Marriott

Team address

Milwaukee Bucks
The Bradley Center
1001 N. 4th St.
Milwaukee, Wis. 53203

Phone: (414) 227-0500

Club mail response

Slow in responding to written requests for information.

Marketing

Poor - The team does not market any souvenirs or collectibles.

Autograph policy

Requests for player autographs can be sent directly to the player's attention at the address listed above. During the year the team sponsors a "One on One" session, which allows fans to greet their favorite team player or coach and possibly obtain an autograph. Each of the 12 regularly-scheduled sessions are held in Section 201 of the Bradley Center and last for 20 minutes. The sessions usually begin at 6:30 p.m., prior to a 7:30 p.m. scheduled game.

Comments

Fans and collectors appreciate the club's "One on One" sessions and would like more of them offered during the season. Also, a brochure or catalog that offered team-related merchandise or collectibles would be welcomed by all Bucks fans.

After the game

Some good sports spots after the game are Saz's and Luke's Sports Spectacular.

Probable visiting team hotel

Hyatt Regency Milwaukee

Team address

Minnesota Timberwolves
Target Center
600 First Ave. N.
Minneapolis, Minn. 55403

Phone: (612) 673-1600

Club mail response

Slow in responding to written requests for information.

Marketing

Fair - The team issues a single-sheet, black-and-white price list that includes 22 team-related items. Sample items from the price list include a Christian Laettner (#32) replica jersey ($45) and a Timberwolves basketball sweatshirt ($50). The team also offers an official NBA All-Star merchandise price list that includes nine items.

Autograph policy

Requests for player autographs can be sent directly to the player's attention at the address listed above, with the exception of Christian Laettner. Laettner autographs one sports trading card for each member of his fan club, if the request is accompanied by an SASE. If you would like to join his fan club, send a check or money order for $24.95 to: Laettner Fan Club, P.O. Box 79, Stillwater, Minn. 55082. The fee includes a monthly newsletter; an official fan club T-shirt; a limited-edition, first-year fan club photo; and a special surprise gift. A portion of the proceeds will be donated to St. Agnes Children's Rehabilitation Center in White Plains, N.Y..

Comments

Collectors and fans would like the Timberwolves to evolve the price list into a merchandise catalog that could include 8x10 color photographs, basketball trading card team sets, limited-edition collectibles, game-used equipment and autographed memorabilia.

After the game

Some good sports spots after the game are Hoops on Hennepin, Hubert's and Mac's Sports Grill and Bar.

Probable visiting team hotel

Marriott City Center

Team address

New Jersey Nets
Brendan Byrne Arena
East Rutherford, N.J. 07073

Phone: (201) 935-8888

Club mail response

Slow in responding to written requests for information.

Marketing

Fair - The team issues a catalog and a calender that offers fans a variety of team-related collectibles, but does not include any autographed memorabilia.

Autograph policy

Requests for player autographs can be sent directly to the player's attention at the address listed above. The team does sponsor an annual evening dedicated to its sponsors and season ticket holders. The evening is attended by many of the team's players, who are obliging to autograph requests.

Comments

Fans and collectors would like the Nets to offer limited-edition collectibles and autographed memorabilia in future catalogs.

After the game

Head into the city and try Legends, Jimmy Weston's and Mickey Mantle's following the game. Gallagher's Steak House and Christo's are also popular restaurants with visiting players.

Probable visiting team hotel

Embassy Suites

Team address

New York Knickerbockers
Madison Square Garden
2 Pennsylvania Plaza
New York, N.Y. 10001

Phone: (212) 465-6499

Club mail response

Fair - The team will respond to your information request usually by mailing you a media guide, with hopes that it will cover any questions you might have. They may also include some team photographs.

Marketing

Fair - The Knicks market merchandise through a variety of New York outlets. Some souvenirs are also available at Madison Square Garden.

Autograph policy

Requests for player autographs can be sent directly to the player's attention at the address listed above.

Comments

Many fans and collectors hope that the Knicks will expand marketing horizons to offer an extensive catalog of souvenirs, limited-edition collectibles and some autographed memorabilia.

After the game

Popular New York sports spots include Jimmy Weston's, Mickey Mantle's, and Runyon's. Planet Hollywood and the Hard Rock Cafe are popular night spots with visiting players.

Probable visiting team hotels

Embassy Suites, Grand Hyatt, Manhattan East Suite Hotels

Team address

Orlando Magic
P.O. Box 76
Orlando, Fla. 32802-0076
Phone: (407) 649-3200

Club mail response

Excellent - A typical reply to an information request can include an Orlando Magic "Fan Pack" - a six page fold-out that includes a team picture, schedule, etc. - and the Orlando Magic "FanAttic," a 24-page product and souvenir catalog.

Marketing

Excellent - Puts almost every other NBA team to shame, and shows what a professional marketing approach can do for a team's popularity. The catalog is current with collector and fan needs, and a dramatic improvement over the "key chain and ashtray" marketing approach of many professional teams. The only thing missing from the catalog is autographed sports memorabilia. For a copy of the "FanAttic" catalog, or to order merchandise, call 1-800-HOT-TEAM. Sample prices from the catalog include a Shaquille O'Neal authentic game jersey ($142.95) and authentic game warmup set ($151.95).

Autograph policy

Requests for player autographs can be sent directly to the player's attention at the address listed above. The players do receive their mail and many, such as Jeff Turner, are outstanding at responding to autograph requests.

Comments

Collectors and fans are hoping that the Magic's approach to product marketing rubs off on other professional teams. Many of us are not fortunate enough to be within visiting distance of our favorite team, and need a way to identify with them. The Magic and the San Jose Sharks have done an excellent job, through their aggressive marketing, in serving their fans coast-to-coast.

After the game

After the game, head to the Sports Dimension or J & B's. Some popular restaurants with players are Pebble's, Hooters and the Olive Garden, all located at Church Street Station. Pinky Lee's is also gaining in popularity. Some popular night spots include the Baja Beach Club, Howl at the Moon, Fat Tuesday's and Sloppy Joes.

Probable visiting team hotel

Omni Hotel

Team address

Philadelphia 76ers
Veterans Stadium
Broad Street and Pattison Avenue
Philadelphia, Pa. 19147

Phone: (215) 339-7600

Club mail response

Slow in responding to written requests for information.

Marketing

Good - The team issues a brochure that contains a variety of team-related merchandise. The team sells black-and-white photographs for $5; they will be signed by your favorite player for an additional charge of $10.

Autograph policy

Requests for player autographs can be sent directly to the player's attention at the address listed above.

Comments

Fans and collectors appreciate that the team offers them an opportunity to have photographs signed. Providing the chance to have other types of collectibles signed, such as basketballs and jerseys, would also be appreciated.

After the game

Some of the finer dining establishments include Bookbinders Seafood House, DiLullo Centro and Cafe Nola.

Probable visiting team hotel

Embassy Suites

Team address

Phoenix Suns
201 E. Jefferson
P.O. Box 1369
Phoenix, Ariz. 85001

Phone: (602) 379-7900

Club mail response

Slow in responding to written requests for information.

Marketing

Good - The Suns offer a 12-page color merchandise catalog that includes a nice selection of clothing and assorted collectibles. To obtain a copy of the catalog, or to order merchandise, call 1-800-821-7151. There is no autographed memorabilia available in the catalog. Sample prices from the catalog include a Charles Barkley (home or road) replica jersey ($43; other players are also available) and a Suns travel bag ($50).

Autograph policy

Requests for player autographs can be sent directly to the player's attention at the address listed above.

Comments

Fans and collectors would like the Suns to add the following merchandise to the catalog: 8x10 color photographs, Suns trading card team sets, limited-edition collectibles, autographed memorabilia and game-used equipment.

After the game

Don and Charlie's and the Pink Pepper Thai restaurant are good places to begin your autograph hunting.

Probable visiting team hotel

Phoenix Hilton Suites

Team address

Portland Trailblazers
700 NE Multnomah St.
Suite 950, Lloyd Building
Portland, Ore. 97232

Phone: (503) 234-9291

Club mail response

Slow in responding to written requests for information.

Marketing

Good - The Blazers issue a 16-page color catalog filled with team-related souvenirs. The catalog includes replica jerseys ($40), authentic Spalding leather basketballs ($100), and an all-leather reversible jacket ($1,000), designed by Jeff Hamilton. Hamilton-designed leather jackets are prominent in professional sports catalogs because of their beautiful patterns and outstanding craftsmanship. To obtain a copy of the catalog, or to order merchandise, call 1-800-395-9525. The catalog does not include any autographed memorabilia.

Autograph policy

Requests for player autographs can be sent directly to the player's attention at the address listed above.

Comments

Fans and collectors would like the Blazers to add the following items to the next catalog: 8x10 color photographs, basketball trading card team sets, limited-edition collectibles, game-used equipment and autographed memorabilia.

After the game

The only real sports spot in town is Champions, located inside the Marriott. Harborside and Esplante are two restaurants popular with players. You may also find some of the players at the Copper Penny or Up Front FX, both very popular night clubs.

Probable visiting team hotel

Portland Marriott

Team address

Sacramento Kings
One Sports Parkway
Sacramento, Calif. 95834

Phone: (916) 928-0000

Club mail response
Slow in responding to written requests for information.

Marketing

Good - The team is issuing a new catalog this year, in conjunction with a new Kings logo. The new color catalog will include 50 different team-related souvenirs, 28 of which are clothing items, but will not contain any autographed memorabilia. The team does operate a gift shop which is open only during games.

Autograph policy

Requests for player autographs can be sent directly to the player's attention at the address listed above.

Comments

Collectors and fans would like the team to add the following items to the next catalog: limited-edition collectibles, game-used equipment and autographed memorabilia.

After the game

After the game, go straight to American Live and stay there. Underneath this one roof are five separate night clubs/ restaurants. Other good dining spots include Fourth Street Grill, Capital Grill and Virga's.

Probable visiting team hotels

Red Lion Hotel, Hyatt Regency/Capitol

Team address

San Antonio Spurs
100 Montana St.
San Antonio, Texas 78203

Phone: (210) 554-7787

Club mail response

Slow in responding to written requests for information.

Marketing

Fair - The team owns and operates the Spurs Shop, which sells a variety of team-related merchandise. Unfortunately for fans and collectors, there is no merchandising catalog available. The team does not sell any autographed memorabilia. Once a year the shop may sponsor an autographed session with a player, but it is a rare occurrence.

Autograph policy

Requests for player autographs can be sent directly to the player's attention at the address listed above.

Comments

It's disappointing to see a team as popular as the Spurs have such limited merchandising. Fans and collectors would like the team to offer a comprehensive catalog of team-related souvenirs and collectibles.

After the game

After the game, start at Champions, then head to Hooters. The Sports Page and Sports Pub are also popular sports spots.

Probable visiting team hotel

Marriott Rivercenter

Team address

Seattle Supersonics
190 Queen Anne Ave. N.
Seattle, Wash. 98109-9711

Phone: (206) 281-5850

Club mail response

Slow in responding to written requests for information.

Marketing

Poor - The Supersonics market no team-related merchandise. There are no team gift shops. Service America - a merchandising vendor, not affiliated with the team - offers a one-page color flier with 14 team-related items. The flier does not contain any autographed merchandise.

Autograph policy

Requests for player autographs can be sent directly to the player's attention at the address listed above.

Comments

It is extremely disappointing that a team as popular as the Sonics has no direct merchandising. The flier of team souvenirs, offered by Service America, is not current with either fan or collector needs.

After the game

Some good sports spots after the game include Charlie Mac's, Swannie's and Sneakers Bar and Restaurant.

Probable visiting team hotel

Stouffer Madison

Team address

Utah Jazz
Delta Center
301 West South Temple
Salt Lake City, Utah 84101

Phone: (801) 325-2500

Club mail response

Good - The team responds timely and accurately to requests for information.

Marketing

Good - The team offers a variety of team-related souvenirs, from buttons to jackets. Sample prices from the price list include golf shirts ($30) and sweaters ($23-$50).

Autograph policy

Requests for player autographs can be sent directly to the player's attention at the address listed above.

Karl Malone has asked that fans seeking autographs from him do not send cards, pictures or objects. He will return a photo with his signature to those who request one. Only those people who include a self-addressed stamped envelope will receive a response.

John Stockton has informed the team that due to the number of requests he receives, he can't sign your cards and/or objects personally. If you write to him he will respond with a printed autographed photo.

Comments

The team made it clear that many players are not signing cards due to those individuals who misuse the privilege and resell the items at shows. Some collectors have had good luck obtaining signatures at the team's training camp during the second week in October. The team's practice site is Dixie College in St. George, Utah. After practice, a trip to the Holiday Inn might prove fruitful.

After the game

In a city like Salt Lake, it is difficult to determine where to head after the game to meet the players. Ask the concierge at the hotel where you are staying.

Probable visiting team hotel

Unsure

Team address

Washington Bullets
USAir Arena
Landover, Md. 20785

Phone: (301) 773-2255

Club mail response

Good - The Bullets respond quickly to fan information requests. This is usually done with a form letter that tells fans how to purchase the team's media guide ($7), The Bulletin ($15, a newspaper published seven times annually), and Jam Session (a magazine for kids, at $10 for four issues per school year).

Marketing

The Bullets marketing of their merchandise and souvenirs is weak compared to other NBA clubs.

Autograph policy

Requests for player autographs can be sent directly to the player's attention at the address listed above.

Comments

Collectors are hopeful that the team will begin to acknowledge the demand for certain types of autographed memorabilia and provide them with a purchasing avenue.

After the game

After the game, start at Tickets, located in the Marriott, then head to the Sports Loft; both are good sports spots. For fine dining, try Sir Walter Raleigh's or Jaspers; both are favorites among many of the players.

Probable visiting team hotel

The Greenbelt Marriott

National Football League

Team address

Atlanta Falcons
2745 Burnette Road
Suwannee, Ga. 30174

Phone: (404) 945-1111

Club mail response

Fair - The team will respond to most written requests for information.

Marketing

Fair - The Falcons have a limited number of souvenirs and team publications available. They do not sell any autographed memorabilia, but they do donate autographed items to charities.

Autograph policy

Requests for player autographs can be sent directly to the player's attention at the address listed above.

Comments

Most collectors and fans are surprised by the limited merchandising by the club.

After the game

Jock "n" Jills is a hot sports spot. Many of the visiting players also make it a point to visit Underground Atlanta before they leave town. Other excellent dining spots include City Grill, Morton's of Chicago/Atlanta, and Pano's and Paul's.

Probable visiting team hotel

Marriott Marquis

Team address

Buffalo Bills
1 Bills Drive
Orchard Park, N.Y. 14127

Phone: (716) 648-1800

Club mail response

Slow in responding to written requests for information.

Marketing

Good - The Buffalo Bills use The Sports Look, a company located in Rochester, N.Y., for the merchandising of team-related souvenirs. The company has a large selection of Bills souvenirs and does sell autographed memorabilia, including 8x10 color photographs, footballs and jerseys. To speak with someone at The Sports Look, call 1-800-836-3313.

Autograph policy

Requests for player autographs can be sent directly to the player's attention at the address listed above.

Comments

Do not bother contacting the club for souvenir or collectible information because all you will receive is a single black-and-white photocopied sheet that is nearly unreadable. The club does a poor job handling fan requests for information on team-related souvenirs.

After the game

Go straight to Jim Kelly's restaurant, the Sports City Grill, with plenty of autograph supplies, and have a great time!

Probable visiting team hotel

Buffalo Hilton

Team address

Chicago Bears
Halas Hall
250 N. Washington Road
Lake Forest, Ill. 60045

Phone: (708) 295-6600 •

• The operator may transfer you to a very frustrating voice mail system, used by the team office, that often traps callers in an endless loop.

Club mail response

Slow in responding to written requests for information.

Marketing

Undetermined - The team has been unresponsive to numerous phone and mail requests for information.

Autograph policy

Requests for player autographs can be sent directly to the player's attention at the address listed above.

Comments

The team needs to implement a better communication system with its fans.

After the game

An obvious choice after any Bears game is America's Bar, owned by "Sweetness" himself - Walter Payton.

Probable visiting team hotels

The Drake, Westin, Hyatt Regency

Team address

Cincinnati Bengals
200 Riverfront Stadium
Cincinnati, Ohio 45202

Phone: (513) 621-3550

Club mail response

Slow in responding to written requests for information.

Marketing

Poor - The team has no gift shop, sells no souvenirs or collectibles of any kind.

Autograph policy

Requests for player autographs can be sent directly to the player's attention at the address listed above.

Comments

It is very disappointing, to collectors and fans, that the Bengals offer no team-related merchandise.

After the game

Barleycorn's, Flanagan's Landing, Willie's Bar and Grill, and the Waterfront Sports Cafe all are good sports spots after the game.

Probable visiting team hotel

The Westin

Team address

Cleveland Browns
Cleveland Stadium
Cleveland, Ohio 44114

Phone: (216) 891-5000

Club mail response

Slow in responding to written requests for information.

Marketing

Poor - The Browns do not offer any team-related merchandise for sale, nor do they have a gift shop. The Browns, like many other NFL teams, refer collectors and fans to Athletic Supply in Dallas - at 1-800-NFL-GIFT - for team souvenirs.

Autograph policy

Requests for player autographs can be sent directly to the player's attention at the address listed above.

Comments

It is very disappointing, to collectors and fans, that the Browns offer no team-related merchandise.

After the game

Grand Slam Grille & Power Play, along with the Rascal House Saloon, are two good places to have some fun after a Browns game.

Probable visiting team hotel

Cleveland Hilton South

Team address

Dallas Cowboys
Cowboys Center
1 Cowboys Parkway
Irving, Texas 75063-4999

Phone: (214) 556-9900

Club mail response

Very Good - Requests for information are promptly and accurately replied to. Your reply may also include a color photograph of the team, a souvenir catalog and an ordering form allowing you to purchase decals, a media guide or additional player or team photographs.

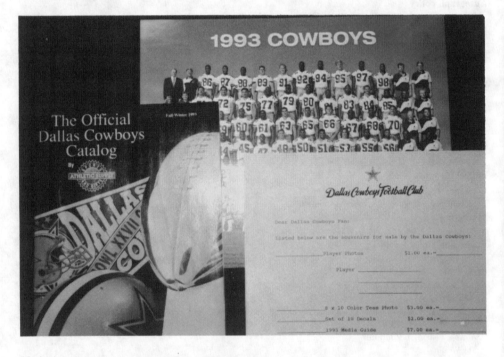

Marketing

Excellent - The club authorizes Athletic Supply of Dallas Inc. to produce "The Official Dallas Cowboys Catalog." The 32-page color catalog includes autographed memorabilia from not only the Cowboys, but from other NFL football teams, too. For example, you can purchase autographed authentic NFL jerseys from Bernie Kosar, Randall Cunningham, Boomer Esiason, Jim Kelly and Warren Moon for $189.99 each; or autographed authentic helmets of Emmitt Smith or Troy Aikman for $319.99 each. To order a catalog, call 1-800-438-4866.

Autograph policy

Requests for player autographs can be sent directly to the player's attention at the address listed above. Also, many of the team's stars frequent the autograph show circuit and do private autograph signings.

Comments

The marketing approach the Cowboys are using seems to work, although some of the catalog items are a bit too expensive for the average collector. Another factor that contributes to the team's success is that the stars on the team are not reclusive; Aikman and Smith make several off-season appearances.

After the game

Dallas is known for its exciting night life. The concierge at your hotel should be able to advise you on some of the better local restaurants and well-known nightclubs. Many of the players prefer heading to the West End, which is a warehouse section that has been renovated into shops, restaurants and night clubs.

Probable visiting team hotel

Hyatt Regency

Team address

Denver Broncos
13655 Broncos Parkway
Englewood, Colo. 80112

Phone: (303) 649-9000

Club mail response

Fair - The Broncos send out a form letter that answers most team inquiries.

Marketing

Fair - The Broncos offer a modest amount of souvenirs, such as media guides ($6), programs, team pictures, yearbooks ($7), player photos (black-and-white only, at $2.50), etc.. The team does not sell any equipment or autographed memorabilia.

Autograph policy

Requests for player autographs can be sent directly to the player's attention at the address listed above. Each player has an individual mailbox at the Broncos facility and is responsible for picking up and responding to his own fan mail.

Comments

Most collectors would like to see the Broncos expand their merchandising to include unique gifts and collectibles, especially autographed memorabilia.

After the game

After the game many of the players head to some of Denver's finest restaurants - Broker Restaurant, Marlowe's, Rock Bottom Brewery and Strings.

Probable visiting team hotel

Westin Galleria

Team address

Detroit Lions
1200 Featherstone Road
Pontiac, Mich. 48057

Phone: (313) 335-4313

Club mail response

Slow in responding to written requests for information.

Marketing

Poor - The Lions offer a minimal amount of team-related merchandise.

Autograph policy

Request for player autographs can be sent directly to the player's attention at the address listed above.

Comments

It is very disappointing, to collectors and fans, that the Lions do not take an aggressive approach in marketing team-related merchandise.

After the game

Reedy's and Lindell Athletic Club are good sports spots to try after the game.

Probable visiting team hotels

Hilton Suites, Omni International

Team address

Green Bay Packers
P.O. Box 10628
1265 Lombardi Ave.
Green Bay, Wis. 54307-0628

Phone: (414) 496-5700

Club mail response

Good - The Packers usually respond quickly and accurately to team inquiries.

Marketing

Good - The Packers market their souvenirs through the Packer Pro Shop. A seven-fold, single-sheet color brochure is available upon request and includes everything from a Packer golf bag ($199.95) to a method of getting your name put on the team's scoreboard ($30-$40). The Packers do not sell any autographed team memorabilia.

Autograph policy

Requests for player autographs can be sent directly to the player's attention at the address listed above. Be sure to include a self-addressed stamped envelope.

Comments

Most collectors would like to see the team expand its merchandising to include more limited-edition items, unique gifts (like the scoreboard idea), and autographed sports memorabilia.

After the game

Unsure

Probable visiting team hotel

Unsure

Team address

Houston Oilers
6910 Fannin St.
Houston, Texas 77030

Phone: (713) 797-9111

Club mail response

Slow in responding to written requests for information.

Marketing

Poor - Bad news for Oilers fans, the gift shop is gone and so is Warren Moon. The Oilers no longer offer team-related merchandise for sale.

Autograph policy

Requests for player autographs can be sent directly to the player's attention at the address listed above.

Comments

The team would not elaborate as to why it no longer has a gift shop. One can only assume it was not a viable undertaking. It is an obvious disappointment to Oiler fans and collectors.

After the game

Head to Shucker's Sports Bar in the Westin Hotel following the game. It is a good place for autograph seekers, considering so many visiting professional teams stay at the hotel while in Houston.

Probable visiting team hotels

Westin Galleria, Stouffer's Presidente

Team address

Indianapolis Colts
7001 W. 56th St.
Indianapolis, Ind. 46224-0100

Phone: (317) 297-2658

Club mail response

Slow in responding to written requests for information.

Marketing

Poor - The Colts offer no team-related merchandise for sale.

Autograph policy

Requests for player autographs can be sent directly to the player's attention at the above address.

Comments

It is very disappointing, to collectors and fans, that the Colts offer no team-related merchandise.

After the game

Following the game, you may want to dine or enjoy a cocktail at the Hyatt Regency, since so many of the professional teams stay at the hotel while in Indianapolis. Many of the players head to the shops, restaurants and night clubs at Union Station. While there, visit Players, Hooters and Rick's Cafe.

Probable visiting team hotel

Hyatt Regency Indianapolis

Team address

Kansas City Chiefs
1 Arrowhead Drive
Kansas City, Mo. 64129

Phone: (816) 924-9300

Club mail response

Very Good - The club is good at providing the requester with exactly what he is looking for. A team photograph or poster will often be included with the team's response.

Marketing

Fair - The Kansas City Chiefs, like the New York Jets, do not offer a catalog of memorabilia exclusively dedicated to the team. All requests are directed to Athletic Supply of Dallas, which can be reached at 1-800-NFL-GIFT, or by mail at 10812 Alder Circle, Dallas, Texas 75238. The team does operate a souvenir stand at the stadium which sells Chiefs merchandise, but it is only open during the season.

Autograph policy

The team does not solicit autographs from its players. Players receive all of their own mail and are responsible for responding, or not responding, to it individually. The Chiefs also discourage fans from mailing in cards or other personal items. The club also acknowledges the huge volume of mail received by Joe Montana, Marcus Allen and Derrick Thomas, and warns fans that it is virtually impossible for them to respond to it personally.

Comments

With players such as Montana, Allen, and Thomas, it's hard to understand why the Chiefs have not begun offering its own catalog of memorabilia. Although the Athletic Supply of Dallas has a wide variety of merchandise, it is a bit expensive for the average collector.

After the game

You may want to first visit Chappell's Bar & Grill - a sports bar/restaurant - before moving on to more expensive dining, such as Bristol Bar and Grill, Cascone's Restaurant and Lounge, Plaza III Steakhouse, or Savoy Grill and Restaurant.

Probable visiting team hotel

Unsure

Team address

Los Angeles Raiders
332 Center St.
El Segundo, Calif. 90245

Phone: (310) 322-3451

Club mail response

Slow in responding to written requests for information.

Marketing

Good - The team issues a 28-page color catalog which contains a variety of team-related merchandise. The catalog offers a nice selection of clothing, authentic jerseys and even an autograph football that has a single, smooth white leather surface that facilitates signature collecting. The catalog, however, does not include any autographed memorabilia. A discounted price is offered to members of the Raiders fan club. Sample pricing from the catalog (for non-fan club members) includes an authentic helmet ($189.99) and an authentic jersey ($99.99). For a copy of the catalog, or to order merchandise, call 1-800-RAIDERS.

Autograph policy

Requests for player autographs can be sent directly to the player's attention at the address listed above. The club usually sponsors an annual "Family Day," held in Oxnard, which gives fans a chance to meet team members. However, this year's scheduled date conflicted with the team's trip to Barcelona for an exhibition game. At the time of this writing, it was still undetermined if the event would be rescheduled.

Comments

Fans and collectors would like to see the Raiders add limited-edition collectibles, game-used equipment and autographed memorabilia to future merchandise catalogs.

After the game

After the game, Legends Sports Bar in Santa Monica is a popular sports spot.

Probable visiting team hotels

Hyatt-Regency Broadway Plaza, Radisson Hotels

Team address

Los Angeles Rams
2327 W. Lincoln Ave.
Anaheim, Calif. 92801

Phone: (714) 535-7267

Club mail response

Slow in responding to written requests for information.

Marketing

Poor - The team issues a single-sheet price list with only a few team-related items. The Rams Gift Shop does carry a wide range of team merchandise, but does not take verbal phone orders. Therefore, you must write or fax your order. The club does offer the Upper Deck Authenticated line of autographed sports memorabilia.

Autograph policy

Requests for player autographs can be sent directly to the player's attention at the above address.

Comments

Collectors and fans would like to see the Rams expand the range of team-related merchandise available through the club. Also, a comprehensive color catalog, with a toll-free phone line, would better serve Rams fans.

After the game

After the game, head to the marina district; many of the players stop at the popular restaurants and night clubs located in this area.

Probable visiting team hotels

Marina del Rey Marriott, Radisson Hotels

Team address

Miami Dolphins
Joe Robbie Stadium
2269 NW 199th St.
Miami, Fla. 33056

Phone: (305) 620-5000

Club mail response

Slow in responding to written requests for information.

Marketing

Fair - The Dolphins issue a color brochure containing about 30 team-related items. The brochure contains no autographed memorabilia, but the team is currently investigating the feasibility of adding some in the future.

Autograph policy

Requests for player autographs can be sent directly to the player's attention at the address listed above. The Dolphins typically schedule a "Family Day" in late July. In the past this event has been in conjunction with a Miami versus Tampa Bay exhibition game. On "Family Day" many players sign autographs at sessions held on the club level of Joe Robbie Stadium.

Comments

Fans and collectors would like to see the Dolphins upgrade the selection of team-related merchandise to include limited-edition collectibles and autographed memorabilia. Carrying the Upper Deck Authenticated line of sports collectibles would be a logical fit since Dan Marino is already affiliated with the company.

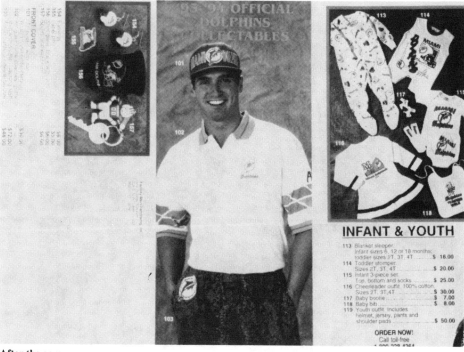

INFANT & YOUTH

113 Blanket sleeper.
Infant sizes 6, 12 or 18 months;
toddler sizes 2T, 3T, 4T ..... $ 18.00
114 Toddler stomper.
Sizes 2T, 3T, 4T ..... $ 20.00
115 Infant 3-piece set.
Top, bottom and socks ..... $ 25.00
116 Cheerleader outfit. 100% cotton.
Sizes 2T, 3T, 4T ..... $ 30.00
117 Baby bootie ..... $ 7.00
118 Baby bib ..... $ 8.00
119 Youth outfit. Includes
helmet, jersey, pants and
shoulder pads ..... $ 50.00

ORDER NOW!
Call toll-free

After the game
Some of the players head to Cap's Place in Fort Lauderdale or over to Joe's Stone Crab Restaurant in South Miami Beach.

Probable visiting team hotels
Sheraton Bal Harbour Resort, Biscayne Bay Marriott

Team address
Minnesota Vikings
9520 Viking Drive
Eden Prairie, Minn. 55344

Phone: (612) 828-6500

Club mail response
Slow in responding to written requests for information.

Marketing
Good - The Vikings issue a three-fold, single-sheet color brochure that contains 31 team-related items. For a copy of the catalog, or to order merchandise, call 1-800-723-6309. The brochure does not contain any autographed memorabilia. Sample prices from the brochure include a Viking Starter jacket ($70) or Viking yearbook ($6.95).

Autograph policy
Requests for player autographs can be sent directly to the player's attention at the address listed above.

Comments
It is very disappointing, to collectors and fans, that the Vikings do not directly offer team-related merchandise.

After the game
Hubert's, Hoops on Hennepin, and Mac's Sports Grill and Bar are all good sports spots after the game. Some of the players also enjoy the barbecued ribs at Rudolph's.

Probable visiting team hotel
Marriott City Center

Team address
New England Patriots
Foxboro Stadium
Route 1
Foxboro, Mass. 02035

Phone: (508) 543-8200

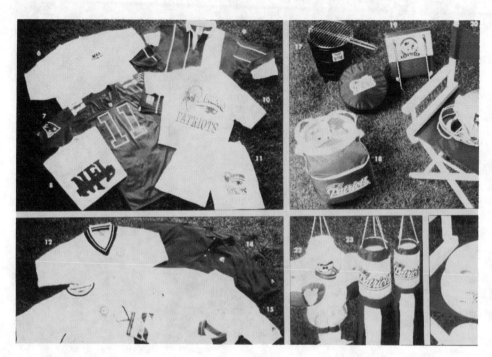

Club mail response

Slow in responding to written requests for information.

Marketing

Good - The team issues a single-sheet color brochure that includes 66 different team-related items. No autographed memorabilia is contained in the brochure. The team's seasonal gift shop is in the process of moving.

Autograph policy

Requests for player autographs can be sent directly to the player's attention at the address listed above.

Comments

Expanding the team's merchandising to include limited-edition collectibles and autographed memorabilia would be useful for both fans and collectors.

After the game

After the game, head downtown to the Faneuil Hall Marketplace and shop or try one of the many restaurants housed in the 19th-century warehouses. Ye Olde Union Oyster House, Anthony's Pier 4 and Jimmy's Harborside are popular dining spots.

Probable visiting team hotel

Marriott Hotels

Team address

New Orleans Saints
6928 Saints Drive
Metairie, La. 70003

Phone: (504) 733-0255

Club mail response

Slow in responding to written requests for information.

Marketing

Poor - The Saints do not directly market team-related merchandise. There is a gift shop in the Superdome that has a selection of souvenirs.

Autograph policy

Requests for player autographs can be sent directly to the player's attention at the address listed above.

Comments

It is very disappointing, to fans and collectors, that the Saints do not directly offer team-related merchandise.

After the game

Most enthusiastic fans, and many visiting players, head to the shops and restaurants along Bourbon Street after the game.

Probable visiting team hotel

Unsure

Team address

New York Giants
Giants Stadium
East Rutherford, N.J. 07073

Phone: (201) 935-8222

Club mail response

Good - The club answers information requests promptly and specifically. The team makes no effort to entice their fans with direct marketing pieces, such as schedules, or information on how to acquire tickets.

Marketing

Poor - The club produces no Giants-specific catalogs, and has no interest in directing fans to where they can obtain team specific merchandise. If there is a place at the stadium that sells merchandise or souvenirs, the team doesn't inform its fans of it.

Autograph policy

"We're not interested in publicizing how people can obtain player's autographs." - director of Public Relations
Requests for player autographs can be sent directly to the player's attention at the address listed above.

Comments

I can't believe that a team, which won the Super Bowl in 1990 and showed so many positive signs on the field last season, has so little to offer its fans in the way of merchandising. Additionally, I don't understand the lack of a strong direct-marketing effort to increase the club's exposure and provide greater public awareness of the players and team.

After the game

After the game, head into Manhattan and take your pick of the largest saturation of good restaurants and hot night clubs to be found anywhere in the world.

Probable visiting team hotel

Embassy Suites

Team address

New York Jets
1000 Fulton Ave.
Hempstead, N.Y. 11550-1099

Phone: (516) 538-6600

Club mail response

Good - A typical Jets reply to an information request can include a Jets bumper sticker, key chain, team photograph, a color poster of Joe Namath - c/o Champion Sports - or a one-page photocopied information letter.

Marketing

Poor - The New York Jets rely on outside sources for their product marketing. Typically, fans seeking NFL merchandise are advised to call 1-800-NFL-GIFT. Used and autographed equipment is not available through the team. Items available directly from the team include yearbooks ($9.95) and Gameday programs ($5).

Autograph policy

Requests for player autographs can be sent directly to the player's attention at the address listed above. The team accepts no responsibility for items sent and will not forward mail addressed only to the Jets or Public Relations Office; letters must have a player's name.

Comments

The Jets show little interest in improving souvenir and team product offerings. It's unfortunate for fans and collectors who follow the team that more material is not available to them. With popular players such as Boomer Esiason and Ronnie Lott, it's difficult to understand why the team doesn't make more of a concerted effort to enhance its product marketing.

After the game

Ask the concierge at the hotel where you are staying what places he recommends.

Probable visiting team hotel

Embassy Suites

Team address

Philadelphia Eagles
Broad Street and Pattison Avenue
Philadelphia, Pa. 19148

Phone: (215) 463-2500

Club mail response

Slow in responding to written requests for information.

Marketing

Poor - The Eagles do not directly market team-related merchandise.

Autograph policy

Requests for player autographs can be sent directly to the player's attention at the address listed above.

Comments

It is very disappointing, to fans and collectors, that the Eagles do not directly offer any team-related merchandise.

After the game

After the game, the Dock Street Brewing Company attracts a good crowd. Some of the finer dining spots include Bookbinders Seafood House, Cafe Nola, DiLullo Centro and La Famiglia.

Probable visiting team hotels

Sheraton Society Hill, Embassy Suites

Team address

Phoenix Cardinals
P.O. Box 888
Phoenix, Ariz. 85001

Phone: (602) 379-0101

Club mail response

Good - The team responds to information requests with a small direct mail package.

Marketing

Good - A free merchandise catalog is available by calling 1-800-NFL-GIFT. Local souvenirs are sold through Merle Harmon's Fanfare, 2152 Fiesta Mall, Mesa, Ariz. 85210. Only a media guide is available directly from the club at a cost of $5.

Autograph policy

Request for player autographs can be sent directly to the player's attention at the address listed above. ONE item per envelope per player - Please!

If you send a check or money order for $25, payable to Cardinal Charities, along with a football, to Player Relations at the above address, the team will have your football signed and returned. Like most NFL teams, the Cardinals provide jerseys and game footballs for local charity functions. Requests for these items should be sent in writing to the Community Relations director.

Comments

Collectors and fans appreciate the generous charity efforts made by the Cardinals. Expanding these efforts to include other types of autographed memorabilia would be beneficial to collectors. A souvenir catalog dedicated to just the Cardinals, and available through the team, would also be helpful.

After the game

After the game, you might want to try Don and Charlie's, Harry & Steve's (even though it's primarily a baseball hangout) and the Pink Pepper Thai restaurant.

Probable visiting team hotel

Phoenix Hilton Suites

Team address

Pittsburgh Steelers
300 Stadium Circle
Pittsburgh, Pa. 15212

Phone: (412) 323-1200

Club mail response

Very Good - The team usually responds promptly and with the information requested. Additionally, the team does an excellent job forwarding player mail during the off-season.

Marketing

Poor - Unlike the Penguins, the Steelers limit specific team merchandising to media guides ($5), yearbooks ($8) and player or team black-and-white photographs ($2-$3). No autographed memorabilia is sold through the team.

Autograph policy

Requests for player autographs can be sent directly to the player's attention at the address listed above. Be sure to address the specific player on the outside of the envelope. For example, Attention: Barry Foster.

Comments

An organization with tremendous marketing potential, the Steelers need to become more aggressive in product merchandising. Collectors are starved for souvenirs, especially limited-edition collectibles and autographed memorabilia.

After the game

When the game's over, head south across the river to the Pittsburgh Sports Garden (corner of Smithfield and East Carson streets) and wait an hour or so to see which players arrive there.

Probable visiting team hotel

Pittsburgh Vista

Team address

San Diego Chargers
Jack Murphy Stadium
P.O. Box 609609
San Diego, Calif. 92160-9609

Phone Number: (619) 280-2111

Club mail response

Fair - Unpredictable, depending upon which individual receives your request.

Marketing

Poor - The club's marketing of team products, gifts and souvenirs is weak compared to other NFL teams.

Autograph policy

Requests for player autographs can be sent directly to the player's attention at the address above.

Comments

It's disappointing to collectors that the Chargers put little effort into marketing team-related product and souvenirs. With an emerging star like Junior Seau, it's hard to believe that the club doesn't recognize the financial viability of such a task.

After the game

Most of the players will choose to dine at an area restaurant with a view of the bay. Mister A's Restaurant, or The Boathouse, on Harbor Island, might be good places to begin your autograph hunt.

Probable visiting team hotel

Marriott Hotel and Marina

Team address

San Francisco 49ers
Marie P. DeBartolo Sports Centre
4949 Centennial Blvd.
Santa Clara, Calif. 95054-1229

Phone: (408) 562-4949

Club mail response

Good - A typical reply to an information request usually will include a copy of the San Francisco 49ers Official Merchandise Catalog. Although this single-sheet, three-fold color brochure is small, it does contain some nice items. The only piece of autographed memorabilia offered in the catalog is a Montana lithograph (includes an embossed impression of actual cleat worn in Super Bowl XXIV) for $200, which is also marketed by Upper Deck Authenticated and is listed in its 1993 Preview Catalog for $299.95.

Marketing

Good - Although the catalog is nice, it needs to be expanded and updated to meet fan and collector needs. An expanded offering of autographed memorabilia would also be helpful to the market. Jerry Rice and Steve Young are willing signers for other merchandisers; why not offer similar items through the team? Sample prices from catalog include a custom authentic 49ers jersey by Wilson ($110) and a 49ers denim jacket ($150). To obtain a merchandise brochure, or to order an item, call 1-800-359-4937.

Autograph policy

Requests for player autographs can be sent directly to the player's attention at the address listed above.

Comments

The collectors of autographed sports memorabilia would like to see the San Francisco 49ers take a more active role in merchandising products through the team, rather than through alternative sources. The benefits are obvious - less authenticity concerns and better quality collectibles.

After the game

Although San Francisco is a big city, the athletes, specifically those from visiting teams, can't resist a trip down to Fisherman's Wharf, where there are outdoor seafood stands, dozens of seafood restaurants, shopping and bay cruises.

Probable visiting team hotels

Parc 55, Hilton, Westin St. Francis, Grand Hyatt

Team address

Seattle Seahawks
11220 NE 53rd St.
Kirkland, Wash. 98033

Phone: (206) 827-9777

Club mail response

Poor - Written requests for information are often unanswered.

Marketing

Undetermined - In previous years the team had issued a catalog of team-related merchandise for sale, but has discontinued it. It is still undetermined which independent vendor will resume the sale of team merchandise.

Autograph policy

Requests for player autographs can be sent directly to the player's attention at the address listed above.

Comments

Ogden Entertainment Services, an independent vendor, has done an excellent job with Seattle Mariners merchandise. It is hoped it or a similar vendor will offer the Seahawks line of team-related collectibles and souvenirs.

After the game

Some interesting sports spots to try after the game are Charlie Mac's, Sneakers Bar and Restaurant, and Swannie's. Weather permitting, the waterfront area, Piers 52-70, offer a nice selection of shops and restaurants. The Seattle Space Needle, with its two revolving restaurants at top, is always worth a visit.

Probable visiting team hotel

Stouffer Madison

Team address

Tampa Bay Buccaneers
One Buccaneer Place
Tampa, Fla. 33607

Phone: (813) 870-2700

Club mail response

Slow in responding to written requests for information.

Marketing

Poor - The team was contacted by phone for the information I requested, at which time I was informed that "the team is not in the merchandising business." However, a limited number of basic souvenir items (hats, shirts, jackets) are available at the ticket office. Sample prices from the price list include T-shirts ($19.17) and windbreakers ($31.95).

Autograph policy

Requests for player autographs can be sent directly to the player's attention at the address listed above.

Comments

Considering the market potential, both in dollars and exposure, it is difficult to believe that a team like the Tampa Bay Buccaneers chooses not to participate in an aggressive merchandising effort.

After the game

After the game, Clancy's and Players are both good sports spots. Hurricanes and Beachnuts are two hot night clubs.

Probable visiting team hotel

Tradewinds

Team address

Washington Redskins
P.O. Box 17247
Dulles International Airport
Washington, D.C. 20041

Phone: (703) 478-8900

Club mail response

Slow in responding to written requests for information. Also, phone requests for information can be extremely disconcerting, with the club's personnel showing little interest whatsoever in the needs of the caller.

Marketing

Poor - The Redskins do not sell any team-related merchandise.

Autograph policy

Requests for player autographs can be sent directly to the player's attention at the address listed above. The team does a good job forwarding player mail during the off-season.

Comments

With a team as popular as the Redskins, it's hard to believe that it does not offer any team-related merchandise. The team has to become conscious of collector and fan needs.

After the game

Tickets, which is located in the Marriott, and the Sports Loft are popular sports spots after the game. For fine dining, try Sir Walter Raleigh's or Jaspers.

Probable visiting team hotel

Greenbelt Marriott

National Hockey League

Team address

Mighty Ducks of Anaheim
1313 S. Harbor Blvd.
Box 3232
Anaheim, Calif. 92803

Phone: (714) 704-2700

Club mail response

Slow in responding to written requests for information.

Marketing

Excellent - The team issues a beautiful 24-page color merchandise catalog. Fans and collectors are treated to a wide variety of team-related merchandise, including authentic game jerseys ($180), duck masks ($20) and an inaugural season poster ($10). The Ducks also have a fantastic selection of limited-edition collector items, such as an inaugural game ticket ($45), commemorative ticket and puck display ($200), and autographed memorabilia.

The autographed memorabilia includes an inaugural game roster sheet ($125); commemorative ticket ($175); official goalie stick ($350); official jersey and commemorative ticket (framed); inaugural season tickets, single-sheet, framed ($400); and an inaugural team puck set ($700). All of these items are signed by all 25 opening day players. Some are even signed by the coach, team chairman and president. To obtain a copy of the catalog, or to order merchandise, call 1-800-2-MIGHTY.

Autograph policy

Requests for player autographs can be sent directly to the player's attention at the address listed above.

Comments

With the exception of game-used equipment, 8x10 color photographs and some hockey trading card team sets, this catalog has it all. The team has done a sensational job at meeting fan and collector needs.

After the game

Popular restaurants with the players include Benihana of Tokyo, Casa Maria, and Cattleman's Wharf.

Probable visiting team hotel

Embassy Suites Brea

Team address

Boston Bruins
Boston Garden
150 Causeway St.
Boston, Mass. 02114

Phone: (617) 227-3206

Club mail response

Slow in responding to written requests for information.

Marketing

Undetermined - The team has been unresponsive to numerous attempts, made by both mail and phone, at obtaining information about Bruins-related merchandising.

Autograph policy

Requests for player autographs can be sent directly to the player's attention at the address listed above.

Comments

The team needs to implement a better communication system with its fans.

After the game

Some good sports spots after the game are Sports Saloon, Champions Bar, T's Pub, or fight the crowd at the Bull & Finch Pub ("Cheers"). Players' favorite dining areas include Anthony's Pier 4, Jimmy's Harborside and Ye Olde Union Oyster House. Also be sure to roam the shops of Faneuil Hall Marketplace; most of the visiting players make it a must stop before they leave town.

Probable visiting team hotel

Marriott Copley Place

Team address

Buffalo Sabres
Memorial Auditorium
Buffalo, N.Y. 14202

Phone: (716) 856-7300

Club mail response

Slow in responding to written requests for information.

Marketing

Good - The Sabres issue a down-sized, 12-page color merchandise catalog. The catalog includes more than 90 different team-related items. Collectors and fans can obtain a catalog, or order merchandise, by calling 1-800-333-PUCK, Ext. 227. The Sabres sell no autographed memorabilia. Sample prices from the catalog include 8x10 glossy photos ($4) and Sabres trading card team sets ($4).

Autograph policy

Requests for player autographs can be sent directly to the player's attention at the address listed above.

Comments

The Sabres merchandise catalog contains many items that can be autographed, including a nice selection of 8x10 color photographs, trading card team sets and pucks. Adding some game-used equipment and autographed memorabilia to the team catalog would delight many collectors.

After the game

After the game, head straight to Jim Kelly's Sports City Grill and bring plenty of autograph supplies.

Probable visiting team hotel

Buffalo Hilton

Team address

Calgary Flames
Saddledome
P.O. Box 1540
Station "M"
Calgary, Alberta, Canada T2P 3B9

Phone: (403) 261-0475

Club mail response

Slow in responding to written requests for information, but prompt and courteous with phone responses.

Marketing

Good - The team issues a 12-page catalog that contains a wide variety of team-related merchandise. The catalog contains 124 different team-related items, from pucks ($3.50) to Flames player photos (8x10, $4.95). There is no autographed memorabilia included in the catalog, but the team does sell authentic Calgary game-worn jerseys, each with a letter of authenticity. Flames game-worn jerseys range in price from $249 (Reese, Musil, etc.) to $899 (Fleury). All questions concerning these jerseys should be directed to the Flames Sport Shop, 7517 Flint Road S.E., Calgary, Alberta, Canada T2H 1G3.

Autograph policy

Requests for player autographs can be sent directly to the player's attention at the address listed above.

Comments

The team is genuinely concerned with meeting the needs of Flames fans and collectors. Look for an aggressive future merchandising effort by this club.

After the game

After the game, head straight to Yankee Doodles on 11th Avenue. It is probably the most popular sports bar in town. For fine dining, head to Fourth Street and take your pick of the many fine restaurants.

Probable visiting team hotel

The Westin Hotel

Team address

Chicago Blackhawks
Chicago Stadium
1800 W. Madison St.
Chicago, Ill. 60612

Phone: (312) 733-5300

Club mail response

Slow in responding to written requests for information.

Marketing

Good - The team uses HawkQuarters as its official team store and merchandiser. HawkQuarters has an excellent team store located at 325 North Michigan Ave. For those who can't visit, the team issues a 16-page color sportswear catalog that includes a variety of souvenirs. Sample prices from the catalog include an authentic game jersey ($179.95, no lettering or nameplate) and a limited-edition jacket ($149.95).

Autograph policy

Requests for player autographs can be sent directly to the player's attention at the address listed above.

Comments

HawkQuarters does an excellent job in merchandising to fans and collectors. The only areas to improve upon would be to carry individual color photographs, limited-edition collectibles and autographed memorabilia. Some game-used products would also be a treat.

After the game

Some hot sports spots are America's Bar and Michael Jordan's.

Probable visiting team hotel

The Drake

Team address

Dallas Stars
North Texas Ice Arena
10101 Cowboys Parkway
Irving, Texas 75063

Phone: (214) 467-8277

Club mail response

Slow in responding to written requests for information.

Marketing

Good - The Stars offer fans a three-fold, single-sheet color brochure that includes 106 different items. The brochure is current with fans' needs and offers collectors some limited-edition collectibles, including glassware, pins, coins, etc.... There is no autographed memorabilia available in the catalog. Sample prices from the catalog include souvenir pucks ($5) and an inaugural season all-leather jacket ($1,000).

Autograph policy

Requests for player autographs can be sent directly to the player's attention at the address listed above.

Comments

The only merchandising suggestion for the Stars is to offer autographed memorabilia and possibly some game-used equipment for collectors.

After the game

After the game, try one of the town's finer nightclubs.

Probable visiting team hotel

Hyatt Regency

Team address

Detroit Red Wings
600 Civic Center Drive
Joe Louis Arena
Detroit, Mich. 48226

Phone: (313) 396-7544

Club mail response

Good - The Red Wings respond timely and accurately to team inquiries for information.

Marketing

Good - The team markets a wide variety of merchandise and collectibles through a six-fold, single-sheet color brochure and arena souvenir shops. The brochure includes everything from baby bibs to boxer shorts. The team does not sell any autographed memorabilia. Sample prices from the brochure include a full leather jacket ($1,000) and an authentic customized jersey ($150).

Autograph policy

Requests for player autographs can be sent directly to the player's attention at the address listed above.

Comments

Collectors would like to see the Red Wings offer more limited-edition collectibles and autographed memorabilia.

After the game

Reedy's Saloon and Lindell AC (Athletic Club) are combination sports bars and restaurants. The Whitney restaurant at 4421 Woodward is one of the finer dining establishments in the city.

Probable visiting team hotel

Omni International

Team address

Edmonton Oilers
Northlands Coliseum
7424 -118 Avenue
Edmonton, Alberta, Canada T5B 4M9

Phone: (403) 474-8561

Club mail response

Good - The Oilers do a good job in answering team inquiries with the information requested.

Marketing

Fair - The Oilers have a single-sheet mail order brochure that includes 40 products. They range in diversity from CCM authentic pro game jerseys to an Oilers baby bottle. Sample prices from the brochure include a souvenir logo puck ($3) and an Oilers team pennant ($4).

Autograph policy

Requests for player autographs can be sent directly to the player's attention at the address listed above.

Comments

Collectors and fans would like to see the Oilers expand product offerings to include more equipment, limited-edition items and autographed memorabilia. It would also be beneficial to have a catalog which shows each item that is available for sale - not just a description. Collectors also have an interest in any materials or souvenirs relating to the Gretzky years with Edmonton.

After the game

Ask the concierge at the hotel where you are staying.

Probable visiting team hotel

Edmonton Hilton

Team address

Florida Panthers
100 NE 3rd St.
10th Floor
Fort Lauderdale, Fla. 33301

Phone: (305) 768-1900

Club mail response

Slow in responding to written requests for information.

Marketing

Very Good - The team markets its collectibles and merchandise through "Pantherland" - The Florida Panthers Hockey Club, out of Miami, Fla.. The "Pantherland" catalog has a nice mix of souvenirs and high-priced collectibles. Autographed limited-edition lithographs are available in the catalog. Sample prices from catalog include a custom leather jacket ($990) and an official Panthers inaugural pin set ($14.99).

Autograph policy

Requests for player autographs can be sent directly to the player's attention at the address listed above.

Comments

The Panthers are off to a good start both on and off the ice. Team merchandise is extremely popular, and, because it's the team's inaugural year, is highly collected. Collectors would like to see more inexpensive autographed memorabilia for sale, such as photographs, pucks and sticks.

After the game

Unsure

Probable visiting team hotel

Don Shula's Hotel

Team address

Hartford Whalers
242 Trumbull Drive
Hartford, Conn. 06013

Phone: (203) 728-3366

Club mail response

Slow in responding to written requests for information.

Marketing

Good - The Hartford Whalers issue a four-fold, single-sheet, color brochure that contains 61 items. The catalog offers a nice selection of merchandise, from Whaler hockey pucks ($5), to Whalers authentic jerseys ($140). To obtain a copy of the catalog, or to order merchandise, call 1-800-218-6126.

Autograph policy

Request for player autographs can be sent directly to the player's attention at the address listed above.

Comments

Collectors and fans would appreciate it if color photographs, hockey trading cards, official hockey sticks and some limited-edition collectibles were added to the Whalers' line of merchandise. Any game-used equipment or autographed hockey memorabilia would also be a welcome addition.

After the game

Some good sports spots after the game include Chuck's Cellar, Margaritaville and the Civic Pub.

Probable visiting team hotel

The Goodwin Hotel

Team address

Los Angeles Kings
Great Western Forum
3900 W. Manchester Blvd.
Box 17013
Inglewood, Calif. 90306

Phone: (310) 419-3160

Club mail response

Slow in responding to written requests for information.

Marketing

Very Good - The Kings issue a black-and-white brochure that contains team-related merchandise. The club also owns and operates four "Slap Shot" gift shops located in Westchester (1-310-215-8580), Santa Anna, Sherman Oaks and West Covina. These shops offer a variety of collectibles, including autographed memorabilia. The shops also carry the Upper Deck Authenticated line of autographed collectibles. The team does occasionally carry game-used equipment. The stores annually sponsor the team's "Locker Room Sale." Used player equipment, such as skates and sticks (but no jerseys), is auctioned off at the end of the season. This year's event was held June 4-5.

Autograph policy

Requests for player autographs can be sent directly to the player's attention at the address listed above. There are two events that all Kings fans and collectors should familiarize themselves with. The first is "Tip a King," which is usually held in March at a ticket price of $50. Fans and collectors who purchase tickets then tip their favorite player $1 per autograph or $2 for a picture with the player. The second event is "Skate with the Kings," which is typically held in January. For $30 per ticket a fan can skate with his favorite player and possibly obtain an autograph.

Comments

Both fans and collectors appreciate the many ways the Kings acknowledge their support, and sincerely hope that all the great events in place now will continue for years to come.

After the game

After the restaurant, many of the players go to the Manhattan Beach Pier to the Sunset Restaurant. Talia's is also a popular eatery after the game. Many of the players staying at the hotel also visit Harry O's and OB's, both located not far from the Radisson.

Probable visiting team hotel

Radisson Hotels International

Team address

Montreal Canadiens
Montreal Forum
2313 St. Catherine St. W.
Montreal, Quebec, Canada H3H 1N2

Phone: (514) 932-2582

Club mail response

Good - Mail responses can be slow, but will be answered accurately.

Marketing

Good - The Canadiens issue a 16-page color products catalog filled with a variety of team-related merchandise. The catalog does not include any autographed memorabilia.

Autograph policy

Requests for player autographs can be sent directly to the player's attention at the above address.

Comments

Both fans and collectors would like to see the Canadiens add limited-edition merchandise, game-used equipment and autographed memorabilia to the catalog.

After the game

After the game, you may want to try visiting one of the 10 La Cage aux Sports restaurants located in the city. For fine dining try Le St. Amable, Chez La Mere Michel, and Les Chenets.

Probable visiting team hotel

Sheraton Center

Team address

New Jersey Devils
Byrne Meadowlands Arena
P.O. Box 504
East Rutherford, N.J. 07073

Phone: (201) 935-6050

Club mail response

Slow in responding to written requests for information.

Marketing

Good - The team issues a single-sheet color price list that includes 48 items. Sample prices from the list include a Starter satin jacket ($90) and an authentic game jersey ($199). To obtain a copy of the price list, or to order merchandise, call 1-800-DEVILS-5. The team does not sell autographed memorabilia.

Autograph policy

Request for player autographs can be sent directly to the player's attention at the above address.

Comments

Both collectors and fans would like to see the price list upgraded to a merchandise catalog that includes 8x10 color photographs, authentic hockey sticks, hockey trading card team sets, limited-edition collectibles, game-used equipment, and autographed memorabilia.

After the game

Bazooka's is a good sports spot after the game. For finer dining, some of the players staying at the hotel go to Barelli's or Lantanos. The closest popular night club to the hotel is Ashley's, which is in Clifton.

Probable visiting team hotel

Embassy Suites

Team address

New York Islanders
Nassau Coliseum
Uniondale, N.Y. 11553

Phone: (516) 794-4100

Club mail response

Slow in responding to written requests for information.

Marketing

Good - The Islanders issue a five-fold, single-sheet color brochure with more than 20 team-related clothing items inside. There is no autographed team-related merchandise or other types of souvenirs included in the brochure. Sample prices from the catalog include a replica jersey ($65) and a wool hat ($20). To obtain a copy of the catalog, or to order merchandise, call the number listed above.

Autograph policy

Requests for player autographs can be sent directly to the player's attention at the address listed above.

Comments

The Islanders need to expand the merchandising brochure to include many other types of souvenirs and collectibles, such as 8x10 color photographs, hockey trading card team sets, hockey sticks, limited-edition collectibles and some game-used equipment.

After the game

After the game, you may want to start at Pitchers, located inside the Marriott. Bright Fellows, Sprats and Buttle's are popular night spots with players.

Probable visiting team hotel

Long Island Marriott

Team address

New York Rangers
Madison Square Garden
4 Pennsylvania Plaza
New York, N.Y. 10001

Phone: (212) 465-6000

Club mail response

Slow in responding to written requests for information.

Marketing

Undetermined - The team has been unresponsive to mail and phone requests for information.

Autograph policy

Requests for player autographs can be sent directly to the player's attention at the address listed above.

Comments

The team needs to implement a more efficient communication system with its fans.

After the game

New York, like Los Angeles, has a volatile social atmosphere. You are better off asking the concierge at the hotel where you are staying which places are the current popular night spots.

Probable visiting team hotel

Manhattan East Suite Hotels

Team address

Ottawa Senators
301 Moodie Drive
Suite 200
Nepean, Ontario, Canada K2H 9C4

Phone: (613) 726-0540

Club mail response

Slow in responding to written requests for information.

Marketing

Very Good - The team issues an eight-page, black-and-white catalog of team-related merchandise. The Ottawa Senators Collectibles catalog includes autographed photographs, pucks, jerseys and skates. The club also sells game-used sticks and jerseys. Sample prices from the catalog include autographed game-used sticks (Daigle, $275; Yashin, $225) and autographed game-worn jerseys (Daigle, $1,700; Yashin, $1,400). To order merchandise, or to obtain a copy of this catalog, call 1-800-461-2979.

Autograph policy

Requests for player autographs can be sent directly to the player's attention at the address listed above.

Comments

The team needs to implement a more effective communication system for its fans.

After the game

Hurley's and O'Toole's are popular restaurants frequented by players. The hotter night spots are all in the market area.

Probable visiting team hotel

The Westin Hotel

Team address

Philadelphia Flyers
The Spectrum
Pattison Place
Philadelphia, Pa. 19148-5291

Phone: (215) 336-3600

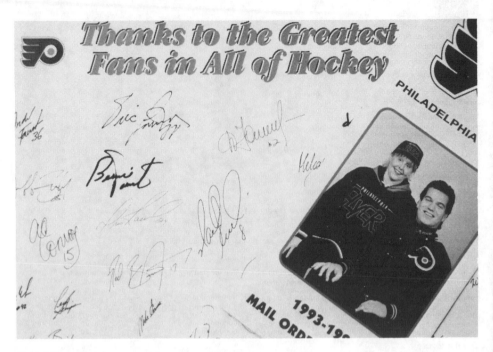

Club mail response

Good - The team responds in a timely and efficient manner to information requests.

Marketing

Good - The team produces a two-fold, single-sheet color mail order catalog that has a small offering of clothing and souvenirs. There is no autographed material available in this catalog. Sample prices from the catalog include a Flyers home replica jersey ($60) and an Eric Lindros action poster ($5).

Autograph policy

Requests for player autographs can be sent directly to the player's attention at the address listed above. Some players, such as Eric Lindros and Mark Recchi, will respond with a color postcard bearing a facsimile autograph, but all the items you sent will be returned unsigned. Many other Flyers, such as Kevin Dineen, are excellent at responding to autograph mail requests.

Comments

Many fans and collectors would like to see the team's mail order catalog expanded to include more souvenirs, limited-edition items and autographed memorabilia.

After the game

Numerous fine dining establishments include Bookbinders Seafood House, Cafe Nola, DiLullo Centro and La Famiglia.

Probable visiting team hotel

Sheraton Society Hill.

Team address

Pittsburgh Penguins
Civic Arena
Pittsburgh, Pa. 15219

Phone: (412) 642-1800

Club mail response

Slow in responding to written requests for information.

Marketing

Excellent - The Pittsburgh Penguins issue a 12-page color catalog dedicated to authentic autographed memorabilia. Every autographed item offered for sale was witnessed by an independent national accounting firm employee, has a numbered hologram attached to the product and comes with a "Certificate of Authenticity." To obtain a copy of the catalog, or to order merchandise, call 1-800-8-GO-PENS. In Pittsburgh dial 412-391-PENS. From autographed goalie gloves to autographed golf balls, this catalog has it all. Sample prices from catalog include an authentic autographed Lemieux hockey stick ($169.95) and an autographed Lemieux baseball ($49.95).

Autograph policy

Requests for player autographs can be sent directly to the player's attention at the address listed above.

Comments

The Penguins Authentic Memorabilia Catalog represents the finest offering of autographed team merchandising by any professional team. The catalog has set the standard by which all followers will be measured. It is professionally done - creative, colorful and well-designed. It is a dream come true for collectors.

After the game

After the game, head straight to the Pittsburgh Sports Garden and bring plenty of items to have autographed. Many autograph collectors are also successful at obtaining signatures after the game outside of the players' entrance to the arena. Just a quick note to Lemieux fans: don't bother waiting for Mario here because he uses a different exit of the arena. When you're finished at the Pittsburgh Sports Garden head to a late hours sandwich place called Parmani Brothers; it's a favorite with many of the players.

Probable visiting team hotel

Pittsburgh Vista

Team address

Quebec Nordiques
Colisee de Quebec
2205 Ave. du Colisee
Quebec City, Quebec, Canada G1L 4W7

Phone: (418) 529-8441

Club mail response

Very Good - The team replies promptly and accurately to information requests.

Marketing

Good - The team offers a single-sheet, three-fold color brochure offering a variety of souvenirs and collectibles. There is no autographed memorabilia for sale in the brochure. Sample (Canadian) prices from the brochure include 8x10 color photos ($6) and authentic jerseys ($170 each).

Autograph policy

Requests for player autographs can be sent directly to the player's attention at the address listed above.

Comments

Many collectors and fans would like to see the Nordiques brochure expanded to include limited-edition collectibles and autographed memorabilia.

After the game

Ask the concierge at the hotel where you are staying to recommend a good place to go after the game.

Probable visiting team hotels

Unsure

Team address

St. Louis Blues
5700 Oakland Ave.
St. Louis, Mo. 63110-1397

Phone: (314) 781-5300

Club mail response

Good - The team responds timely and accurately to team inquiries for information.

Marketing

Very Good - The Blues have an eight-page color gift catalog that is available at 1-800-BLUES-16. The catalog offers a variety of merchandise, most of which is clothing. The team also operates five Bluenote Sports Shops in the St. Louis area which sell a limited supply of game-used sticks and jerseys. The team is currently developing new ideas that address the collectible concept, and should have more information over the next few months. Sample prices from the catalog include a pro "game issue" CCM jersey ($200, with name and number) and a media guide ($8).

Autograph policy

Requests for player autographs can be sent directly to the player's attention at the address listed above. Collectors should keep in mind that next season the team will be moving to Kiel Center and the address will change.

Comments

Collectors and fans like the marketing direction taken by the Blues, particularly the offering of game-used equipment for sale. The Bluenote Sports Shops are also convenient for customer needs. More limited-edition items, and autographed memorabilia, would be helpful to collectors.

After the game

It's always worth dropping by Charlie Gitto's Pasta House to see who's there. Ozzie's Restaurant/Sports Bar might also prove worthwhile. Fine dining stops should include Dierdorf and Hart's, Gitto's On The Hill, and Tony's.

Probable visiting team hotel

Adam's Mark.

Team address

San Jose Sharks
525 West Santa Clara St.
San Jose, Calif. 95113

Phone: (408) 287-7070

Club mail response

Excellent - The team responds promptly and accurately to information requests.

Marketing

Excellent - Typical of a new organization, the Sharks marketing is more attune to the needs of the collector and the fan. No "ashtray and key chain" marketing approach here; instead, an eight-page full color team catalog offers a wide variety of clothing, souvenirs and collectibles. No autographed memorabilia is available in the catalog, but when a fan purchases a San Jose Sharks authentic team jersey ($160), or shell parka ($110) directly from the team, the club will have it autographed by the designated player. There are also many inaugural season (1991-92) collectibles still available through the club. If you are interested in these items contact (408) 982-5930.

Autograph policy

Requests for player autographs can be sent directly to the player's attention at the address listed above.

Comments

Collectors and fans appreciate the effort the club puts forth to have certain items autographed. The only comment concerning the merchandise catalog is to possibly include autographed memorabilia in future printings.

After the game

Sports City Cafe, Gordon Biersch and the Tide House are all good sports spots after the game. Some of the players' favorite dining spots are Paula's or Emile's.

Probable visiting team hotel

Fairmont Hotel

Team address

Tampa Bay Lightning
Mack Center
501 E. Kennedy Blvd.
Suite 175
Tampa, Fla. 33602

Phone: (813) 229-2658

Club mail response

Slow in responding to written requests for information.

Marketing

Undetermined - The team has been unresponsive to mail and phone requests for information.

Autograph policy

Requests for player autographs can be sent directly to the player's attention at the address listed above.

Comments

The team needs to implement a better communication system with its fans.

After the game

Clancy's and Players are both good sports spots to hit after the game. A favorite dining spot with players is Brunello's, not too far from the Tradewinds. As far as night spots, Hurricane and Beachnuts are two good choices.

Probable visiting team hotel

Tradewinds

Team address

Toronto Maple Leafs
Maple Leaf Gardens
60 Carlton St.
Toronto, Ontario, Canada M5B 1L1

Phone: (416) 977-1641

Club mail response

Slow in responding to written requests for information.

Marketing

Very Good - The Maple Leafs issue a 12-page color brochure which includes a wide variety of team-related merchandise. Parkhurst Ice Authentics and LeafSport offer a wide selection of autographed hockey memorabilia. LeafSport, located at Maple Leaf Gardens, is the team's official gift shop. Should you wish to order a catalog or merchandise, they can be reached at 1-416-596-3360. The team also allows collectors and fans to order game-used hockey sticks from their favorite Maple Leafs players; for prices and availability you must call the team.

Autograph policy

Requests for player autographs can be sent directly to the player's attention at the address listed above.

Comments

The Maple Leafs are doing a fine job meeting the needs of fans and collectors.

After the game

After the game, a favorite player spot is Alice Fazooli's Italian Crabshack Saloon. Fisherman's Wharf and the Whistling Oyster are also good dining spots.

Probable visiting team hotel

The Westin Hotel

Team address

Vancouver Canucks
Pacific Coliseum
100 N. Renfrew St.
Vancouver, B.C., Canada V5K 3N7

Phone: (604) 254-5141

Club mail response

Slow in responding to written requests for information.

Marketing

Undetermined - The team has been unresponsive to phone and mail requests for information.

Autograph policy

Requests for player autographs can be sent directly to the player's attention at the address listed above.

Comments

The team needs to implement a better communications system with its fans.

After the game

After the game, head to Sportscasters and stay there. This sports bar and restaurant is only about four blocks from The Westin Bayshore.

Probable visiting team hotel

The Westin Bayshore

Team address
Washington Capitals
USAir Arena
Landover, Md. 20785

Phone: (301) 386-7000

Club mail response
Slow in responding to written requests for information.

Sea Watch - Black band with white face, date. ITEM #26....$34.95

Hair Twisties - Available in Capitals Lightning, Flyers, Penguins, Panthers and Mighty Ducks. ITEM #7....$5.00

Earrings - ITEM #27....$8.00
Necklace - ITEM #28....$8.00

▲ 20ᵗʰ **Anniversary Hat** - Two-tone red and blue twill (Black also available. Not pictured). One size. Please specify color. ITEM #18....$15.00

▲ 20ᵗʰ **Anniversary Tee** - 100% cotton available in black or red. Specify color. Adult Sizes M, L, XL. ITEM #19....$17.00

◄ Logo pins - All teams available, sold

Marketing
Good - The Capitals issue a three-sheet color brochure that includes 58 different team-related items. Some sample prices from the brochure include an authentic pro jersey ($195, includes patch and lettering) and a yearbook ($7). To order a copy of the catalog, or merchandise, dial 1-202-432-SEAT.

Autograph policy
Requests for player autographs can be sent directly to the player's attention at the address listed above.

Comments
The Capitals need to expand the team's brochure to include 8x10 color photographs, hockey trading card team sets, hockey sticks, limited-edition collectibles, game-used equipment and autographed memorabilia.

After the game
The Tickets lounge in the Marriott is a good sports spot after the game, as is the Sports Loft. Sir Walter Raleigh's and Jaspers are also popular restaurants frequented by players.

Probable visiting team hotel
The Greenbelt Marriott

Team address
Winnipeg Jets
Winnipeg Arena
15-1430 Maroons Road
Winnipeg, Manitoba, Canada R3G 0L5

Phone: (204) 783-5387

Club mail response
Slow in responding to written requests for information.

Marketing

Undetermined - The team has been unresponsive to phone and mail requests for information.

Autograph policy

Requests for player autographs can be sent directly to the player's attention at the address listed above.

Comments

The team needs to implement a better communication system with its fans.

After the game

The Bank, Market Club, Norma Jean's and Rolling Stone are all popular night spots and are located near The Westin Hotel. For dining, many players choose The Forks, which is also close to the The Westin Hotel.

Probable visiting team hotel

The Westin Hotel

These are some of the offerings from various pro teams

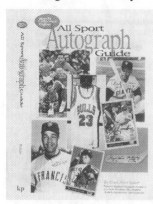

Chapter 12

Beginner's Gallery

Players can be reached for autographs through their teams.

You can add these 100 sports autographs to you collection for less than $1 each. All it takes is a card and two stamps - one stamp for the letter to send to the player, in care of his team, and one stamp for the self-addressed, stamped envelope he can use to send your card back to you.

The players were chosen at random from cards included in several Topps packs, which were purchased to obtain a variety of players from each of the four sports. Response time was generally between one to four weeks, but each player responded. All autograph responses are assumed to be authentic, but the inclusion of a player in this section does not imply or guarantee that he will respond to your request. Signature quality varies due to card surfaces and ink characteristics.

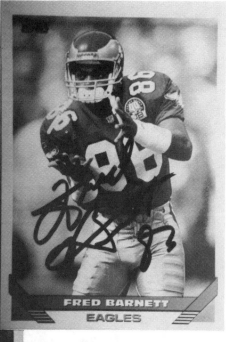

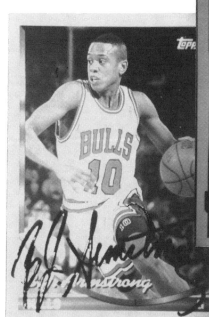

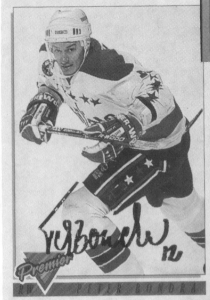

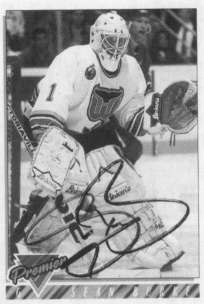

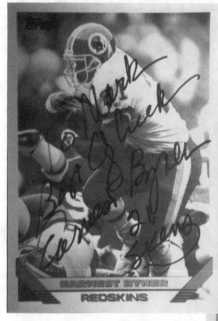

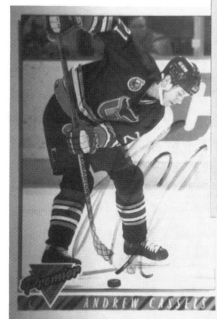

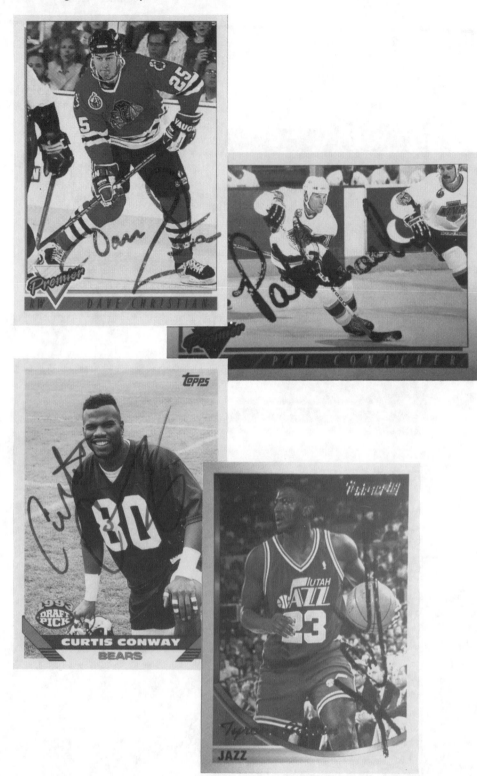

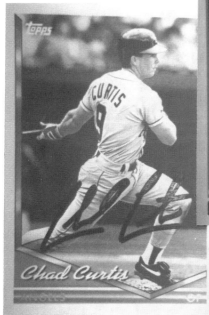

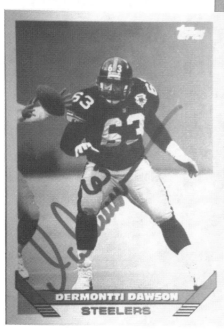

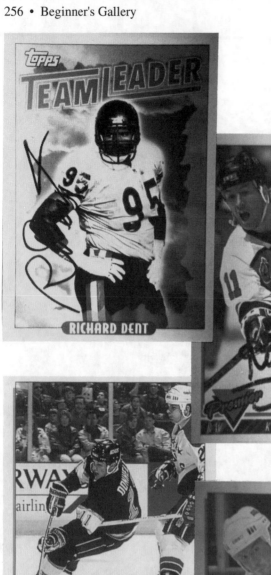

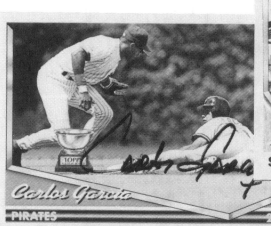

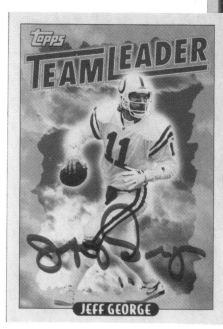

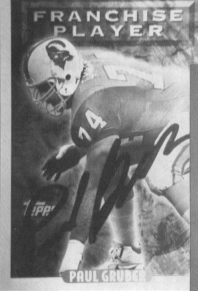

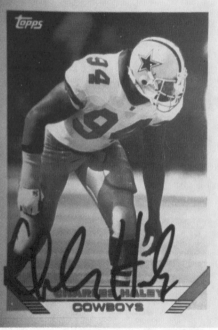

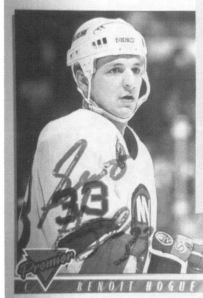

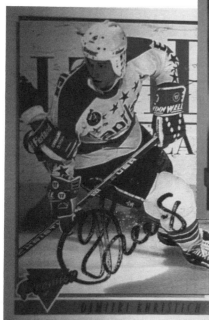

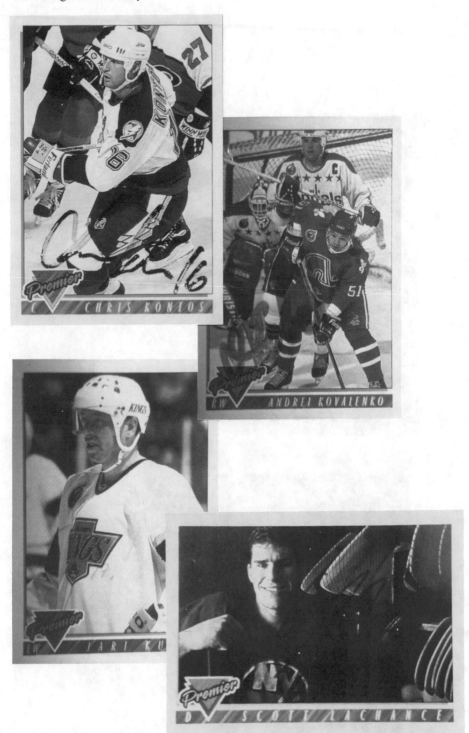

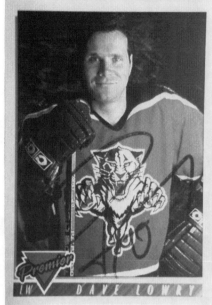

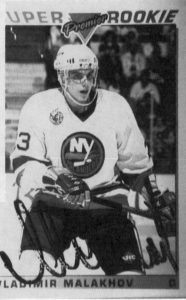

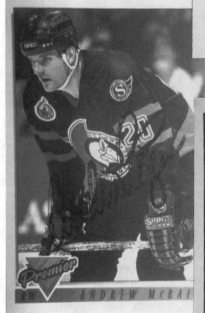

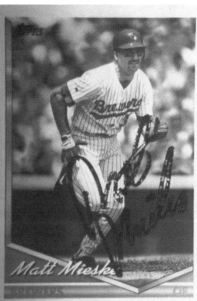

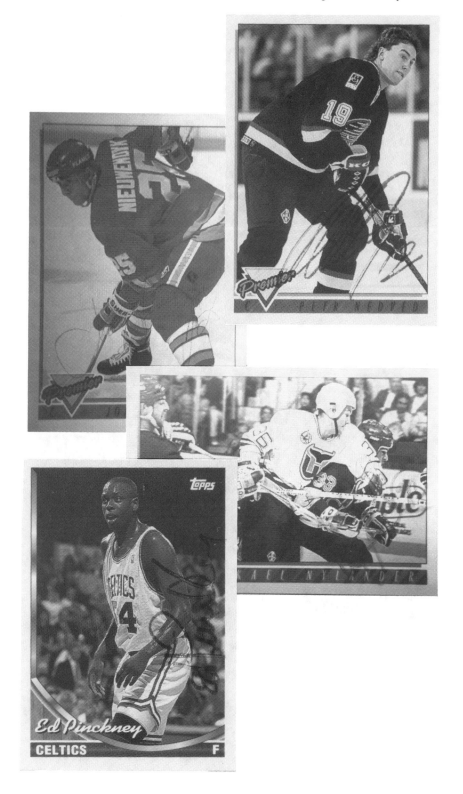

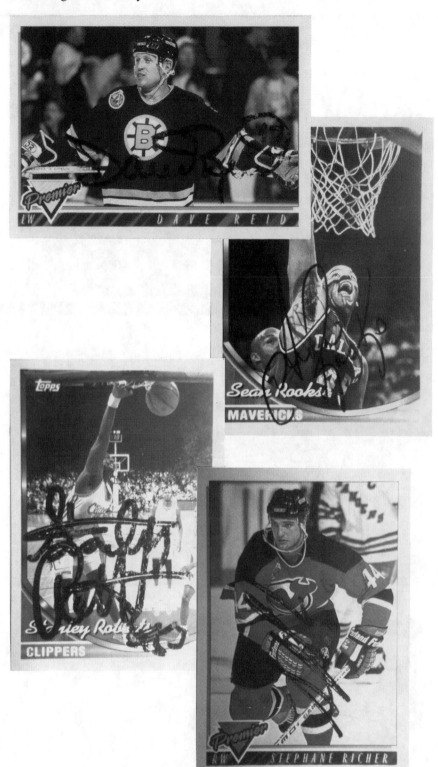

ALEXANDER SEMAK

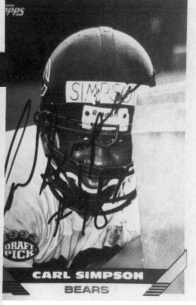

CARL SIMPSON

BEARS

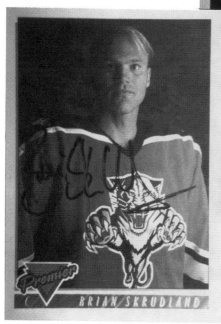

BRIAN SKRUDLAND

CHRIS SPIELMAN

DWIGHT STONE

STEELERS

MATT STOVER

BROWNS

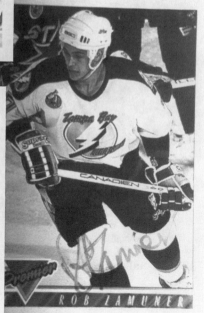

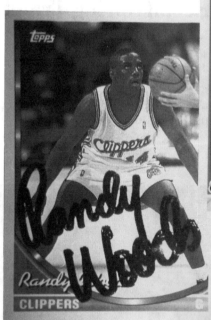

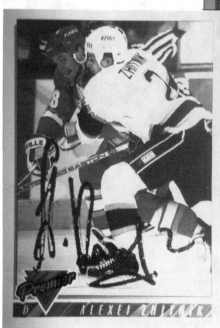

Chapter 13

Baseball Spring Training

An Autograph Collector's Guide

The casual atmosphere in spring training is an opportune time for autographs.

Every autograph baseball collector dreams about the riches of spring training - a warm Arizona breeze, the Florida sunshine, and a cluster of major league superstars and future prospects within speaking, or should I say, stalking distance.

It's been months of rest, and last year's losses have all but been forgotten; an April optimism envelops the players, so much so that some even begin to mingle with the fans. Collectors, frustrated by the inaccessibility of major league ballparks and the unwillingness of so many players to sign autographs, are thrown their first curve ball - a willing signer.

Most players haven't had to deal with autograph collectors at the ballpark since October, so their skin is thick and less sensitive to brash and overwhelming requests.

Yankee owner George Steinbrenner signs during spring training.

The atmosphere is the key factor in an autograph collector's success during spring training. The relaxed surroundings of Florida and Arizona, and the knowledge that the games don't really count, are big factors for the veterans, who are expected to carry the team during the regular season. But it's not so for the unproven rookies, who eagerly await their at bats or a chance to sign an autograph.

A veteran, seasoned in autograph avoidance techniques, realizes his name, when scribbled on a piece of paper, has an associated value. But he's usually relaxed; his position on the team is probably secure.

Most established stars rent condominiums during spring training, so the team hotel does not provide the autograph opportunities that a visiting team's hotel would during the regular season. The solitude of a home cooked meal is preferred by some ballplayers over the risk of being interrupted during dinner at a popular restaurant.

Unlike veteran superstars, many young prospects and minor leaguers are often not recognized in public. After the game, most players, in small groups, usually like to dine at a local restaurant, usually determined by the players' tastes, expense money and salary levels. Time permitting, some players may also visit some of the sports hot spots or nightclubs in the area after dinner.

Many autograph collectors who make the annual pilgrimage to spring training are not from or familiar with these areas, so it is often difficult to determine a player's whereabouts. Therefore, the ballpark or sports complex becomes the collector's logical initial hunting ground.

Players sign most frequently before and after morning workouts, or while walking back and forth to the parking lots. Parking lots, during the regular season, are typically not key autograph areas because of limited or restricted access. Many newer stadiums have private access to the clubhouse from guarded indoor parking areas.

Another key advantage for autograph collectors is that spring training attracts many of the game's legends. Many Hall of Fame inductees remain affiliated in some manner with the game, either as broadcasters, instructors or executives. From Brooks Robinson to Frank Robinson, nowhere other than Cooperstown will you find a greater density of baseball autograph targets.

Spring Training Leagues

Cactus League (Arizona)
California
Chicago Cubs
Colorado
Milwaukee
Oakland
San Diego
San Francisco
Seattle

All the teams in the Cactus League are clustered in the Phoenix area. Most collectors choose to stay in centrally-located Scottsdale.

Most of the league's ballparks have a clubhouse built into the stadium, giving players an unobscured path from the locker room to the playing field. Collectors are advised to concentrate on the players' parking lots or at the several playing fields in each complex.

Grapefruit League (Florida)

East Coast	Central Florida	Gulf Coast
Atlanta	Boston	Baltimore
Los Angeles	Cincinnati	Chicago White Sox
Montreal	Cleveland	Minnesota
New York Mets	Detroit	Philadlephia
New York Yankees	Florida	Pittsburgh
xxx	Houston	St. Louis
xxx	Kansas City	Texas
xxx	xxx	Toronto

With a much larger league, collectors have two choices - drive to the various locations around the state, or stay put and let the teams come to you. Remember that, in addition to spring training, this time of year is also a popular tourist time for Walt Disney World and college spring break crowds.

Cactus League Overview (Arizona)

Team address
California Angels, 2200 W. Alameda, Tempe, Ariz. 85282
Capacity: 9,785
Phone: (602) 431-0801
Team hotel: Hotel Fiesta Inn
Autograph hints: There is limited access around the dugouts, so most of the collectors prefer heading to the bullpens. Studebaker's and Rustler's Roost are the first two restaurants where collectors should begin their autograph search.

Team address
Chicago Cubs, HoHoKam Park, 1235 N. Center St., Mesa, Ariz. 85201
Capacity: 8,963
Phone: (602) 964-4467
Team hotel: Mezona Motor Inn

Autograph hints: Concentrate on the open parking lot before and after games. Before the start of the exhibition season, the team trains at Fitch Park (655 N. Center St. - five blocks from the stadium). Focus your attention in key areas around it. After the game, head to Harry & Steve's Chicago Grill (named for broadcasters Harry Caray and Steve Stone). You won't catch the veterans here, but many of the prospects stop by.

Team address

Colorado Rockies, Hi Corbett Field, 3400 E. Camino Campestre, Tucson, Ariz. 85726
Capacity: 9,500
Phone: (602) 325-2621
Team hotel: unsure
Autograph hints: Concentrate along the low fences at the ballpark. It is a fairly easy park to gain access to players in usual areas, dugouts, etc....

Team address

Milwaukee Brewers, Compadre Stadium, 1425 W. Ocotillo Road, Chandler, Ariz. 85248
Capacity: 5,000 (also 5,000 lawn seats)
Phone: (602) 895-1200
Team hotel: Dobson Ranch Inn
Autograph hints: Collectors will love the easy access to the players, who have to walk from adjacent batting cages and practice fields. After the game, head to Guedo's Taco Shop, China Gate or Tomaso's and see which players you run into. Choose a choice spot at the stadium before the team's 10 a.m. workout.

Team address

Oakland A's, Phoenix Municipal Stadium, 5999 E. Van Buren, Phoenix, Ariz. 85008
Capacity: 8,500
Phone: (602) 392-0074
Team hotel: Doubletree Suites
Autograph hints: Collectors have easy access along railings and the ramp to the clubhouse. The player's parking lot near the left field corner is also a popular spot. After the game, try Honey Bear's Barbeque, the Pink Pony, or Don & Charlie's to see who stops by.

Team address

San Diego Padres & Seattle Mariners, Peoria Sports Complex, 8131 W. Paradise Lane, Peoria, Ariz. 85541
Capacity: to be determined
Phone: (602) 486-2011
Team hotel: unsure
Autograph hints: This is a brand-new, state-of-the-art stadium/training facility that just opened this year, so many of the key autograph areas are still undetermined.

Team address

San Francisco Giants, Scottsdale Stadium, 7208 E. Osborn Road, Scottsdale, Ariz. 85251
Capacity: 10,000
Phone: (602) 990-0052
Team hotel: Scottsdale Plaza Resort
Autograph hints: The new stadium (1992) features a walkway directly from the clubhouse to the field, restricting autograph collector access. A collector's best bet for acquiring signatures after the game might be either of these restaurants - Don & Charlie's or the Pink Pony.

Grapefruit League Overview (Florida)

East Coast

If you're early, you may catch Braves prospects Chipper Jones and Ryan Klesko.

Team address

Atlanta Braves/Montreal Expos, Municipal Stadium, Palm Beach Lakes Boulevard and Congress Avenue, West Palm Beach, Fla. 33402

Capacity: 7,200

Phone: (407) 683-6100 (Braves); (407) 689-9121 (Expos)

Team hotels: Palm Beach Gardens Marriott (Braves); Holiday Inn Singer Island (Expos)

Autograph hints: Many collectors concentrate on the parking lot behind third base or public access areas for autographs. Players must walk through fans in the public access area to reach the clubhouse, making them easy targets. Collectors should arrive early and try to catch the players before morning workouts, which usually begin at 10 a.m. After the game, you may want to dine at Manero's or Chef Mingo's.

Team address

Los Angeles Dodgers, Bud Holman Stadium, 4001 26th St., Vero Beach, Fla. 32961-2887

Capacity: 6,500

Phone: (407) 569-4900

Team hotel: Dodgertown

Autograph hints: Considered a collector and fan paradise, with easy access to players. The players must walk through the crowds, to the various fields, from a centrally-located clubhouse. After the game, you may want to dine at the Patio Restaurant or Mr. Manatee.

Team address

New York Mets, County Sports Complex, 525 NW Peacock Blvd., Port St. Lucie, Fla. 34986

Capacity: 7,347

Phone (407) 871-2115

Team hotel: Radisson Hotel

Autograph hints: A tough ballpark to obtain signatures in because there is no public access area between the field and the clubhouse; players travel through a dugout tunnel. After the game, try dining at Applebee's Dugout Diner, Amici's Cafe, or try shopping at the Orange Blossom or Treasure Coast Malls.

Team address

New York Yankees, Fort Lauderdale Stadium, 5301 NW 12th Ave., Fort Lauderdale, Fla. 33309
Capacity: 7,461
Phone: (305) 776-1921
Team hotel: Palm Aire Hotel
Autograph hints: It can be difficult to obtain tickets, so purchase them upon availability. The majority of the collectors concentrate on players after practice, when the atmosphere is less hectic. Along fences and high railings can be difficult areas for collectors to acquire signatures. After the game, stop by Sonny's Stardust for some barbecued food and a possible autograph or two.

Central Florida

Team address

Boston Red Sox, City of Palms Park, 2201 Edison Ave., Fort Myers, Fla. 33912
Capacity: 7,000
Phone: (813) 334-4700
Team hotel: undetermined
Autograph hints: The new stadium has just hosted its second season as the winter home of the Red Sox. As with any new complex, it will take a few seasons to determine the most successful spots for autographs.

Team address

Cincinnati Reds, Plant City Stadium, 1900 S. Park Road, Plant City, Fla. 33566
Capacity: 6,700
Phone (813) 752-1878
Team hotel: Holiday Inn
Autograph hints: Collectors will find excellent player access along the typical ballpark hot spots - around dugouts, bullpen areas and along railings. After the game, grab a bite to eat at Buddy Freddy's.

Team address

Cleveland Indians, Chain O' Lakes Park, Cypress Gardens Boulevard, Winter Haven, Fla. 33880
Capacity: 4,520
Phone: (813) 293-3900
Team hotel: Holiday Inn
Autograph hints: Collectors will enjoy the excellent access to players, especially along the left-field line. After the game, grab a bite to eat at Christy's Sundown or Harriston's.

Team address

Detroit Tigers, Joker Marchant Stadium, Lakeland Hills Boulevard, Lakeland, Fla. 33801
Capacity: 7,009
Phone: (813) 499-8229
Team hotel: Holiday Inn North
Autograph hints: An average access ballpark for autograph collectors, with players typically signing along railings, near dugouts and box seats.

Team address

Florida Marlins, Carl Barger Baseball Complex, 5600 Stadium Parkway, Melbourne, Fla.
Capacity: 7,200
Phone: (407) 633-9200
Team hotel: undetermined
Autograph hints: As with most new facilities, determining the best spot for collecting autographs may take a few seasons. Most collectors concentrate on the practice fields before or during workouts; you will probably have greater success if you arrive early - 9:30 a.m.

Team address

Houston Astros, Osceola County Stadium, 1000 Osceola Blvd., Kissimmee, Fla. 34744

Capacity: 5,000

Phone: (407) 933-5500

Team hotel: Sol Orlando Village Hotel

Autograph hints: The stadium has good access to players along railings, near dugouts and box seats. Most experienced collectors concentrate on the complex's four practice fields surrounding the stadium, on non-home game days (only days open to the public), from 8:30 a.m. to 2 p.m. After your autograph hunting, try a bite to eat at Fibber McGee's or Calico Jack's.

Team address

Kansas City Royals, Baseball City Stadium, 300 Stadium Way, Baseball City, Fla. 33837

Capacity: 8,000

Phone: (813) 424-2424

Team hotel: Sonesta Villa Resort

Autograph hints: Can be a tough ballpark to work as an autograph collector. There is limited player access, so most collectors concentrate around dugouts and box seats.

Gulf Coast

Team address

Baltimore Orioles/St. Louis Cardinals, Al Lang Stadium, 180 Second Ave. SE, St. Petersburg, Fla. 33701

Capacity: 7,227

Phone: (813) 822-3384

Team hotel: St. Petersburg Hilton & Towers (The Wings nightclub inside the hotel is also popular with players).

Autograph hints: At Al Lang Stadium, player access is fair, so most collectors head to either the Busch Complex (7901 30th Ave., about 10 minutes from the stadium), where the Cardinals work out, or to Twin Lakes Park (Sarasota) to watch the Orioles train. Both sites offer excellent access to players, especially the Busch Complex. After the game, stop by the Hurricane Restaurant, Bern's Steakhouse or Beach Nuts nightclub. While at the stadium, be sure to grab an autographed hot dog bag from legendary singing vendor Tommy Walton.

Team address

Chicago White Sox, Ed Smith Stadium, 12th Street and Tuttle Avenue, Sarasota, Fla. 34237

Capacity: 7,500

Phone: (813) 366-8451

Team hotel: Hampton Inn

Autograph hints: Collectors concentrate their autograph efforts around the four playing fields adjacent to the main stadium. After the game, head to El Adobe, Shells or the Melting Pot for a variety of fine dining.

Team address

Minnesota Twins, Lee County Sports Complex, 14100 Six Mile Cypress Parkway, Fort Myers, Fla. 33912

Capacity: 5,500

Phone: (813) 768-4200

Team hotel: Courtyard Marriott

Autograph hints: Collectors frequent railings and gather near the dugouts and the box seats. After the game, try dining at Pott's Sports Cafe or Luigi's.

It helps if you know a team's training schedule inside out.

Team address
Pittsburgh Pirates, McKechnie Field, 17th Ave. and 9th St. W., Bradenton, Fla. 34205
Capacity: 5,000
Phone: (813) 748-4610
Team hotel: none
Autograph hints: Collectors have limited access between the clubhouse and the field. Most players sign autographs along the railings. After the game, lift your spirits at the Lone Star, the Sarasota Brewing Company or Chili's.

Team address
Philadelphia Phillies, Jack Russell Memorial Stadium, 800 Phillies Drive, Clearwater, Fla. 34615
Capacity: 7,350
Phone: (813) 441-8638
Team hotel: none
Autograph hints: Jack Russell Stadium, with its limited player access, is not a favorite among autograph seekers. The most effective area has been outside the stadium's clubhouse entrance. Most collectors instead opt for Carpenter Complex (Drew Street and Coachman Road, 1.5 miles from the stadium), where, prior to the exhibition schedule, the team works out from 10 a.m. to 2 p.m. This complex offers excellent player access, but once the exhibition schedule begins, major league workouts are not open to the public.

Team address
Texas Rangers, Charlotte County Stadium, 2300 El Jobean Rd., Port Charlotte, Fla. 33949
Capacity: 6,026
Phone: (813) 625-9500
Team hotels: Palm Island Resort, Days Inn
Autograph hints: Collectors congregate near the clubhouse or by the bullpens. During workouts many players are also accessible along railings. The players' parking lot used to be a good spot until fences had to be erected, allegedly because of player automobile damage caused by autograph seekers.

Team address

Toronto Blue Jays, Dunedin Stadium, 350 Douglas Ave., Dunedin, Fla. 34698

Capacity: 6,218

Phone: (813) 733-0429

Team hotel: Ramada Inn Countryside

Autograph hints: Most collectors accumulate along the railings, around box seats and near dugouts. After the game, stop by Sea-Sea Rider's or head to Derby Lane for the dog races. For breakfast, head to Iris's and be sure to have your autograph supplies handy, as many players dine here before workouts begin.

Notes:

Team hotels may vary each year, depending upon rates, or by team, depending upon a club's expenses. Phone numbers may also vary, depending upon a specific service or changes in location. Team training areas or complex access may also change each season, as well as workout schedules. Surrounding area businesses, frequented by players, may vary by night - not all places are open seven days a week - or due to a player's expense level. Fine dining can have a large associated expense. The businesses listed above are only suggestions and have no associated guarantees. Most team training complexes are adjacent to their respective parks.

All visitors to spring training are encouraged to make reservations well in advance to avoid any travel problems. Many major league clubs book months in advance, so finding a strategically-placed hotel for a dedicated autograph seeker may be difficult if not timely addressed.

As a dedicated collector, you must become synchronized with the player's daily schedule. Most players arrive early at training facilities, so that they can have their afternoons free for golf or relaxation.

Know a team's training schedule inside and out, and also observe the routines of many of the players. Keep track of player arrival and departure times, player automobiles, frequented establishments and who each player hangs around with.

All of this information will be useful in developing your autograph strategy. I have become so familiar with the habits of certain players that I can predict what restaurants they will dine at on certain days, what company will join them, how long they will stay, where they will go afterward, and possibly what they might have for dinner.

One of the best places to find a few ballplayers, as well as assorted team personnel, is at the Derby Lane dog track in St. Petersburg, which was one of Pete Rose's favorite hangouts. Many players regularly visit and enjoy the track's atmosphere while in Florida.

In Phoenix, Ariz., the nightly gathering spot is the Pink Pony in Old Scottsdale. Roger Angell, of the New Yorker magazine, once referred to it as "the best baseball restaurant in the land."

As a final note, don't forget to bring a pair of sunglasses, plenty of suntain lotion and a comprehensive package of autograph supplies. Spring training offers baseball fans a wonderful odyssey into our past, and a peak into our future. Enjoy it!

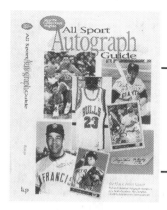

Appendix

Dollars and Sense in Sports Wares

Try going one day without seeing a professional team's logo, or the face of one of its athletes. If the difficulty of this task surprises you, then you will be overwhelmed by the revenues associated with professional team licensing.

Licensing is the official granting of permission to use an image to stimulate sales. The common forms used in licensing are association logos, league logos, team logos, or the visual image, signature, name, or voice of an athlete.

The retail sales of all licensed sports merchandise is projected to be more than $14 billion in 1994 alone. Major League Baseball will account for approximately 30 percent of that figure, and the National Football League about 27 percent.

Since most sports autograph collectors are familiar with trading cards, we will examine briefly their impact. In 1994, sports trading cards sales are expected to fall just short of $3 billion, with 44 percent of the revenue projected to be from the retail sale of baseball cards.

The issue of licensing becomes most perplexing when one tries to determine which entity - the player, the club or the association - owns which image. Simply stated, a player's image of him in his official uniform belongs to the league or to the player's unions, but many details differ.

Baseball

Major League Baseball Properties Inc. was formed in 1987 to centralize licensing efforts that had been previously handled by each individual club. A division of Major League Baseball, MLB Properties now has more than 400 licensees offering almost 3,000 types of team-related souvenirs. Retail sales from licensing, for this division, are expected to reach $4 billion in 1994.

Basketball

The National Basketball Association monitors all its licensing through NBA Properties. The division is believed to have more than 400 licensees who manufacture more than 3,000 types of team-related souvenirs. Retail sales as a result of NBA Properties should reach $3.5 billion in 1994.

Football

If you eliminated the impact of trading cards on this market, the licensing efforts of the NFL would be viewed as most aggressive. NFL Properties was created in 1963 to preserve the league's images and trademarks and to market the sport. This division of the NFL licenses more than 300 manufacturers to produce nearly 3,000 items affiliated with the league.

NFL Properties does not manufacture any items, it only licenses them. This is why you see so many of the same souvenirs in each team's merchandising catalogs. In addition to souvenirs, there are also official corporate sponsors who are allowed to use the NFL logo.

Hockey

NHL Enterprises was started in July of 1992 to centralize the league's licensing arrangements. With its large international appeal, it has a broader market base and is expected over the next five years to show the largest percentage of revenue increase of any of the four major sports. Revenue expectations from licensing from this new division this year are expected to fall just short of $2 billion.

Why is all this important to the sports autographs collector? Simple - if you think for one second that any of these groups listed above, or their respected player associations, will ignore the revenues created by the sale of autographed memorabilia, you're wrong.

All of these groups will make their presence known more aggressively in this market. Also, any increases in licensing fees from any of these groups will increase the retail cost of the official team-related item that you have autographed.

If NHL Enterprises notices an increased interest in the collectors' consumption of autographed player jerseys, you can bet that CCM's licensing agreement ends; it will most likely have to pay an increased rate for its renewal. If this happens, then you would be wise to stock up on a few key jerseys before a price increase occurs.

Hall of Fame Inductees

* indicates deceased members

National Baseball Hall of Fame & Museum

1st Basemen

Cap Anson * 1939
Jake Beckley * 1971
Jim Bottomley * 1974
Dan Brouthers * 1945
Frank Chance * 1946
Roger Connor * 1976
Jimmie Foxx * 1951
Lou Gehrig * 1939
Hank Greenberg * 1956
George Kelly * 1973
Harmon Killebrew 1984
Buck Leonard 1972
Willie McCovey 1986
Johnny Mize * 1981
George Sisler * 1939
Bill Terry * 1954

2nd Basemen

Rod Carew 1991
Eddie Collins * 1939
Bobby Doerr 1986
Johnny Evers * 1946
Frankie Frisch * 1947
Charlie Gehringer * 1949
Billy Herman * 1975
Rogers Hornsby * 1942
Nap Lajoie * 1937
Tony Lazzeri * 1991
Joe Morgan 1990
Jackie Robinson * 1962
Red Schoendienst 1989

Shortstops

Luis Aparicio 1984
Luke Appling * 1964
Dave Bancroft * 1971
Ernie Banks 1977
Lou Boudreau 1970
Joe Cronin * 1956
Travis Jackson * 1982
Hugh Jennings * 1945
Pop Lloyd * 1977
Rabbit Maranville * 1954
Pee Wee Reese 1984
Joe Sewell * 1977
Joe Tinker * 1946
Arky Vaughan * 1985
Honus Wagner * 1936

Bobby Wallace * 1953
Monte Ward * 1964

3rd Basemen

Frank Baker * 1955
Jimmy Collins * 1945
Ray Dandridge 1987
Judy Johnson * 1975
George Kell 1983
Fred Lindstrom * 1976
Eddie Mathews 1978
Brooks Robinson 1983
Pie Traynor * 1948

Outfielders

Hank Aaron 1982
Earl Averill * 1975
Cool Papa Bell * 1974
Lou Brock 1985
Jesse Burkett * 1946
Max Carey * 1961
Oscar Charleston * 1976
Fred Clarke * 1945
Roberto Clemente * 1973
Ty Cobb * 1936
Earle Combs * 1970
Sam Crawford * 1957
Kiki Cuyler * 1968
Ed Delahanty * 1945
Joe DiMaggio 1955
Hugh Duffy * 1945
Elmer Flick * 1963
Goose Goslin * 1968
Chick Hafey * 1971
Billy Hamilton * 1961
Harry Heilmann * 1952
Harry Hooper * 1971
Monte Irvin 1973
Reggie Jackson 1993
Al Kaline 1980
Willie Keeler * 1939
Joe Kelley * 1971
King Kelly * 1945
Ralph Kiner 1975
Chuck Klein * 1980
Mickey Mantle 1974
Heinie Manush * 1964
Willie Mays 1979
Tommy McCarthy * 1946
Joe Medwick * 1968
Stan Musial 1969
Jim O'Rourke * 1945

Mel Ott * 1951
Sam Rice * 1963
Frank Robinson 1982
Edd Roush * 1962
Babe Ruth * 1936
Al Simmons * 1953
Enos Slaughter 1985
Duke Snider 1980
Tris Speaker * 1937
Willie Stargell 1988
Sam Thompson * 1974
Lloyd Waner * 1967
Paul Waner * 1952
Zack Wheat * 1959
Billy Williams 1987
Ted Williams 1966
Hack Wilson * 1979
Carl Yastrzemski 1989
Ross Youngs * 1972

Catchers

Johnny Bench 1989
Yogi Berra 1972
Roger Bresnahan * 1945
Roy Campanella * 1969
Mickey Cochrane * 1947
Bill Dickey 1954
Buck Ewing * 1939
Rick Ferrell 1984
Josh Gibson * 1972
Gabby Hartnett * 1955
Ernie Lombardi * 1986
Ray Schalk * 1955

Pitchers

Grover Alexander * 1938
Chief Bender * 1953
Mordecai Brown * 1949
Jack Chesbro * 1946
John Clarkson * 1963
Stan Coveleski * 1969
Dizzy Dean * 1953
Martin Dihigo * 1977
Don Drysdale * 1984
Red Faber * 1964
Bob Feller 1962
Rollie Fingers 1992
Whitey Ford 1974
Rube Foster * 1981
Pud Galvin * 1965
Bob Gibson 1981
Lefty Gomez * 1972
Burleigh Grimes * 1964
Lefty Grove * 1947
Jess Haines * 1970
Waite Hoyt * 1969
Carl Hubbell * 1947

Catfish Hunter 1987
Ferguson Jenkins 1991
Walter Johnson * 1936
Addie Joss * 1978
Tim Keefe * 1964
Sandy Koufax 1972
Bob Lemon 1976
Ted Lyons * 1955
Juan Marichal 1983
Rube Marquard * 1971
Christy Mathewson * 1936
Joe McGinnity * 1946
Hal Newhouser 1992
Kid Nichols * 1949
Satchel Paige * 1971
Jim Palmer 1990
Herb Pennock * 1948
Gaylord Perry 1991
Eddie Plank * 1946
Old Hoss Radbourn * 1939
Eppa Rixey * 1963
Robin Roberts 1976
Red Ruffing * 1967
Amos Rusie * 1977
Tom Seaver 1992
Warren Spahn 1973
Dazzy Vance * 1955
Rube Waddell * 1946
Ed Walsh * 1946
Mickey Welch * 1973
Hoyt Wilhelm 1985
Early Wynn 1972
Cy Young * 1937

Managers

Walter Alston * 1983
Bucky Harris * 1975
Miller Huggins * 1964
Al Lopez 1977
Connie Mack * 1937
Joe McCarthy * 1957
John McGraw * 1937
Bill McKechnie * 1962
Wilbert Robinson * 1945
Casey Stengel * 1966

Naismith Memorial Basketball Hall of Fame

Nate Archibald 1991
Paul Arizin 1977
Thomas Barlow * 1980
Rick Barry 1987
Elgin Baylor 1976
John Beckman * 1972
Walt Bellamy 1993
Sergei Belov 1992
Dave Bing 1990

Benny Borgmann * 1961
Bill Bradley 1982
Joe Brennan * 1974
Al Cervi 1984
Wilt Chamberlain 1978
Charles Cooper * 1976
Bob Cousy 1970
Dave Cowens 1991
Billy Cunningham 1986
Bob Davies * 1969
Forrest DeBernardi * 1961
Dave DeBusschere 1982
Dutch Dehnert * 1968
Paul Endacott 1971
Julius Erving 1993
Bud Foster 1964
Walt Frazier 1987
Marty Friedman * 1971
Joe Fulks * 1977
Laddie Gale 1976
Harry Gallatin 1991
William Gates 1989
Tom Gola 1975
Hal Greer 1981
Robert Gruenig * 1963
Cliff Hagan 1977
Victor Hanson * 1960
John Havlicek 1983
Connie Hawkins 1992
Elvin Hayes 1990
Tom Heinsohn 1986
Nat Holman 1964
Bob Houbregs 1987
Chuck Hyatt * 1959
Dan Issel 1993
Bill Johnson * 1976
Neil Johnston * 1990
K.C. Jones 1989
Sam Jones 1983
Edward Krause 1975
Bob Kurland 1961
Bob Lanier 1992
Joe Lapchick * 1966
Clyde Lovellette 1988
Jerry Lucas 1979
Hank Luisetti 1959
Ed Macauley 1960
Pete Maravich * 1987
Slater Martin 1981
Branch McCracken * 1960
Jack McCracken * 1962
Bobby McDermott 1988
George Mikan 1959
Earl Monroe 1990
Calvin Murphy 1993
Charles Murphy 1960
Harlan Page * 1962

Bob Pettit 1970
Andy Phillip 1961
Jim Pollard * 1977
Frank Rmsey 1981
Willis Reed 1981
Oscar Robertson 1979
John Roosma * 1961
John Russell * 1964
Bill Russell 1974
Dolph Schayes 1972
Ernest Schmidt * 1973
John Schommer * 1959
Barney Sedran * 1962
Bill Sharman 1975
Christian Steinmetz * 1961
John Thompson * 1962
Nate Thurmond 1984
Jack Twyman 1982
Wes Unseld 1988
Robert Vandivier * 1974
Ed Wachter * 1961
Bill Walton 1993
Bobby Wanzer 1987
Jerry West 1979
Lenny Wilkens 1989
John Wooden 1960

Pro Football Hall of Fame

Quarterbacks

Sammy Baugh 1963
George Blanda 1981
Terry Bradshaw 1989
Dutch Clark * 1963
Jimmy Conzelman * 1964
Len Dawson 1987
Paddy Driscoll * 1965
Dan Fouts 1993
Otto Graham 1965
Bob Griese 1990
Arnie Herber * 1966
Sonny Jurgensen 1983
Bobby Layne * 1967
Sid Luckman 1965
Joe Namath 1985
Clarence Parker 1972
Bart Starr 1977
Roger Staubach 1985
Fran Tarkenton 1986
Y.A. Tittle 1971
Johnny Unitas 1979
Norm Van Brocklin * 1971
Bob Waterfield * 1965

Running Backs

Cliff Battles * 1968
Jim Brown 1971

Earl Campbell 1991
Tony Canadeo 1974
Larry Csonka 1987
Bill Dudley 1966
Frank Gifford 1977
Red Grange * 1977
Joe Guyon * 1966
Franco Harris 1990
Clarke Hinkle * 1964
Paul Hornung 1986
John Henry Johnson 1987
Tuffy Leemans * 1978
Ollie Matson 1972
George McAfee 1966
Hugh McElhenny 1970
Johnny McNally 1963
Lenny Moore 1975
Marion Motley 1968
Bronko Nagurski * 1963
Ernie Nevers * 1963
Walter Payton 1993
Joe Perry 1969
John Riggins 1992
Gale Sayers 1977
O.J. Simpson 1985
Ken Strong * 1967
Jim Taylor 1976
Jim Thorpe * 1963
Charley Trippi 1968
Steve Van Buren 1965
Doak Walker 1986

Ends and Receivers

Lance Alworth 1978
Red Badgro 1981
Raymond Berry 1973
Fred Biletnikoff 1988
Guy Chamberlin * 1965
Mike Ditka 1988
Tom Fears 1970
Bill Hewitt * 1971
Elroy Hirsch 1968
Don Hutson 1963
Dante Lavelli 1975
John Mackey 1992
Don Maynard 1987
Wayne Millner * 1968
Bobby Mitchell 1983
Pete Pihos 1970
Charley Taylor 1984
Paul Warfield 1983

Offensive Linemen

Chuck Bednarik 1967
Roosevelt Brown 1975
Turk Edwards * 1969
Dan Fortmann 1985

Frank Gatski 1985
Forrest Gregg 1977
Lou Groza 1974
John Hannah 1991
Ed Healey * 1964
Mel Hein * 1963
Pete Henry * 1963
Cal Hubbard * 1963
Stan Jones 1991
Walt Kiesling 1966
Bruiser Kinard * 1971
Jim Langer 1987
Larry Little 1993
Link Lyman * 1964
Mike McCormack 1984
Mike Michalske * 1964
Ron Mix 1979
George Musso 1982
Jim Otto 1980
Jim Parker 1973
Jim Ringo 1981
Bob St. Clair 1990
Art Shell 1989
Joe Stydahar * 1967
George Trafton * 1964
Bulldog Turner 1966
Gene Upshaw 1987
Alex Wojciechowicz * 1968

Defensive Linemen

Doug Atkins 1982
Buck Buchanan * 1990
Willie Davis 1981
Art Donovan 1968
Len Ford * 1976
Joe Greene 1987
Deacon Jones 1980
Bob Lilly 1980
Gino Marchetti 1972
Leo Nomellini 1969
Merlin Olsen 1982
Alan Page 1988
Andy Robustelli 1971
Ernie Stautner 1969
Arnie Weinmeister 1984
Bill Willis 1977

Linebackers

Bobby Bell 1983
Dick Butkus 1979
George Connor 1975
Bill George * 1974
Jack Ham 1988
Ted Hendricks 1990
Sam Huff 1982
Jack Lambert 1990
Willie Lanier 1986

Ray Nitschke 1978
Joe Schmidt 1973

Defensive Backs

Herb Adderley 1980
Lem Barney 1992
Mel Blount 1989
Willie Brown 1984
Jack Christiansen * 1970
Ken Houston 1986
Dick Lane 1974
Lary Yale 1979
Emlen Tunnell * 1967
Larry Wilson 1978
Willie Wood 1989

Placekicker

Jan Stenerud 1991

Hockey Hall of Fame

Forwards

Sid Abel 1969
Jack Adams * 1959
Syl Apps 1961
George Armstrong 1975
Ace Bailey * 1975
Dan Bain * 1945
Hobey Baker 1945
Bill Barber 1990
Marty Barry * 1965
Andy Bathgate 1978
Jean Beliveau 1972
Doug Bentley * 1964
Max Bentley * 1966
Toe Blake 1966
Mike Bossy 1991
Frank Boucher * 1958
Dubbie Bowie * 1945
Punch Broadbent * 1962
John Bucyk 1981
Billy Burch 1974
Bobby Clarke 1987
Neil Colville 1967
Charlie Conacher 1961
Bill Cook * 1952
Yvan Cournoyer 1982
Bill Cowley 1968
Rusty Crawford * 1962
Jack Darragh * 1962
Scotty Davidson * 1950
Hap Day 1961
Alex Delvecchio 1977
Cy Denneny * 1959
Marcel Dionne 1992
Gordie Drillon * 1975
Graham Drinkwater * 1950

Woody Dumart 1992
Tommy Dunderdale * 1974
Babe Dye * 1970
Phil Esposito 1984
Arthur Farrell * 1965
Frank Foyston * 1958
Frank Frederickson * 1958
Bob Gainey 1992
Jimmy Gardner * 1962
Bernie Geoffrion 1972
Eddie Gerard * 1945
Rod Gilbert 1982
Billy Gilmour * 1962
Si Griffis * 1950
George Hay * 1958
Bryan Hextall * 1969
Tom Hooper * 1962
Gordie Howe 1972
Syd Howe * 1965
Bobby Hull 1983
Harry Hyland * 1962
Dick Irvin * 1958
Busher Jackson * 1971
Aurel Joliat * 1947
Duke Keats * 1958
Ted Kennedy 1966
Dave Keon 1986
Elmer Lach 1966
Guy Lafleur 1988
Newsy Lalonde * 1950
Jacques Lemaire 1984
Herbie Lewis * 1989
Ted Lindsay 1966
Mickey MacKay * 1952
Frank Maholvich 1981
Joe Malone * 1950
Jack Marshall * 1965
Fred Maxwell * 1962
Lanny McDonald 1992
Frank McGee * 1945
Billy McGimsie * 1962
Stan Mikita 1983
Dickie Moore 1974
Howie Morenz * 1945
Bill Mosienko * 1965
Frank Nighbor * 1947
Reg Noble * 1962
Buddy O'Connor * 1988
Harry Oliver * 1967
Bert Olmstead 1985
Lynn Patrick * 1980
Gilbert Perreault 1990
Tom Phillips * 1945
Joe Primeau * 1963
Bob Pulford 1991
Frank Rankin * 1961
Jean Ratelle 1985

Henri Richard 1979
Maurice Richard 1961
George Richardson * 1950
Gordie Roberts * 1971
Blair Russel * 1965
Jack Ruttan * 1962
Fred Scanlan * 1965
Milt Schmidt 1961
Sweeney Schriner * 1962
Oliver Seibert * 1961
Babe Siebert * 1964
Darryl Sittler 1989
Alf Smith * 1962
Clint Smith 1991
Hooley Smith * 1972
Tommy Smith * 1973
Barney Stanley * 1962
Nels Stewart * 1962
Bruce Stuart * 1961
Fred Taylor * 1947
Harry Trihey * 1950
Norm Ullman 1982
Jack Walker * 1960
Marty Walsh * 1962
Harry Watson * 1962
Cooney Weiland * 1971
Harry Westwick * 1962
Fred Whitcroft * 1962

Defensemen

Leo Boivin 1986
Dickie Boon * 1952
Butch Bouchard 1966
George Boucher * 1960
Harry Cameron * 1962
King Clancy * 1958
Dit Clapper * 1947
Sprague Cleghorn * 1958
Art Coulter 1974
Red Dutton * 1958
Fernie Flaman 1990
Bill Gadsby 1970
Herb Gardiner * 1958
F.X. Goheen * 1952
Ebbie Goodfellow * 1963
Mike Grant * 1950
Wilf Green * 1962
Joe Hall * 1961
Doug Harvey 1973
Red Horner 1965
Tom Horton * 1977
Harry Howell 1979
Ching Johnson * 1958
Ernie Johnson * 1952
Tom Johnson 1970
Red Kelly 1969
Jack Laviollette * 1962

Jacques Leperrier 1987
Sylvio Mantha * 1960
George McNamara * 1958
Bobby Orr 1979
Lester Patrick * 1947
Pierre Pilote 1975
Didier Pitre * 1962
Denis Potvin 1991
Babe Pratt * 1966
Marcel Pronovost 1978
Harvey Pulford * 1945
Bill Quackenbush 1976
Kenny Reardon 1966
Art Ross * 1945
Serge Savard 1986
Earl Seibert 1963
Eddie Shore * 1947
Joe Simpson * 1962
Allan Stanley 1981
Jack Stewart * 1964
Hod Stuart * 1945
Gordon Wilson * 1962

Goaltenders

Clint Benedict * 1965
Johnny Bower 1976
Frankie Brimsek 1966
Turk Broda * 1967
Gerry Cheevers 1985
Alex Connell * 1958
Ken Dryden 1983
Bill Durnan * 1964
Tony Esposito 1988
Chuck Gardiner * 1945
Eddie Giacomin 1987
George Hainsworth * 1961
Glenn Hall 1975
Riley Hern * 1962
Hap Holmes * 1972
J.B. Hutton * 1962
Hughie Lehman * 1958
Percy LeSueur * 1961
Harry Lumley 1980
Paddy Moran * 1958
Bernie Parent 1984
Jacques Plante * 1978
Chuck Rayner 1973
Terry Sawchuck * 1971
Billy Smith 1993
Tiny Thompson * 1959
Vladislav Tretiak 1989
Georges Vezina * 1945
Gump Worsley 1980
Roy Worters 1969

Key starting pitchers from the Atlanta Braves' World Series teams of the early 1990s include Steve Avery, Tom Glavine and John Smoltz.

What will baseballs signed by Atlanta Braves prospects Javier Lopez, Ryan Klesko and Chipper Jones be worth some day?

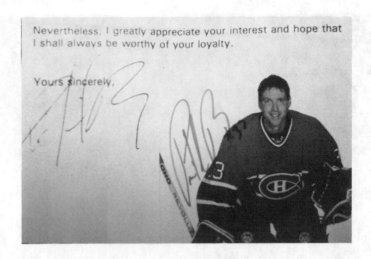

Upper Deck Authenticated certifies that autographed memorabilia is genuine, including *Sports Illustrated* memorabilia such as signed magazine covers and equipment. Score had the "Yankee Clipper," Joe DiMaggio, sign 2,500 baseball cards for the company's 1992 Series I packs. Patrick Roy sends a form letter thanking fans for their loyalty, but says he doesn't have time to answer each individual autograph; his response, however, includes a facsimile signature. At the right of that signature is a photo with a genuine signature.

May 31, 1994

Mark Baker
Box 2492
Liverpool, NY 13089

Dear Mark:

This is in response to a letter requesting your individual
trading card be signed.

The request is appreciated; however, the smooth glossy material
covering some cards make them very hard to write on. In
addition, due to an exclusive contract with the Classic Trading
Card Company, it is preferable no other trading cards be signed
at this time. As you can imagine many are resold for a profit.
Because of the vast amount of cards received for Shaquille's
signature it's not possible to personalize each and every one
of them. Surely you can understand this dilemma.

Enclosed is an autographed postcard that we hope you will
accept to accommodate your request. I am also returning the
trading card to you and trust that you're pleased and satisfied
with the substitution.

We are working expeditiously to form the SHAQPAQ Fan Club for
you and other fans as well. Information and details will be
available in the near future.

Thank you for your continued interest and support of Shaquille.

Sincerely,

Lucille Harrison
Secretary

LH:lh
enclosures (2)

P.O. Box 951840 · Lake Mary, FL 32795-1840 · (407) 444-2838 · Fax (407) 333-8868

Dear Fan,

I want to personally thank you for
your recent letter. My first season in
the NBA was great and it is because
of fans like you that I love playing this
game every night. As you can imagine, I am receiving hundreds of pieces
of mail every day and I am unable to
answer each piece individually. I did
however want to send you this autographed picture postcard as a thanks
to you for taking the time to write.
Thanks again for your support and
keep on cheering for the Magic.

Sincerely,

Shaquille O'Neal

Photo by Barry Gossage

**Shaquille O'Neal has been receiving so much mail since he entered the NBA he has
a fan club secretary who sends out a postcard with a facsimile signature. O'Neal
shies away from signing mail-in basketball cards for two reasons - some cards are
too glossy, so they are difficult to sign, and he's under an exclusive contract with
Classic Trading Card Co.. But Shaq has made some card show appearances.**

Acknowledgments

Foremost, I would like to thank everyone at Krause Publications for their confidence and support of this project, especially Mark K. Larson, Nathan Unseth, Pat Klug, Bob Lemke, Hugh McAloon, Chris Williams, Tom Nelsen, and Marge Larson.

Also, and on behalf of everyone who collects sports autographs, a special thanks goes to Dave Miedema for his dedication to the hobby.

I owe a great deal of gratitude to all of the professional teams that responded so generously with their time and support of this project. I would especially like to acknowledge the following individuals: Michael Wisniewski (ARA Services - Chicago Cubs), Herk Robinson (Kansas City Royals), Mark Geddis (Florida Marlins), Catherine Philbin (Los Angeles Dodgers), Mark Bingham (New York Mets), Mike Sadek (San Francisco Giants), Cindy McManus (Baltimore Orioles), Joe Billedeaux (Pittsburgh Pirates), Mary Ellen Pitts (Montreal Expos), Charlie Taylor (Atlanta Falcons), Lee Remmel (Green Bay Packers), Eileen Normile (Kansas City Chiefs), Pat Hanlon (New York Giants), Jeffrey Twist, Wayne Levi (Boston Celtics), Bill Jamieson (Detroit Red Wings), Bill Tuele (Edmonton Oilers), Jennifer Corey (Philadelphia Flyers), Denise La Rue (Quebec Nordiques), Jeff Trammel (St.Louis Blues) and Matt Levine (San Jose Sharks).

A special word of appreciation goes to the staff of the United States Postal Service - Bayberry Branch, Liverpool, N.Y. 13089 - which handles thousands of letters each year for me.

To Mark Solak, an outstanding broadcaster and good friend, thank you for all your help, especially regarding the Pittsburgh Penguins.

To Tom Novak, Patrick Roy's biggest fan, thanks for your help.

To Mike Horvath and Jeff Buis at Heroes Legends, in North Syracuse, N.Y., thank you!

To Deniese White, thank you very much for the autograph samples.

To Tom Gilhooly, now a Gaylord Brothers employee, thanks for your assistance.

To Leon Ghezzi, and his wonderful daughter Kristin, thanks for helping at work.

To my parents, Mr. and Mrs. Ford W. Baker, thanks for your love and support.

To Aaron, Elizabeth, and Rebecca, for your wonderful smiles and hugs that melt a father's heart.

Finally, to Alison Long, whose assistance, support, warmth, and friendship has meant so very much to me.

About the author

A resident of central New York, Mark Allen Baker possesses a bachelor's degree from State University of New York at Oswego. His post graduate work has included study at the Rochester Institute of Technology, George Washington University and the Massachusetts Institute of Technology, primarily in the area of computer graphics. His articles, artwork and photography have appeared in more than 40 periodicals, including *Computer Graphics World*, *Computer Pictures*, *CFO*, *Public Relations Journal*, *Personal Computing*, *Topps Magazine*, *Antique News*, and *Sports Collectors Digest*.

During his career, Baker has worked in a variety of finance, marketing, sales and executive positions for the General Electric Corp., Genigraphics Corp., and Pansophic Systems Inc. Baker's work has primarily centered around the design, development and manufacture of computer-based imaging systems.

Baker was awarded a lifetime membership to the National Baseball Hall of Fame for the research he did for his first book, titled the Baseball Autograph Handbook.

An acknowledged researcher and collector, Baker has been quoted in several publications, including *USA Today* and *Sports Illustrated*.

Additional biographical data can be found in several professional directories, including Who's Who in the East.

Books by the author

Baseball Autograph Handbook, first edition, 1990, by Krause Publications, 288 pages.
Baseball Autograph Handbook, second edition, 1991, by Krause Publications, 352 pages.
Team Baseballs, first edition, 1992, by Krause Publications, 544 pages.

Selected Bibliography

Associated Features Inc. *The Complete Handbook of Pro Basketball*. New York, N.Y.: Signet, 1993.

Associated Features Inc. *The Complete Handbook of Pro Football*. New York, N.Y.: Signet, 1993.

Baker, Mark A. *Sports Collectors Digest Baseball Autograph Handbook*. Iola, Wis.: Krause Publications Inc., 1990.

Baker, Mark A. *Sports Collectors Digest Baseball Autograph Handbook, second edition*. Iola, Wis.: Krause Publications Inc., 1991.

Baker, Mark A. *Sports Collectors Digest Team Baseballs*. Iola, Wis.: Krause Publications Inc., 1992.

Benjamin, Mary A. *Autographs: A Key to Collecting*. New York, N.Y.: R.R. Bowker, 1946; revised edition, 1963.

Berkeley, Edmund, editor, Herbert Klinghofer and Kenneth Rendell, coeditors. *Autographs and Manuscripts: A Collector's Manual*. New York, N.Y.: Charles Scribner's Sons, 1978.

Bowden, Glen. *Collectible Fountain Pens*. Glenview, Ill.: Glen Bowden Communications.

Carvalho, David N. *Forty Centuries of Ink, or a Chronological Narrative Concerning Ink and Its Background*. New York: Banks Law Publishing Co., 1904.

Clapp, Anne F. *Curatorial Care of Works of Art on Paper*. Oberlin: Intermuseum Conservation Association, 1973.

Doloff, Francis W. and Roy I. Perkinson. *How to Care for Works of Art on Paper*. Boston, Mass.: Museum of Fine Arts, 1971.

Forensic Science Handbook. R. Saferstein, editor. Englewood Cliffs, N.J.: Prentice-Hall Inc., 1982.

Giamatti, A. Bartlett. *Take Time for Paradise: Americans and their games*. New York, N.Y.: Summit Books, 1989.

Gorman, Jerry and Kirk Calhoun. *The Name of the Game*. New York, N.Y.: John Wiley & Sons Inc., 1994.

Harrison, Wilson R. *Suspect Documents: Their Scientific Examination*. London: Sweet and Maxwell, 1958.

Kathpalia, Yash Pal. *Conservation and Restoration of Archive Materials*. Paris: UNESCO, 1973.

Larson, Mark K. *Sports Collectors Digest The Complete Guide to Baseball Memorabilia*. Iola, Wis.: Krause Publications Inc., 1992.

Lawerence, Cliff. *Official P.F.C. Pen Guide*. Dunedin, Fla.

National Baseball Hall of Fame and Museum Inc.. National Baseball Hall of Fame & Museum Yearbook, 1991.

Nickell, Joe. *Pen, Ink, & Evidence*. Lexington, Ky.: The University Press of Kentucky, 1990.

Rand McNally & Co. *The Official Baseball Atlas*, Rand McNally & Co., 1994.

Reichler, Joseph, editor. *The Baseball Encyclopedia, 6th edition*. New York, N.Y.: Macmillian Publishing Co., 1985.

Rosen, Alan and Doug Carr. *Mr. Mint's Insider's Guide to Investing in Baseball Cards and Collectibles*. New York, N.Y.: Warner Books Inc., 1991.

Saferstein, Richard. *Criminalistics: An Introduction to Forensic Science*. Englewood Cliffs, N.J.: Prentice-Hall Inc., 1987.

The National Hockey League. *Official Guide & Record Book 1993-94*. Chicago, Ill.: Triumph Books, 1993.

The Sporting News. *Complete Hockey Book 1993-94*. St. Louis, Mo.: The Sporting News Publishing Co., 1993.

The Sporting News. *The Complete Baseball Record Book.* St. Louis, Mo.: The Sporting News Publishing Co., 1993.

Smith, Ken. *Baseball's Hall of Fame.* New York, N.Y.: Tempo Books, 1981.

Valerio, Anthony. *Bart: A. Bartlett Giamatti, A Life by Him and about Him.* New York, N.Y.: Harcourt Brace Jovanovich, 1991.

Periodicals

Sports Collectors Digest, Krause Publications Inc., 700 East State St., Iola, Wis. 54990.

The Autograph Collector's Magazine, P.O. Box 55328, Stockton, Calif. 95205.

The Autograph Review, 305 Carlton Road, Syracuse, N.Y. 13207.

Additional

Source material and notes

Preface
Financial information quoted from required documentation provided to the Securities and Exchange Commission. Additional information provided by the Shareholders Relations Office of the Score Board Inc., Cherry Hill, N.J..

Upper Deck Authenticated is a division of the Upper Deck Co., and affiliated with McNall Sports Entertainment. Upper Deck is a trademark of the Upper Deck Co..

Authenticated is a trademark of Authentics Ltd. Copyright 1992 - Authentics Ltd. Quotation provided to the author by Ernest Byner from correspondence in April 1994.

Forward
Inspiration provided by James Fennimore Cooper. A special thanks to the staff at the National Baseball Hall of Fame and Library, especially Patricia Kelly and William J. Guilfoile, and to the families of Joseph Wheeler Sewell and A. Bartlett Giamatti - my heartfelt thanks for allowing me to share in the lives of two very special people. To Ted Williams, Stan Musial, Bob Feller and Bobby Doerr, thank you for sharing some tender moments with me.

Chapter 1
Inspiration provided by A. Bartlett Giamatti, Jackie Robinson, Gale Sayers and the children who choose to follow the dreams of these wonderful men.

Chapter 2
Reference material courtesy of Bleachers Sports Bar and Restaurant, Liverpool, N.Y.. A special thanks to Mark Solak for the Pittsburgh Penguins memorabilia. Price quotes courtesy of Penguins Authentic Memorabilia.

Chapter 4
(see bibliography)

"Sharpie" is a registered trademark of the Sanford Corp. of Bellwood, Ill..

Nation's Business - "Mighty Battle of the Pens," November 1946.

Additional source material available in "Forensic Science International."

Additional source material provided by Parker and Paper Mate, a division of the Gillette Co.

Chapter 5
"Signature Rookies" copyright Signature Rookies of Factoryville, Pa.. Autographed single-signature baseballs quoted from advertisements in the March 18, 1994, issue of Sports Collectors Digest.

A special thanks to the Syracuse Chiefs, MacArthur Stadium, Syracuse, N.Y. 13208, especially Tex and John Simone.

Chapter 8
All prices quoted from Gaylord Brothers Archival & Storage Materials & Conservation Supplies 1994 Catalog No. 4. Gaylord Bros., P.O. Box 4901, Syracuse, N.Y. 13221-4901.

Chapter 10
Addresses courtesy of Major League Baseball, National Basketball Association, National Football League and the National Hockey League.

Upper Deck Authenticated is a registered trademark of the Upper Deck Co..

Additional source material provided by the San Francisco Giants, New York Knickerbockers, Leaf/Donruss and the Official Dallas Cowboys Catalog.

"Sports City Grill" is a registered trademark.

Chapter 11
Merchandising material referenced was provided directly by the specific professional organization or its designated vendor. All material and pricing is subject to change.

Merchandising data courtesy Major League Baseball Properties, NBA Properties, NFL Properties, and NHL Enterprises. All retail projections are estimates based upon known industry data.

Chapter 12
Sports trading cards courtesy of, and copyright 1994, by the Topps Co. Inc., Duryea, Pa. 18642. Licensing provided to Topps by Major League Baseball, National Basketball Association Properties Inc., National Football League Quarterback Club Inc. and National Hockey League, and by the Major League Baseball Players, Major League Baseball Properties, National Hockey League Players Association and National Hockey League Enterprises.

Players were chosen at random. All autograph requests were sent through the mail and addressed to the player's attention at their respective clubs. All autograph requests included a self-addressed stamped envelope for the player's convenience.

All requests were mailed during the months of March and April 1994. Signature quality varies due to card surfaces and ink characteristics. All autograph responses are assumed to be authentic. The inclusion of specific responses in this section in no means implies or includes any guarantees.

Chapter 13
Team addresses and information courtesy of the specific club referenced.

Additional source material is provided by certain major league baseball players who will remain nameless, as to not agitate their teammates or current ball club.

Additional material provided by USA TODAY Baseball Weekly and The Official Baseball Atlas by Rand McNally.

* All professional teams and individual team member marks reproduced in this product are trademarks which are the exclusive property of those respective teams and the associations which represents the athlete.

Player/Team Index

FULL HOUSE

Football, Basketball & Hockey Price Guide

Updated values for all NFL, NBA and NHL sportscards. Packed with more cards, more prices and more photos than any other single price guide in this growing field. Contains over 240,000 current values for card and sets from 1935 to date.

$14⁹⁵

plus $2.50 shipping

Complete Guide to Baseball Memorabilia

Contains everything from programs to magazines, autographs, plates, books, balls, bats, gloves,pennants, pins, cachets, yearbooks, statues, uniforms and ticket stubs are listed and priced to help you identify, buy and sell with confidence.

$16⁹⁵

plus $2.50 shipping

Standard Catalog of Baseball Cards

The most comprehensive baseball card price guide available. Coverage begins with early tobacco cards in 1886 and is complete through new issues of 1994. You'll browse through more than 150,000 cards, 450,000 prices and 2,500 photos.

$34⁹⁵

plus $2.50 shipping

Sportscard Counterfeit Detector

Trained counterfeit detector Bob Lemke and veteran sportscard dealer Sally Grace have compiled the M.O.s of wily counterfeiters so you won't be fooled. Includes over 200 known phony cards plus 800 detailed, close-up photos.

$17⁹⁵

plus $2.50 shipping

From Ruth to Ryan: Unbeatable Card Buys

Dollars-and-sense advice on what types of cards to add to your collection. Presents valuable buying tips from hobby experts, and chronicles the history and rarity of baseball cards from 1900 to 1993. Recommends singles-to-full sets.

$6⁹⁵

plus $2.50 shipping

Krause Publications

700 E. State St., Iola, WI 54990-0001